*Audacious Reforms*

THE JOHNS HOPKINS UNIVERSITY PRESS

*Baltimore and London*

# *Audacious* *Reforms*

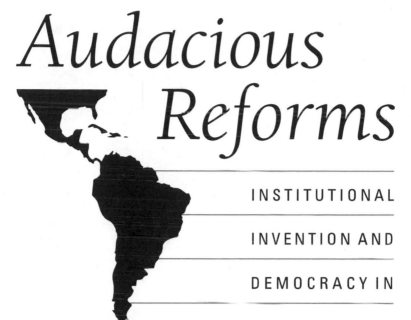

INSTITUTIONAL

INVENTION AND

DEMOCRACY IN

LATIN AMERICA

Merilee S. Grindle

The Johns Hopkins University Press
2715 North Charles Street
Baltimore, Maryland 21218-4363
www.press.jhu.edu

Library of Congress Cataloging-in-Publication Data will be found at the end of this book.
A catalog record for this book is available from the British Library

ISBN 0-8018-6420-8
ISBN 0-8018-6421-6 (pbk.)

In remembrance of

*June Duncan Serrill*
*Douglas Edward Serrill*

# Contents

# Figures, Tables, and Boxes

## Figures

## Tables

## Boxes

# Acknowledgments

**M**y central interest in this book is to understand more fully how reforms happen in the "real world." During a trip to several Latin American countries in 1996, I was struck by the extent to which the distribution of power within formal democracies was being discussed and altered, often at high levels within government. This raised an intriguing question: why would politicians be experimenting with changes that would diminish their control over political resources? As I began to explore this question in greater depth, my interests expanded to a more general interest in how institutional change occurs and what its consequences are for how politics gets done within a country.

I was fortunate to be able to explore these ideas with many of the people who had been the architects of new institutions and the initiators of reform activities in Latin America. In Venezuela, Carlos Andrés Pérez, Carlos Blanco, and Ramón Velásquez were among those who shared their experiences from the "real world" with me. I also had an opportunity to discuss decentralization with Eduardo Fernández while he was visiting Cambridge. In Bolivia, Gonzalo Sánchez de Lozada offered his perspectives about how a radical change in center-local political structures took place, and Carlos Hugo Molina and José Guillermo Justiniano recounted their experiences on the team that devised Popular Participation. In Argentina, I was able to discuss constitutional reform with Raúl Alfonsin, Alberto García Lema, and Ricardo Gil Lavedra, among others. More broadly, I spoke with many participants in the reform process, academics in each country who had studied and written about the reforms, and observers and critics of politics in the country, a total of some eighty-seven people. I owe deep appreciation to these individuals for the time and valuable insights they provided.

In each country, there were individuals who were extraordinarily helpful in orienting me to national and local politics and who helped arrange interviews with a variety of important actors in the reform process. In Venezuela, I am particularly grateful to Janet Kelly, Juan Carlos Navarro, Rafael de la Cruz, Aníbal Romero, Gustavo Velásquez, Francisco Arrocha, Subdelia Sevilla

Paez, José Manuel Rodriguez, and Arístides Moreno. Mosés Naím was also helpful in putting me in contact with those who had been close to the policy reforms of the Pérez period. In Bolivia, Manuel Contreras, Ramiro Ortega Landa, Ronald Maclean, and Nico van Niekerk were generous with their time and assistance in arranging interviews and access to data for me. George Gray Molina was a good friend who not only shared his work with me but also provided important insights into the process of reform in Bolivia. In Argentina, I could not have carried out the research without the kind and assiduous assistance of Luis Moreno Ocampo, Christian Gruenberg, and Roberto de Michele. In addition, I'd like to thank Hugo Carranza and José María Ghio for their interest in my work and their assistance. My friend Malka Rohr made every trip to Buenos Aires a delight.

Several Kennedy School students were central to the research and production of the book. During the early stages of the work, Amy Gray and Darnes Tavera offered able research assistance. Juan Sadurní spent a summer collecting and assessing often elusive data in the process of producing important tables and figures. Sebastian Popik generated important bibliographic material on the Argentine case and took up an exploration of that case with energy, enthusiasm, and intelligence. Robert Taliercio provided valuable insights and missing data for the project. Kathleen O'Neill also provided helpful comments. More generally, students and colleagues at the Kennedy School provided a wonderful intellectual environment for those of us who are intrigued by how things work out in practice.

Also at the Kennedy School, I am very grateful to the Innovations in State and Local Government program and to its director and executive director, Alan Altshuler and Bill Parent, for providing a grant that helped fund the field research activities. Rebecca Tolk Clark was important in helping produce the manuscript.

As always, I am enormously thankful to Steven, Alexandra, and Stefanie Grindle for their forbearance and for their willingness to believe, as I do, that research about how things happen in the world is both interesting and important.

# Abbreviations

## Venezuela

| | |
|---|---|
| AD | Acción Democrática |
| COPEI | Comité de Organización Política Electoral Independente |
| COPRE | Presidential Commission for the Reform of the State |
| FIDES | Intergovernmental Fund for Decentralization |
| MAS | Movimiento al Socialismo |
| MEP | Movimiento Electoral del Pueblo |
| PCV | Partido Comunista de Venezuela |
| URD | Unión Republicana Democrática |

## Bolivia

| | |
|---|---|
| ADN | Acción Democrática Nacionalista |
| ASP | Asemblea por la Soberanía de los Pueblos (Assembly for People's Sovereignty) |
| CEPB | Confederación de Empresarios Privados de Bolivia |
| COB | Central Obrera Boliviana |
| CONDEPA | Conciencia de Patria |
| CSUTCB | Confederación Sindical Unica de Trabajadores de Bolivia (rural unions) |
| DDCs | Departmental Development Corporations |
| FSTMB | Federación Sindical de Trabajadores Mineros de Bolivia |
| IU | Izquierda Unida Party |
| MBL | Movimiento Bolivia Libre |
| MIR | Movimiento de Izquierda Revolucionaria |
| MNR | Movimiento Nacionalista Revolucionario |
| MRTKL | Movimiento Revolucionario Tupac Katari de Liberación (Katarista Party) |
| NPE | Nueva Política Económica |
| OTBs | Territorial Base Organizations |
| UCS | Unión Cívica de Solidaridad |
| UDP | Unidad Democrática y Popular |

UDAPSO      Social Policy Analysis Unit

**Argentina**
FREPASO    Frente del Pais Solidario
MODIN      Movimiento por la Dignidad y la Independencia Nacional
UCS        Unión Cívica Radical

*Audacious Reforms*

# Audacious Reforms

## Democratizing Latin America

*Why would politicians promote reforms that*
*limit their power? How are new institutions created?*
*What implications does the invention of new*
*institutions have for the political process?*

Most politics is the politics of incrementalism, of coping, of limping from crisis to crisis, or of adjustment at the margins. Periodically, however, this normal politics is punctuated by the creation of new institutions that alter the way in which public problems are manifested and resolved, the way in which political actors calculate the costs and benefits of their activities, and the ways in which social groups relate to the political and policy process. The invention of new institutions, of new ways of doing politics, is the subject of this book. In it, I examine three decisions to redistribute power downward in Latin America's political systems and explore why such decisions were made and what consequences they had for doing politics.

- In 1989, citizens of Venezuela voted in elections for governors and mayors for the first time in the country's history. Moreover, for the first time since a democratic regime had been introduced in 1958, Venezuelans had the option of voting for candidates by name rather than by party list. They were able to do so because a series of reforms mandated the popular election of regional and local leaders and instituted changes in the electoral law. Prior to these changes, governors were selected by the president as a form of party-based patronage in a highly centralized political system dominated by a small circle of party leaders and the president. Municipal presidents had been selected by local councils from among their members, usually in accord with the majority party's claims for leadership.[1]

- Four years after these events in Venezuela, Bolivia's national congress passed the Law for Popular Participation. This law created 311 municipalities, provided for the election of mayors and municipal councillors, and mandated that 20 percent of government revenue be assigned to local governments for development investments. Although the country had never been integrated enough for the highly centralized political system to exert effective control throughout Bolivia's vast and isolating terrain, the Popular Participation Law provided both legitimacy and resources for large numbers of local communities to deal with deplorable municipal services, low levels of education and health, and devastating conditions of poverty. In 1995, many citizens in small towns and remote rural villages had their first experience of voting for mayors and councillors.

- In Argentina, citizens of the capital city, Buenos Aires, went to the polls in 1996 to elect a mayor for the first time. They did so in the aftermath of a broad set of constitutional changes instituted in 1994 that included, among other things, the political autonomy of the capital city and the possibility of re-election for incumbent presidents. The mayoral election, as predicted, brought the Radical Party to power in the city, while national politics continued to be dominated by the Peronist Party, led by Carlos Menem. Among the first activities of the new mayor was to set in place the structure for decentralizing the city's management. These changes ensured that the weight of the capital city of three million inhabitants would be greater in national politics than it had been in the past, and simultaneously opened up greater potential for political estrangement between the city and national political leaders.

Deliberate acts by the beneficiaries of political power to divest themselves of some of that power are puzzling phenomena. Indeed, from the perspective of normal politics, it is important to emphasize what politicians were giving up. In Venezuela, Bolivia, and Argentina, political power had traditionally been achieved and maintained through centralization of decision making and the careful calculation of resource distribution based on patronage and clientelism. Thus, with institutional invention, central politicians were giving up extensive patronage prerogatives, great capacity to dominate their party hierarchies, significant control over resources that allowed them to appease divergent interests and maintain political stability, and the capacity to allocate government programs and projects for electoral advantage. Rules of the game that were well institutionalized and clearly beneficial to central political leaders were exchanged for uncertainty and the risks attendant upon increased political competition. Most prior efforts to decentralize government in Latin America foundered precisely because of such uncertainty and loss of power; despite rhetoric, clear efficiency gains, and elaborate plans, political leaders had a long history of rebelling against efforts to dilute their power.[2]

This book is about audacious institutional invention in democratic settings. For my purposes, audacious reforms are those for which there are no obviously compelling answers to the question, "Why would politicians, concerned about the electoral consequences of their actions, choose such a change?" Thus, these reforms call into question many conventional assumptions about the motivations of political actors. They force us to inquire into why particular decisions are made and to question the insights of theories that purport to explain political behavior. Second, these innovations are notable for the creation of new rules about the distribution of power. Most theoretical discussions of institutions explain change in terms of path dependence, evolution, and "stickiness." But there are numerous examples of situations, such as those explored here, in which dramatically new rules of the game are substituted for those that have been in place for long periods. Thus, institutional creation raises interesting questions about political agency—the capacity to bring about change—and the embeddedness of political structures. Third, audacious reforms have consequences for political behavior that cannot be reliably anticipated. Political actors are propelled into uncharted territories by these changes; new institutions are surrounded by uncertainty about their impact on political competition, party dynamics, and political incentives. As a result, theories that predict political behavior in stable institutional environments may not be particularly useful when institutions are newly created.

Reforms that are audacious in these ways thus provide interesting opportunities to ask three questions about where institutional change comes from and what consequences are likely to flow from it. The first and possibly most arresting question relates to the motivations of politicians: *Why would rational politicians choose to give up power?* In the cases discussed here, politicians made deliberate decisions to expand the extent to which citizens and other politicians had the capacity to check the power of chief executives and executive and party bureaucracies. They decided to share power downward in their political systems, introducing the possibility of opening up political competition to new voices, new interests, and new demands, thus creating opportunities for new paths to political power. As we will see, it is not at all obvious why they would decide to do so; in each case, decision makers had other ways out of the political dilemmas they faced that were less drastic in the sense that these dilemmas did not require the creation of new institutions and certainly did not require them to relinquish power. Yet they chose audacious responses to the issues and problems they faced. How can we understand what motivated them?

Added to the puzzle of the motivations that lie behind the choices that politicians make is the need to explain the particular way the politicians in the three countries chose to relinquish power—they created new institutions that would be binding on them and other politicians in the future. A second important question, then, is: *What accounts for the selection of some institutions rather than others?* This question is clearly linked to the initial question about the motivations of politicians, but it also probes into questions of intentionality and agency in political life. In this book, institutions are the rules of the game that structure action and signal rational behavior.[3] Indeed, in most research, institutions are taken as independent or intermediary variables in the sense that they either cause or structure action. If it is possible to isolate founding moments of new institutions, however, it should be possible to explore the extent to which they are artifacts of deliberate efforts to deal with transaction costs or principal-agent problems, as some theorists have proposed, or are instead contingent outcomes of political conflict, as others have argued.

Given new institutions that allocate power differently within a political system, a third question relates to the consequences of institutional choice for politics: *How does the introduction of new institutions alter the nature of political interactions?* In the specific cases of Venezuela, Bolivia, and Argentina, how did institutional creation affect the behavior of political parties, politicians, and citizens? What kinds of political learning occurred as these actors adjusted to new rules of the game for political contestation? Were new conflicts introduced into the political systems of these countries as a result of institutional change? How did the new institutions affect other institutions within the political system? These questions encourage us to consider how institutional choice is linked to outcomes in political history. They raise the issue of whether these outcomes are best understood as new equilibria or as temporary results of political contests that will be reversed, altered, or further institutionalized through ongoing conflict.

## The Problem of Democracy in Latin America

The changes introduced in Venezuela, Bolivia, and Argentina were democratizing: they increased opportunities for citizens to participate in political decision making. In the context of Latin American politics, this is a significant kind of reform. Democratization continues to be a concern of citizens, political activists, and scholars throughout the region. In the late 1970s, most of Latin America's governments were dominated by authoritarian—usually military—dictators. Indeed, only Venezuela and Colombia had been able to maintain democratic regimes in power through the economic and social turbulence of the 1960s and 1970s. Beginning with the transition to democratic government in Ecuador in 1978, however, the region was marked by widespread changes from authoritarian to democratic regimes.[4] By 1990, only Mexico and Cuba had not joined the democratic club, and both countries were under mounting internal and external pressure to do so. Authoritarianism was partly revived in Peru under the presidency of Alberto Fujimori in 1992, but even there, democratic trappings were retained, and few considered that the military alternative carried with it reasonable solutions to the problem of governance and stability in the country. In Mexico, the pressure to democratize increased substantially in the 1990s. By the end of the decade, competitive elections had become routine phenomena.

This transition to democratic political systems in Latin America in the 1980s and 1990s is laudable. It is all the more impressive because these transitions took place and took root in countries that were undergoing severe and prolonged economic crisis and disruptive and often conflict-ridden transitions to more market-oriented economies whose future would be tied to the globalization of the world economy. This period of political and economic change in Latin America makes for good storytelling. It is replete with heroes and villains, new-style technocrats and old-style politicians, innovations and resistance, major reforms and legislative gridlock, great sacrifice and astounding scandal, peace accords and contestation, strikes and negotiated settlements. By the end of this turbulent period, major gains had been made in the reach of democratic politics throughout the region.

Despite these accomplishments, observers of Latin America's political systems continue to be deeply critical of the extent of democracy in the region. They frequently note that the majority of its democratic governments are very imperfect: they exclude large portions of the population and maintain institutions of governance that are neither fully legitimate in the eyes of citizens nor fully observed by those who have access to power and influence. While recognizing the positive nature of the region's rejection of authoritarian rule, and while anticipating that democratic government is both more legitimate and more effective in resolving the region's deep problems of economic and social injustice, they nevertheless point to the many ways in which democracy is not fully developed. In fact, as Aníbal Romero has pointed out, scholars and commentators frequently hyphenate their references to Latin America's democratic systems, referring to them as "exclusionary," "frozen," "crisis-prone," "semi-," "restricted," "hybrid," or "tutelary" democracies.[5]

Behind this unwillingness to credit political systems in the region as fully democratic are some inescapable realities: in a wide range of countries, many citizens are excluded from public debate and the reach of public services; in some, large numbers of citizens absent themselves from elections and profess extreme cynicism about political and governmental institutions and about politicians and public officials; and in many countries, the routine operation of these institutions is partisan, corrupt, inefficient, and unresponsive.

Moreover, throughout democratic Latin America in the 1980s and much of the 1990s, centralization of decision making continued to be a marked characteristic of how public policies were determined. Several of the region's notable transitions to democracy were the result of elite bargains or pacts, with little participation of ordinary citizens, and these new systems continued to generate decisions based on behind-the-scenes negotiation among the same elites. Despite regular elections, clientelism continued to hold many political parties together and reinforced centralization and the winner-take-all nature of access to political power, public resources, and public positions. Centralization of decision making increased in the decade of the 1980s, when major changes in economic policies were undertaken in almost all countries in the region. In the development of plans for stabilization and structural adjustment, policy making was dominated by presidents and their elite technocratic teams, with little input, if any, from legislatures, political parties, major interest groups, or even line ministries associated with the spending side of government activity.[6] Thus, while countries reinstituted democratic regimes, policy making generally remained as remote from citizens as it had been under prior authoritarian systems.

In addition, party systems in many countries continued to suffer from centralization and elite domination, and party leaders lost touch with the populations they professed to represent. In other cases, parties were little more than loose coalitions formed around particular personalities. Voting was often characterized by high levels of abstention, and public opinion polls repeatedly demonstrated that the public mood toward politics was one of cynicism, apathy, and distrust. Moreover, because many citizens had "checked out" of involvement in public life, pressures to hold institutions and officials accountable were often minimal. Reports of corruption and misuse of public resources abounded. Despite widespread belief among citizens that democratic government was essential for the development of the region, day-to-day government in hyphenated democracies continued to be carried on in an atmosphere of rejection and alienation.[7]

This was the unpropitious but familiar context in which democratizing reforms were introduced in Venezuela, Bolivia, and Argentina—politics that were centralized, unresponsive, urban- and elite-biased, and remote from the concerns of most citizens. In all three countries, a set of pre-reform institutions entrenched a status quo that privileged national decision makers, centralized parties, and issues of national import, while marginalizing local participation and influence over decision making, the responsiveness of parties and politicians to their constituencies, and the salience of locally relevant issues. Thus, the changes involved important reconfigurations of political power, reversing historical trends toward ever-greater centralization of control.

- In Venezuela, the introduction of state and local elections reversed an eighty-year trend toward increasing political centralization. Indeed, the political history of the country and the political imaginations of its people had been deeply affected by political turmoil throughout the nineteenth century and into the twentieth, when the focus of strife had been over a unitary or federalist structure of political power, and in which federalism generally meant local warlord control and internecine violence among regional armies and their leaders. Dictatorships of the twentieth century were recognized and even applauded for bringing centralized control and political peace to the country. The democratic system introduced in 1958 was accompanied by the concentration of power in two highly centralized political parties. The president of the country managed an extensive patronage system that reached throughout the national territory and that responded to the political objectives of a handful of party leaders in Caracas.
- In Bolivia, a similar history of conflict between unitarists and federalists fed fear of violence and even the dissolution of the country. The Revolution of 1952 spawned a hegemonic political party intent

on national integration of a dispersed and subsistence-oriented rural economy. In the 1980s, new political parties emerged to challenge control over a prebendal system in which the president and party leaders controlled a national system of patronage and the distribution of development resources along clientelistic lines. Not only did the Popular Participation Law destroy a large part of the control by national political leaders over this political and economic patronage, but it also recognized the claims to citizenship and participation of the ethnic minorities that composed 55 percent of the country's population who had been marginalized from political power since the time of the Spanish conquest.

• For many observers, political autonomy for Buenos Aires was an idea whose time had come. The capital city included some 10 percent of the population of the country and was the center of its economic, political, and social life. Historically, the city had been prized by both unitarists and federalists because it dominated the national economy. From the time of independence, much political discourse centered on the opposition of Buenos Aires and *la provincia,* composing the rest of the country. Bonairenses enjoyed numerous advantages of living in a wealthy, cosmopolitan, and exciting city but were also aware that its fate depended on the whims of politicians elected elsewhere and officials beholden to party machines they did not control. Political autonomy offered an avenue for resolving some of these issues but, at the same time, robbed national political leaders of control over the city's budget, lucrative and politically important jobs and contracts, and the certainty that a presidentially appointed mayor would reflect the party and policy preferences of the country's leaders.

In other ways as well, Venezuela, Bolivia, and Argentina reflected characteristics of many Latin American countries. When new political institutions were introduced, these countries were characterized by a set of newly introduced market-oriented policies. Political leaders, acquiring power through imperfect democratic institutions, faced a set of challenges that related to the capacity of market institutions to generate economic growth and the capacity of political institutions to be legitimate sources of decision making, conflict resolution, and response to societal demands. At the same time, constrained economic growth limited the resources available to politicians to resolve such problems. Moreover, the institutions of these states did not work particularly well in contributing to the equity, effectiveness, or efficiency of state actions. Indeed, there were many signs that the state was "unwell"—large fiscal deficits, inability to collect taxes, high levels of social protest, and low levels of voter mobilization.[8] These conditions raised real questions about the extent to which the authority of the state was accepted as legitimate by citizens. The need for institutional change was clear; the political sources of it were unknown.

## Investigating Audacious Reforms

In the decade and a half following the economic crisis of the early 1980s, Latin American countries were a laboratory of economic policy change and political transition. Indeed, of all the areas of the world, with the possible exceptions of the states of Eastern Europe and the former Soviet Union, no other experienced such fundamental changes during this period. Economic development strategies that had been in place in some countries as far back as the 1930s were discarded in favor of new strategies that placed considerably less emphasis on state-guided development and considerably more emphasis on the market as the engine of growth in the economy. And as we have seen, countries that had suffered under authoritarian rule as far back as the 1960s introduced or returned to democratic political structures, even as unpopular stabilization and structural adjustment measures were imposed. In addition, decentralization was widely advocated as a panacea for many economic, social, and political problems. Interestingly, it was adopted as policy in a significant number of countries.[9] The period was transformative; changes rarely viewed as possible were introduced in country after country, redefining the nature of economics and politics in the region.

Over the past two decades, numerous studies have sought to explain these kinds of reforms. Of particular interest have been changes in economic policies and the institutional arrangements that surround economic policy making. Scholars have been intrigued by the question of why governments might choose to adopt harsh stabilization and structural adjustment measures that carry with them significant burdens for large portions of society and for politically important groups. This question has seemed especially important to understand reform initiatives in fragile or transitional democracies.[10] Various studies have highlighted the role of rent-seeking interests in entrenching inappropriate development policies in the past, the distributional consequences of reform, the way in which crises enhance opportunities for reform, and the activities of political entrepreneurs and technocratic

"change teams" in altering decision-making dynamics to be more friendly to
reform initiatives.

This literature has provided some interesting ideas about why self-
regarding politicians are occasionally interested in promoting major economic reforms. Some scholars, for example, have argued that severe crisis or
post-election honeymoons permit reform-oriented leaders an opportunity to
introduce policy change; others, that pressure from international financial
institutions leaves countries little choice but to reform; and still others, that
politicians promote policies that are favored by powerful economic groups
and technocratic advisers. Some have also favored explanations about the
electoral calculations behind change initiatives.[11] These explanations of economic policy reforms, however, do not necessarily provide helpful insights
into why politicians might be interested in promoting *political* reforms that
impinge significantly on their own power and that open the policy preferences of incumbents to increased contestation. Indeed, in the throes of attempting to introduce major economic policy reforms, politicians typically
concentrated power in the executive and in the economic ministries or technocratic teams that had been appointed to design policy packages and negotiate conditionalities with international financial institutions. Moreover, economic reform leaders typically introduced their reforms through the use of
executive decree powers rather than through legislative processes.[12] Although
many have grappled with finding explanations for why self-regarding and
electorally sensitive leaders became advocates of politically costly economic
policy reforms, these explanations are not convincing in accounting for why
politicians might give up power in the political arena.

Scholars who have been primarily concerned with political reform have
focused most of their attention on the recent emergence of democratic regimes. The literature on transitions from authoritarian systems has emphasized the factors behind a global "wave" of democratization beginning in the
mid-1970s, the sins of the authoritarians while in power, the defection of
economic elites from authoritarian coalitions, the emergence of new actors in
civil society such as nongovernmental organizations and a variety of identity
and citizenship groups, and the role of traditional political parties and labor
organizations in pressing for a return to power.[13] Scholars have highlighted
the frequent convergence of interest in extracting the military from power
and the equally frequent divergence of interest in how political power is to
be shared in post-transition democracies. Indeed, we have learned a great
deal about why and when major political transitions are likely to occur and
the role of political elites and civil society organizations in those historically

important changes. More recently, attention has begun to focus on the tensions being confronted by the new democracies, including their institutional weaknesses.[14] As part of this concern about the fragility of new systems, a number of scholars have turned their attention to issues of administrative and political decentralization and their anticipated impact on equity and efficiency in government.

While the transitions literature has provided important insights into the dynamics of regime change and post-transition literature has revealed important "fault lines" in new democracies, this work has not been noted by those whose primary concern is with more abstract discussions of institutions. Particularly at the theoretical level, research on institutions has emphasized continuity and evolutionary change rather than institutional creation. In economics, institutions such as property rights and contracts, and such regimes as legal systems and government policies, are understood to evolve over time to lower transaction costs, offset problems of incomplete information, and encourage greater efficiency in the functioning of markets.[15] In political science, researchers generally understand institutions as enduring and slowly evolving constraints and structures that channel and influence political activities and determine the outcome of political conflict and policy choices. For example, a number of scholars have been intrigued by the ways in which electoral rules can shape the structure of party politics and the stability and instability of electoral and governing coalitions.[16] In this literature, the choices of electoral institutions are generally assumed to be a given, and the task for analysts is to assess how they have led to enduring patterns of political competition and policy making. Although the transition and post-transition literature is sometimes very relevant to the question of how new institutions are selected, there are precious few explicit efforts to understand how and when institutional creation occurs instead of the more common process of institutional evolution.

To respond adequately to questions about the motivations of political actors, the selection of new institutions, and their consequences, empirical work can seek to uncover the dynamics of a process of change: How and when did issues of institutional reform emerge? Who were the principal actors in the reform initiatives? What caused these actors to champion or oppose change? How did they attempt to exert influence over the choices to be made? How were reform proposals adopted and legitimized? How did political actors respond in the presence of new rules of the game? These are the questions that underlie the case studies in the following chapters.

All three of the countries I chose for analysis have undertaken reform.

Some might argue that it would be more appropriate to compare reformers and non-reformers in order to explore the conditions that facilitate and constrain change. The study of reform initiatives, however, raises some difficulties with this methodological choice. Reform happens sporadically in a political system. To study reform is, in fact, to study a moving target. Whether a country is a reformer or a non-reformer can be altered by political events at any moment, in that today's non-reformer often becomes tomorrow's case about extraordinary change. Choosing cases along a reform-non-reform dimension, therefore, is problematic, as it assumes a stable equilibrium that does not exist.

Even accepting that it is both plausible and useful to select cases that share a reformist outcome, what factors led to the choice of Venezuela, Bolivia, and Argentina? In part, I thought that the kinds of reforms adopted in these countries were interesting in and of themselves. Moreover, it seemed to me that they also represented a range of types of political decentralization occurring in other countries of the region. More tellingly, these countries shared some important institutional similarities. Each had a historical trajectory toward centralization of power, a tradition of executive dominance in politics, and principal political parties that identified themselves with nationalist causes but that were held together by patronage and clientelism. There are, of course, many differences among the three countries in their levels of economic and political development. These differences are also important; in fact, looking across them, I hoped to be able to identify some common dynamics in the process of change that held in spite of the differences. If such similarities did emerge, they might suggest wider patterns of reform than those represented by three cases.

In fact, important commonalities in the dynamics of political reform did emerge from reconstructing the process on the basis of the written record and interviews with central figures in the reforms. First, in all three countries, the introduction of political change was not preceded by extensive public debate or controversy about its merits. Indeed, there was considerable ambiguity about who would be winners and losers in the new structures of power. Citizens, interest groups, and political parties were generally unprepared for the ways in which these new institutions altered the incentives and dynamics of public action and electoral competition. Moreover, the manner in which the reforms were introduced emphasized that they were "chosen" by political actors rather than "pushed" on decision makers by societal interests or international pressures.[17] The case studies in chapters 3–8 reveal the extent to which political leaders were concerned about the sustainability of the unusually fragile or newly introduced democratic political systems. In the perspectives of such reformers, these systems were facing serious crises of legitimacy.

- Venezuela's modern democracy, born of resistance to dictatorship in the 1930s and 1940s and consolidated in a highly celebrated political pact in 1958, was threatened by the oligarchic control that aged party leaders exercised over the political system and policy making. Abstentionism in national elections had reached unprecedented levels in the 1980s. In an unusual display of spontaneous violence, the citizens of the capital city, Caracas, had taken to the streets on February 27, 1989, in an expression of extreme dissatisfaction with economic and political conditions in the country. Riots left three hundred people dead, two thousand wounded, and $175 million worth of damage to the economy of the city.[18] National political leaders were shocked by the dimensions of the violence and deeply concerned about the continued viability of democratic government in the country.

- Democratic government had returned to Bolivia in 1982, after decades of strife and military rule and in the immediate aftermath of numerous coups, counter coups, and aborted elections between 1978 and 1982. The structure of the major political parties was boss-driven and centralized. Among the stronger institutions in the country was a highly mobilized union sector whose traditions encouraged confrontation with government. A drastic program of economic adjustment and restructuring brought heightened social protest in its wake. Simultaneously, the country's ethnic populations mobilized to demand political recognition of their cultural identities. Thus, the changes that restructured national-local relationships in 1994 were introduced by a democratic government facing considerable political vulnerability and risk.

- Argentina returned to democratic rule in 1983, after seven years of harsh military rule. The military had stepped into political power in 1976 to confront a scene of political violence and instability created by leftist guerrilla groups and extensive mobilization among the country's militant labor unions and student groups. Harsh repression, including the torture, disappearance, and murder of as many as thirty thousand people, followed in the wake of the coup. In 1983, the military could only attempt to negotiate a return to the barracks after not only failing to manage the economy but also suffering a humiliating defeat to Great Britain in a war over the Malvinas (Falkland Islands). President Raúl Alfonsín was elected with a clear mandate to govern and dedicated his administration to the consolidation of democracy in the country. Despite overwhelming support for democratic institutions by citizens of Argentina, this task was made more difficult by deep tensions related to the culpability of the military for its actions during the "dirty war," by deep economic crisis and instability, and by the revival of bitter political rivalries between the two main political parties.

Second, in each of the three cases, politicians had a range of options they could have pursued to respond to the institutional crises they faced. In fact, the solutions the reformers chose had the imprimatur of influential "design teams." They were attractive reform options largely because they offered a readily available response at a critical moment when larger issues of political sustainability loomed in importance for political leaders. Thus, the recommendations of presidentially appointed design teams figure significantly in explaining why particular institutional innovations were chosen.

- In Venezuela, the initial idea for state and local elections was worked out within a national commission composed of modernizing technocrats and representatives of the most important groups in the country—the church, the private sector, unions, and the parties—but with little fanfare and no significant political demands from organized groups or citizens more generally. Then, Carlos Andrés Pérez adopted the direct election of governors and mayors as a campaign promise in 1988 and joined in a challenge to other presidential contenders to sign an agreement that, if elected, they would pursue the same reform. This campaign promise, along with other actions, helped drive a wedge between Pérez and the majority faction of his party, which favored "politics-as-usual" to the redistribution of power that its candidate proposed.
- The promise of Popular Participation in Bolivia emerged as part of a campaign platform that favored decentralization and was worked out between 1991 and 1993 within a think tank created by presidential candidate Gonzalo Sánchez de Lozada. After winning the election, the president constituted a working group composed of lawyers

and technocrats to devise a law that would put municipalization into effect. This group worked after hours, often in conjunction with the new president, to draft a law that would subsequently be introduced into the national legislature and passed with only cursory discussion because of the support of the president's coalition in congress. While the reform team consulted about the contents of the law with some organized groups in the country during their three months of activity, discussions focused on technical details and the "workability" of the reform, not on whether the reform should or should not be carried out. This had already been decided by the president and was one of the major priorities of his term of office.

- The political autonomy of Buenos Aires was the result of a political pact between two central figures of modern Argentine history, Raúl Alfonsín, the president elected when democracy was restored in the country, and Carlos Menem, who as president had empowered an exceptional team led by Domingo Cavallo to bring economic stability and growth to the country. The pact was then the basis for the constitutional changes agreed to in 1994. Behind the pact, however, was nearly a decade of discussions among a group of public intellectuals and politicians. Initially called together to serve on a presidential advisory council, they continued to discuss ways in which the constitution should be altered and were active participants in the negotiations that led to the changes. While there was broad public agreement that many of the constitutional changes would be good for the country, they cannot be linked to specific proposals pressed upon the government or the political parties by reformist groups in society.

Finally, the institutional reforms in Venezuela, Bolivia, and Argentina introduced major changes in the way politics got done in those countries. In each case, the consequence of institutional change was the reemergence of conflict about power and resource allocation, played out in the context of new rules of the game. These new institutions, however, provided opportunities for new voices to emerge and for new strategies of political contestation to be introduced. They offered the potential for greater accountability and responsiveness from government at the same time that they also created opportunities for the creation of new political machines and the survival of clientelism. New institutions did not, in any of the cases, put conflict over the distribution of power to rest.

- In Venezuela, the capacity of the ruling Acción Democrática (AD) Party or its traditional challenger, COPEI, to capture a significant number of state governorships or local mayoralities was extremely unclear, given the highly centralized organization and highly constrained internal democracy in both parties. For these parties, winning local elections meant having to be concerned, for the first time in their histories, with the political "attractiveness" of candidates for office at local and regional levels. Moreover, the reforms opened up the possibility that popularly elected governors and mayors—particularly of economically important states and large cities—could use their periods in office to launch themselves on national-level political careers. Moreover, the emergence of new political parties around locally popular candidates could not be discounted.

- In Bolivia, municipalization opened up opportunities for new political careers and new political alliances. The slow response of national leaders of the main political parties to grasp the significance of the new rules of the game increased the degree of unpredictability. Indeed, the vacuum created by new rules and new sources of political power, and ambiguity about their meaning, allowed some communities to acquire unprecedented bargaining power with political parties that had long run roughshod over localities in their preference for corporatist structures of political mediation and control. The local elections of 1995 featured a number of local political alliances, often involving very strange bedfellows from the perspective of national politics. Moreover, great uncertainty surrounded the impact of reform because of the remoteness and low level of education found in a large number of the country's municipalities. The risk of ensuring that municipal authorities would become effective managers of development resources was immense in a country in which 47 percent of the population was rural and some 40 percent of those who lived in rural areas spoke only an indigenous language.[19]

- If political autonomy for Buenos Aires allowed for presidential re-election in Argentina, it also opened up an arena for major challenges to presidential leadership. The mayor of the largest city would necessarily be a national political figure, and one who had the potential, through access to the national media concentrated in the capital city, to represent opposition parties. Moreover, because of the introduction of first- and second-round elections, which would increase the importance of forming electoral coalitions, the mayor would be in a position to advance or hinder the chances of presidential and congressional aspirants. By providing an important outlet for dissent and the potential for a new platform for national politics, the political independence of Buenos Aires opened a Pandora's box of political consequences only partly understood by the actors who negotiated for it. Institutional crisis continued to be a theme in Argentine democracy.

The common dynamics that emerged in the case studies—changes that were (a) led by chief executives concerned about system legitimacy, (b) significantly influenced by the ideas of change teams closely linked to the executive branch of government, and (c) introducing new political incentives and political actors—are relevant for the hypotheses introduced in chapter 2. There, I outline alternative hypotheses to respond to the questions posed about motivations, choice, and consequences. These hypotheses are derived from two major explanatory traditions in political science, one that draws on economics for insights and one that draws on sociology. The two traditions provide strikingly different ways of explaining the same events.

In chapters 3–8, I present case studies to assess the usefulness of the hypotheses. For each case, I devote one chapter to exploring the related questions of the decision to cede power and the reasons behind the particular choices made. In a second chapter I deal with the political consequences of new institutions. Each account of reform begins with an analysis of the principal political institutions in the country in the pre-reform period and then moves on to consider the process of reform and its aftermath. The discussion of the pre-reform institutional context is important to highlight the significant characteristics and path dependencies that the reforms altered. They signal the degree of contextual change that needs to be explained in each case. In the final chapter, I draw comparative lessons from the cases and the light they shed on the hypotheses.

The findings suggest that several hypotheses, drawn from distinct traditions of political inquiry, are best able to provide convincing responses to the questions posed in this book. In terms of the first question, historically embedded conflicts over the definition of the nation and the state, the traditional ways in which political issues are contested, concerns about system legitimacy, and the ways in which political elites frame issues are important factors that lie behind efforts to alter the rules of the game. The case studies thus indicate that the motivations for institutional invention must be understood from theoretical perspectives that stretch beyond the immediate concerns of electoral politics and political support building. Approaches derived from microeconomics do not provide theoretical tools for doing this. Moreover, neither economic nor sociological approaches provide sufficient insight into the role of political leadership in introducing change. The cases are clear in indicating the extent to which leaders were critically important actors. At a theoretical level, however, political leadership remains a black box.

In explaining the content of the choices, the "new institutionalist" thinking in political economy derived from economics is useful; sociological approaches to political economy tend to ignore the extent to which self-conscious problem-solving surrounds efforts to introduce new institutions. The cases indicate the extent to which deliberate efforts at institutional engineering are important ways in which new rules of the game are identified. Once identified through the work of design teams, they were taken up by political leaders as responses to the specific problems they confronted. The responses to the first two questions thus combine to suggest that statecraft clearly makes a difference in the institutional life of countries.

In terms of the third question, both traditions of political explanations prove partly useful. The consequences of institutional invention reintroduced more familiar kinds of short-term electoral and support-building rationality that are found in economic approaches to politics. Politicians and parties were newly constrained by rules of the game that influenced their strategic calculations. Nevertheless, conflict also emerged around efforts to undo or further alter the new institutional context, as those who draw on sociological theory would predict. The rules of the game are new, but the conflicts of the past were not buried with the old institutional order, nor was the legitimacy of the new order safe from controversy. Despite continued conflict over the scope of change, however, democratic openings were secured in each country. This assessment of institutional invention therefore provides some hope that the future of Latin America's democracies may be brighter than their past.

# Explaining the Unexpected

The institutional innovations introduced in Venezuela, Bolivia, and Argentina between 1989 and 1994 significantly redistributed political power in those countries These changes were democratizing: they increased opportunities for citizens to participate in political decision making, and they were deliberately chosen by political leaders whose power would be constricted as a consequence of their actions. Innovations of this nature are not the stuff of normal politics, when relatively stable institutions form the context within which political decisions get made and when politicians are expected to behave in fairly predictable ways.

This chapter takes up three questions related to the origin and consequences of significant institutional innovation. Each of the questions—*Why would rational politicians choose to give up power? What accounts for the selection of some institutions rather than others? How does the introduction of new institutions alter the nature of political interactions?*—raises important theoretical issues. In particular, the study of politics, the explanation of institutions, and the relationship between politics and institutions are issues of contention between social scientists who draw insights from economic theory and those who draw primarily on sociological theory.[1] How useful are economic and sociological perspectives on politics in accounting for events in Venezuela, Bolivia, and Argentina? In the following pages, I consider how each would respond to the central questions posed for the case studies and the hypotheses each would propose to account for experiences of democratizing reform.

Political analysts who have looked to economics for inspiration have been motivated to develop a general theory of politics that is deductive, powerful, and rigorous. They draw on a tradition that stretches back to Adam Smith and that has been applied to studies of development in the work of Robert Bates, Dani Rodrik, Alberto Alesina, Barbara Geddes, Anne Krueger, and many others. From this perspective, rational choice and new institutionalist approaches provide one avenue for responding to the three questions.[2] Rational choice theory poses interesting assertions about the motivations of politicians; new institutionalist approaches provide explanations for institutional change by drawing on economic concepts of transaction costs and principal-agent dilemmas. These perspectives, rooted in the theory and tools of microeconomics, provide a basis for making predictions about how the incentives created by institutions structure the rational behavior of political actors and how behavior is likely to be changed through the introduction of new institutions. Because of a concern to develop a general theory of politics, neoclassical approaches seek explanations and predictions that hold across a wide range of empirical cases. Their central concern, therefore, is to explain similarities rather than differences among cases.

Those who draw on sociology to explain politics counter economic approaches by insisting that political behavior is always deeply rooted in context and specificity and that theory must be able to evoke, explore, and explain this complexity and specificity if it is to be useful.[3] Although the tradition traces its roots to Karl Marx and Max Weber and other "grand" theorists, those scholars who currently pursue research through this perspective generally seek to generate middle-range rather than grand theory and deep rather than broad knowledge. A variety of theoretical orientations fit comfortably within this tradition, but they are drawn together by an appreciation of the role of structures of power and conflict in political behavior. In the cases of audacious reform of interest here, scholars in this tradition would reject *ex ante* assumptions about motivations as inappropriate and uninteresting; they would explore questions of institutional choice by investigating the conflicts surrounding such choices; and they would be deeply interested in exploring how new institutions unleash conflicts over the distribution of power in a society. They would further insist that political institutions—party and electoral systems, the structure of interest representation, formal allocations of power within government—are central to explaining why outcomes of conflict differ across countries and why the study of political history is primarily a study of how similar issues in collective life work out differently in distinct contexts. Thus, political science rooted in economics and comparative political institutionalism rooted in sociology provide strikingly dissimilar ways to explain politics. In this book, I am interested in exploring the utility of hypotheses derived from each perspective in responding to the three issues under consideration here.

## The Motivations of Politicians

Why would politicians choose to give up power? It makes sense, in posing this question, to assume that the politicians in the three cases were purposive and rational in the sense that they took deliberate actions in order to achieve particular goals; we should assume that they did not act randomly or unthinkingly. At the same time, it is important to inquire into the motivations that surrounded politicians' actions when they set new institutional dynamics in place. They were not acting as other politicians had acted before them nor, as we will see, were they always acting in accord with their own past behavior. Even more important, they were acting historically, in the sense that their actions altered the institutional structures within which future political decisions would be made and future politicians would act. How well do major approaches to politics allow us to understand why prominent political actors would make such decisions?

Rational choice approaches to the study of politics deal directly with the issue of the motivations of politicians. Extrapolating from basic assumptions about the behavior of economic actors, they assert that political actors, like *homo economicus,* act to maximize their utility, generally assumed to reflect their self-interest.[4] Preferences are taken as given and, in theory at least, must be asserted *ex ante.* In practice, rational choice approaches generally posit a set of reasonable first-order preferences for the subjects of their research. Thus, for example, in seeking to explain the behavior of politicians, it is usually asserted that politicians will naturally prefer more power to less power, survival in office to defeat, reelection to loss, or influence to irrelevance.[5] Voters will naturally prefer politicians who provide benefits that improve their individual welfare to those who do not. Bureaucrats will naturally prefer higher budgets to lower ones, more discretion to less, more opportunities to promote their own welfare to fewer, or career promotion to demotion. These individuals are distinct from economic actors only in that they are conceptualized as interacting in a *political* market in which competition is about power to provide or receive benefits from public policy, public investments, and resources controlled by government.

Indeed, based on everyday perceptions that most of us have about politics, this seems a reasonable way to explain or predict the motivations behind the choices that politicians, voters, bureaucrats, and other political actors make, and they stand up to a considerable amount of empirical testing. Thus, it is not particularly surprising to learn that politicians design or support public policies to increase their opportunities for winning elections or that they encourage or tolerate inefficient organizations in government if these organizations contribute to their ability to control resources that are in turn used to "buy" electoral support. Looking at the world through the maximizing eyes of the self-interested politician, these are highly rational behaviors. Armed with the basic assumption of rationality and some reasonable assertions about preferences, rational choice approaches make predictions about political behavior in terms of the choices made during elections, in the design of public policies, and in the implementation of these policies.

While this approach is rooted in assumptions about the motivations of generic individuals, it is not blind to the context in which political behavior occurs. Context, in terms of the particular constraints imposed by political institutions or incentive systems, shape the opportunities available to political actors to pursue their preferences. In this way, politicians become strategic actors who accumulate information about the options available to them and select actions that are most likely to allow them to maximize power, votes, influence, or political survival.[6] From the perspective of research, given assumptions about the preferences of political actors, knowledge of the context in which they operate is important to the capacity to explain and predict the choices they make. Preferences are taken as given; actions reveal strategic choices about how to achieve those preferences within given institutional contexts.[7]

The interests of voters or constituencies in democratic systems are accorded considerable importance in rational choice political economy because they constrain the choices available to politicians and compel them to make decisions that are characteristically geared toward electoral gains. Moreover, because of periodic elections, politicians must discount the future heavily.[8] Thus, it is reasonable for politicians to sacrifice choices that will pay off in the longer term to those that have shorter-term positive advantages for them. The political marketplace makes such choices highly rational. In some cases, so powerful is the need of politicians to trade policy benefits for votes that policy making can be captured by particular interests extorting preferential treatment in return for supporting politicians through votes or resources for electoral campaigns.[9]

Individuals are the unit of analysis in rational choice approaches to the explanation of political behavior. But because, empirically, much political activity involves the behavior of groups, Mancur Olson and others have explained how and when self-interested individuals will act collectively to achieve their goals.[10] They will do so when they can be assured that the energy exerted by acting as a group will pay off efficiently in terms of individual benefits received. For reasons having to do with the potential for free-riders to benefit from group action without expending the energy necessary to cooperate, groups tend to coalesce around very specific interests that, if achieved, will not provide benefits to those outside the group. Politically, this translates into the tendency for exchanges between politicians and a multitude of interest groups, each of which is pursuing a narrowly focused and usually immediate benefit. The task for the politician, then, becomes that of parceling out public policy or public resources to a large number of competing groups, each of which has some capacity to punish the provider. The larger purposes of government, such as "the national welfare," are difficult to achieve, given the exchange relationships between politicians and interests.

The rational choice approach to understanding politics offers one set of responses to questions about the motivations behind institutional creations in Venezuela, Bolivia, and Argentina. If we assume that the politicians who made choices to create new institutions were acting both rationally and strategically, then we must assume that they were acting on the basis of some set of preferences that can be asserted without reference to empirical observation. One possibility, of course, is to assert that politicians prefer less power to more power, a statement that is fully compatible with the approach. They might prefer honorable mention in history books or pursuit of democratic values or the act of creation itself to power or reelection or survival in office. At the same time, however, asserting such preferences as a generalizable basis for political action cannot be, by any reasonable standard, either intellectually satisfying or likely to be verified across a range of cases or observations.

More plausibly, given the importance of maximizing favorable electoral outcomes in rational choice theory and the importance of context in explaining strategic actions, it could be hypothesized that politicians would cede some of their power in order to achieve more immediate advantage over opponents or achieve other immediate goals they considered more important, or that they would respond to the overwhelming pressure of those who supported power-sharing in exchange for electoral support. Rationally, of course, these situations might encourage politicians to find strategic alternatives to creating new institutions. The creation of new institutions would commit them to a power-sharing solution far into the future, while more short-term pacts or agreements might achieve the immediate electoral needs without compromising incumbents through time. Nevertheless, the hypothesis that politicians trade long-term institutional change for immediate electoral advantage should be retained as a plausible explanation to be tested in the case studies.

Another plausible hypothesis asserts the opposite: politicians might prefer less immediate power to more power in the future. In studies exploring the creation of independent central banks or independent boards of tax agencies or monetary boards, for example, the invention of new institutions has been explained by the desire of politicians to signal commitment to economic policy reform or to lock in the policy choices they have put in place against the capacity of future incumbents to alter them.[11] In the first case, that of signaling commitment, the message is aimed at domestic and international economic agents to convince them that the policy choices made will remain stable, unaffected by the immediate electoral needs of (implicitly, other) politicians.[12] In the second case, the target is future politicians who might seek to undo a set of policy reforms and thus undermine the preferences of current incumbents.[13] The purpose of preferring these choices over that of maximizing power in the present is to reduce uncertainty about future choices, particularly those that might be made by other politicians.

This hypothesis, focusing on preferences for future power, has provided important insights into choices about institutions that constrain politicians' influence over economic policy and should be proposed as a potential explanation for the creation of new political institutions. Nevertheless, explanations that rely on signaling or locking-in preferences for the future appear to fit the creation of economic-policy institutions better than the creation of more democratic political institutions. In the former case, new institutions generally reduce the risk of change by constricting participation and rights to be involved in decision making and increasing the extent to which policy making is a technical rather than a political process. In the latter case, by creating rules to enhance participation, reforms increase ambiguity and risk about decision making in the future. They generally expand the number of people who are making decisions about the distribution of political power, the number of political offices available, and the possibility that distinct parties or interests can capture or claim these positions. Thus, they increase the competition over future possibilities to maintain power or influence policy. Similarly, democratizing changes do not lock in a set of policy preferences but rather increase the potential for widely varying policy choices and outcomes. When new political institutions are democratizing, they increase the uncertainty of their creators and increase the number of competitors for power in the future.

In a larger sense, however, a rational choice response to the question of why politicians would cede power poses limitations for this inquiry because it requires that motivations be posited *ex ante*. A general theory of politics (the objective of the rational choice approach) is most appropriate in stable institutional contexts in which the objective is to explain the behavior of the generic politician, voter, bureaucrat, or interest-group member. But the particular cases explored in this book are about choices that caused important disjunctures in how politics was done. A rational choice approach, then, may fail to be predictive of precisely the kinds of choices that make a difference in political life. Although it takes individuals as the unit of analysis, the approach can be faulted for not taking individuals seriously enough, in the sense that individuals can be agents of history and not simply captives of the "games" that are in play. Indeed, if we are dealing with actions that shape, in fundamental ways, the future politics of a country, then issues of motivation must be the objects of research.

Comparative institutionalism, which draws on sociology for analytic tools and on history for empirical insights, provides an alternative approach for inquiring into the motivations of politicians.[14] Researchers who follow this tradition view political actors as embedded within historical contexts that shape their behavior; they take groups, classes, interests, or other collectivities as primary units of analysis but insist that their behavior always be understood within institutional settings.[15] These scholars place conflict at the center of political analysis in ways that differ significantly from an economic perspective. In rational choice theory, conflict exists when two or more individuals simultaneously seek preferences that cannot be achieved through joint action. Comparative institutionalists, in contrast, view conflict as an ongoing process through which groups compete for predominance in particular economic, social, and policy arenas and in which prior conflicts shape the nature of current conflicts and determine the issues that are contested. Thus, "institutional factors can shape both the objectives of political actors and the distribution of power among them in a given polity."[16] Embeddedness is a key concept that makes it possible to analyze particular conflicts as ones that are historically rooted and inherently evolving.[17]

Comparative institutionalists would agree with rational choice enthusiasts that there are regularities in political behavior and policy choice that can be observed. They part company with rational choice, however, because of their insistence that these regularities are the result of complex institutions that shape the motivations, orientations, and options available to political actors, who are understood primarily as groups, classes, interests, or collectivities. To understand them as generic individuals pursuing generic preferences is to miss the role of institutions and history more generally in shaping the preferences and strategies of collective actors. Thus, institutions are much more than contexts that shape rational strategic action. Political actions are embedded in historically evolved institutions that are, in turn, the site of ongoing struggles to define public policy and distributions of economic and political power. This perspective allows comparative institutionalists to explain how similar policy problems—the provision of health care in modern industrial countries, for example—have generated distinct solutions; they are results of the way institutional contexts have shaped how groups and interests contest for influence over policy, that is, how they have learned to engage in conflict.[18]

Comparative institutionalists tend to be most interested in explaining the particular ways in which particular institutions shape particular outcomes. Research focused on this goal is, by necessity, deeply concerned with the historical record, with the knowledge of group activities, and with the interaction of collectivities that coalesce and conflict around policy and other choices. As a result, comparative institutionalists tend to produce research that is rich in depth and complexity rather than in breadth and parsimony. Their work emphasizes the importance of institutions and the conflicts among interests as factors that shape history. In doing so, they assert that institutions mediate political conflict but are, at the same time, shaped by the outcome of political conflicts.

Comparative institutionalist analyses are, in general, more concerned with the factors that shape the actions of collectivities than they are with explaining the logic of individual choice. Nevertheless, researchers in this tradition have also been concerned with "statecraft," the ways in which individual political actors or political entrepreneurs maneuver within institutional contexts to build coalitions, engineer consensus, negotiate, and bargain to generate new policies, new legislation, and, presumably, new institutions. Some individuals are motivated to bring about change while others resist it. Motivations can draw on ideas, collective identities, group interests, and values as well as on self-interest, and some are more skilled in the use of political resources, as well as having greater or lesser access to these resources, than others. Thus, while collectivities and conflict among them are the principal engines of particular histories, the characteristics of individuals in leadership roles can be a focus of analysis in this approach. Their ideas, values, and objectives are subject to empirical research and do not need to be taken as given.[19]

In practice, a comparative institutionalist approach to understanding the choices made in Venezuela, Bolivia, and Argentina would be less interested in the decision makers than it would be in describing and analyzing political struggles taking place within complex institutional spaces over the allocation of political power. Specific political actors—for example, presidents—would tend to be viewed as leaders of movements, parties, or interests that were actively engaged in using their institutional positions and resources to promote change; their resources and tactics would be contrasted with those who were actively engaged in resisting it. This approach would be concerned with how these leaders and collectivities were advantaged or disadvantaged by the institutional setting of politics and the skills they brought to tasks of forming coalitions, managing conflict, negotiating, bargaining, and leading. Struggles over the distribution of political power would be distinct in each case because of the differences among countries in terms of how their political, social, and economic institutions mediate conflict and in the ability of leaders to act effectively to make change occur. Moreover, the contingencies of a particular historical context would be called upon to explain why change occurred or did not occur at a particular time. Thus, one hypothesis derived from this approach would focus on the conflict of group interests and how this is reflected in the choices of leaders: politicians reflect the pressure for change exerted by historically situated groups that seek to enhance their access to power through institutional change. Another hypothesis derived from the same approach would focus on the capacity of existing institutions to resolve conflict in a society. In cases in which existing institutions do not provide satisfactory rules to mediate conflict, groups and their leaders may propose new rules; consensus and conflict will develop around the creation of new rules that are more able to deal with societal conflict. Institutional crisis can therefore generate pressure for change.

By taking history and context seriously, a sociological approach to explaining politics provides rich explanations about why things worked out the way they did and about why outcomes of political conflict differ from country to country. It is an approach that allows for empirical enquiry into the motivations of political actors. At the same time, however, it tends to produce rich

---

**Why Would Rational Politicians Choose to Give Up Power?**

*Hypotheses about the motivations of politicians:*

*Rational Choice*
• Politicians choose to cede power in order to achieve short-term electoral advantage.
• Politicians choose to cede power in order to maximize their power in the future.

*Comparative Institutionalism*
• In choosing to cede power, politicians reflect the pressures for change exerted by historically situated groups that seek to enhance their access to power through institutional change.
• In choosing to cede power, politicians and the social groups they represent seek solutions to deep or sustained institutional crises that reveal the incapacity of the political system to mediate political and economic crisis.

BOX 1

---

descriptions and "thick" or detailed analysis of historically rooted changes in political life in ways that make general theory elusive and are more likely to explain why outcomes are different than why they are similar.

Two distinct approaches to explaining political behavior suggest four alternative hypotheses for why politicians would choose to give up power (see Box 1). The first two hypotheses differ from the second two in terms of their underlying assumptions about how preferences are derived (maximizing utility vs. historically created), the foundation of social action (individuals vs. groups), the origins of conflict (individual preferences vs. historically evolved group interests), and the influence of institutions on actions (strategic context vs. embedded experience). The case studies provide an opportunity to assess these hypotheses.

## The Creation of Institutions

It is important to explain something about the content of the choices that were made in Venezuela, Bolivia, and Argentina. Why did politicians select the particular mechanisms they did for sharing power? Again, political economy traditions that draw from economics and sociology provide distinct answers to this question, although both are more able to explain how institutions evolve than how they periodically appear and disappear. In the case of economic approaches to politics, institutions emerge as responses to particular kinds of problems—transaction costs and principal-agent asymmetries. In the case of comparative institutionalism, institutions evolve from conflicts over the allocation of resources in society, and these institutions explain why patterns of power and wealth endure through time as characteristics of particular societies.

In economics-based approaches to politics, the focus on individual self-interest and action in rational choice theory has been criticized for its failure to explain institutions. The theory deals with institutions only as a strategic arena for individual choice; it has not generated an understanding of how institutional contexts emerge and change.[20] Led by Douglass North and others, a "new institutionalist" perspective seeks to address this shortcoming.[21]

One variant of the new institutionalism takes as a founding insight the idea that all exchanges involve transaction costs.[22] North and his colleagues have been centrally concerned with explaining economic development and the evolution of institutions that raise or lower transaction costs. In economics, transaction costs, such as acquiring information or enforcing rules, decrease the efficiency of exchange relationships; a critical insight in North's approach is that institutions are not simply a result of efforts to lower the transaction costs of market exchanges but also a function of political and social interests and differences in the allocation of power in a society. Thus, he argues that institutions "are not necessarily or even usually created to be socially efficient; rather they, or at least the formal rules, are created to serve the interests of those with the bargaining power to devise the rules. In a zero-transaction-cost world, bargaining strength does not affect the efficiency of outcomes, but in a world of positive transaction costs it does."[23] Based on the assumption of microeconomic rationality, institutional change is promoted when actors with power perceive that their interests can be better achieved through alternative sets of rules.[24]

Extrapolating from this explanation of institutions that affect economic interactions, transaction costs are present in political exchanges such as those between politicians and voters or politicians and interest groups. Politicians often do not have full information on the activities and interests of important constituencies nor the time or ability to acquire such information. They may also face conflicting demands from different interest constituencies. Voters and particular constituencies may not have full information on the behavior of the public officials they want to respond to their concerns. Nor do they necessarily know how many votes or how much campaign money is efficient for getting what they want from the politicians. Legislators do not necessarily have information on the preferences of other legislators. The difficulty of acquiring such information increases the risks of making choices for politicians, voters, campaign contributors, and others. To lower these transaction costs, implicit or explicit rules of the game emerge that allow politicians and voters to act on the basis of incomplete information without undue risk or without having to invest heavily in collecting information.

In this way, institutions such as electoral systems, political parties, and rules or procedures in legislatures emerge over time. At the same time, however, these rules structure the interactions of citizens, politicians, and would-be politicians by providing incentives and sanctions to behave in certain ways and by distributing bargaining power differentially. The behavior of political actors becomes predictable over time as it conforms to these incentives, sanctions, and power relationships. Moreover, these rules and procedures structure the way other transaction costs problems are treated. When such problems emerge and, over time, generate pressures for changes or greater stability in how they are dealt with, legislation is introduced, debated, and voted upon according to the rules that have evolved over time for dealing with legislation, debates, and votes. Over time, institutions accommodate to important changes in the nature of transactions, such as those caused by technological innovation. Over time also, history demonstrates certain "path dependencies" that result from the way power relationships lock in certain distributional biases as institutions evolve along fairly predictable lines in accommodating to changes in technology, the availability of information, and the influence of other institutions (which are also evolving).[25] "Discontinuous change" occurs much less frequently and is generally a result of revolution or conquest.

A second new institutionalist approach also uses the tools of microeconomics to explain the creation of new institutions. An "institutional design" perspective is explicitly theoretical and non-empirical in that it posits characteristic problems faced within organizations or institutions, typically of a principal-agent nature, and seeks to develop rules and organizational principles that allow for the efficient solution of these problems.[26] Principal-agent problems abound in political life—in the relationship between the voter and the representative, the politician and the bureaucrat, the bureaucratic superior and subordinate, the policy maker and the implementer. The essential problem is that the principal (in these cases, the voter, the politician, the bureaucratic superior, and the policy maker) does not have sufficient information or control over the actions of the agent (the representative, the bureaucrat, the subordinate, and the implementer) to ensure that his or her commands are actually being carried out. This creates a moral hazard for the principals in that they cannot be certain about the motivations or actions of those entrusted with carrying out their promises or wishes.

The task for institutional design, then, is to find ways to structure this difficult relationship in ways that minimize the principal-agent problem. Characteristically, work in this field has focused attention on the incentive structures that surround the actions of agents; it is concerned with ensuring that agents have incentives that encourage them to be attentive to the wishes of the principals and efficient in responding to them. In solving principal-agent problems, the institutional designer asks: How can rules, procedures, and incentive structures be created that ensure that agents *commit* to the goals of the principal?[27] Often, the issue is posed in terms of the principal's desire to ensure future commitment to particular policy or institutional preferences.

Approaching the issue of institutional creation through an institutional design perspective is intriguing because it suggests that history and process are not important nor is path dependence a constraint. With this perspective, explaining the creation of new institutions at particular moments becomes that of demonstrating how political actors self-consciously design new rules of the game through a process of analysis, much as an engineer would analyze a particular problem relating to say, weight-bearing capacity, and then design a structure that solves the particular problem. Indeed, the "reengineering" approach to organizational change is based on similar assumptions; the reorganization of New Zealand's public sector in the 1990s, for example, was significantly influenced by such a design experience.[28] For our cases, this approach suggests that new institutions were created because a group of institutional designers identified a set of ongoing principal-agent problems that they wished to solve, self-consciously designed new ways to resolve them, and then put them into effect.

Of course, many would balk at such a direct and uncomplicated explanation of institutional choice. They would raise a set of questions about what drove the institutional designers to the table in the first place and what authorization they had to solve the problems they identified. They would argue that such a rational problem-solving perspective cannot explain away conflict over goals and the allocation of power. They might insist that, while rational problem-solving may contribute to political outcomes, it does not tell the whole story. Nevertheless, this institutional design perspective introduces the possibility of analytically informed problem solving on the part of those who create new institutions and is certainly an interesting alternative hypothesis to explore through the case studies.

What, then, of hypotheses derived from comparative political institutionalism? Comparative institutionalists generally argue that political actions are shaped by institutions, which are in turn shaped by the actions of political agents. In fact, however, like those who adopt an economic approach to politics, they tend to focus much more on how actions are shaped by institutions than they do on the transformative effect of action on institutions.[29] This reiterates quite realistically the dynamics of everyday politics, in which political actions take place in comfortable institutional settings, as suggested by the concept of embeddedness. New institutions are descendants of older institutions, altered to accommodate new power relationships or the consequences of conflicts over policy. Thus, comparative institutionalists have adopted the use of path dependence as a concept to explain continuity, just as new institutionalists in economic analysis have adopted the concept of embeddedness.[30]

Analytically, in exploring the question of why particular institutional solutions are chosen, comparative institutionalists would hypothesize that conflicts and differences in the power of collectivities would lead to an outcome in which new rules of the game are negotiated or imposed on society. New rules thus evolve out of past conflicts and past structures of power. Comparative institutionalists would seek insight into the relationship between context and choice: Under what conditions is it likely that new institutions will be created? Under what conditions will those who favor change be more likely to be successful than those who oppose it? Under what conditions is agency possible in political history? As a hypothesis to explain the choice of institutions, then, comparative institutionalism suggests that new institutions come into being as a result of historically embedded conflicts about the distribution of power and benefits in a society and can be understood as negotiated or imposed resultants of contestation among interests.

Thus, economic and sociological approaches to the study of politics suggest at least three hypotheses about the content of the choices made to create new institutions (see Box 2). They differ primarily in terms of the kind of problems that require institutional solutions (transaction costs, principal-agent dilemmas, or who has access to power) and the dynamics through which solutions are sought (bargaining, formal analysis, or conflict). While the new institutionalism that focuses on transaction costs and comparative institutionalism agree on the importance of path dependence, the institu-

**What Accounts for the Selection of Some Institutions Rather Than Others?**

*Hypotheses about the creation of institutions:*

*New Institutionalism—Transaction Costs*
• Institutions chosen are path dependent efforts to lower the transaction costs of doing politics.

*New Institutionalism—Institutional Design*
• Political actors self-consciously design new institutions to solve principal-agent problems through a process of "engineering" new structures of accountability and incentives.

*Comparative Institutionalism*
• The choice of institutions is a result of historically embedded conflict among social collectivities about the distribution of power in society and can be understood as negotiated or imposed outcomes of that contestation.

BOX 2

tional design approach suggests that the content of innovation is unconstrained by prior choices.

## The Consequences of New Institutions

New institutions in Venezuela, Bolivia, and Argentina introduced new rules and new incentives into national and local politics. These institutions may have altered long-existing power relationships, introduced new sources of conflict, resolved some long-standing problems, or altered the motivations of political actors in important ways. In each of the cases, then, the story of new institutions is only partly told if it explains no more than their creation. I am particularly interested in the extent to which new institutions affected the behavior of political parties, influenced the issues that emerged in electoral contests, and altered the dynamics of political careers. Again, alternative hypotheses to explain a variety of possible outcomes can be derived from distinct theoretical approaches to explaining politics.

To begin with theory derived from economics, a rational choice explanation of the consequences of introducing new institutions would focus on how a new set of constraints on the options available to politicians, bureaucrats, and citizens would lead to new strategies for achieving their preferences. Politicians, for example, would have to adjust their efforts to maximize power, survive in office, or win elections. While the approach may not provide particularly interesting insights about the motivations of politicians in changing the rules of the game in ways that increase their vulnerability to the actions of others, it does suggest that given institutional change, political actors will revert to activities that are rational in terms of their predictable preferences for more power rather than less, more electoral advantage rather than less, more career stability rather than less, and so forth. If voters at local levels have greater capacity to influence the outcome of electoral contests, for example, then politicians will expend more energy in attempting to attract their votes. This approach, then, presents a hypothesis that, given institutional change, political activity can be understood on the basis of normal expectations about individual preferences, the constraints faced by individuals in particular institutional contexts, and the strategies that they select rationally (given the information they possess about their options) to pursue their preferences.

An alternative way of understanding the consequences of institutional creation from the perspective of economic analysis can be derived from the transaction-costs concerns of the new institutionalism. If, as hypothesized, new institutions are created in response to transaction-costs problems, then it can be predicted that new institutions will, in fact, lower the costs of doing politics. The problematic nature of politics—that transaction costs accrue to individuals or interests rather than to something as abstract as the market—could be explored through research into whose transaction costs of doing politics are lowered and, even, whose might be increased by institutional change. An interesting follow-on hypothesis would be that even in cases in which institutional disjuncture occurs, path dependence would reassert itself as an explanation for the subsequent evolution of institutions.[31]

The institutional design literature offers a similarly interesting hypothesis for understanding the political consequences of institutional creation. If the institutions created in Venezuela, Bolivia, and Argentina were created with an eye toward how they could resolve principal-agent problems, then we should find evidence that they created more accountability in the political systems of these countries in the sense of ensuring a closer link between what principals want and what agents do. Considering the institutional inventions from this perspective would also encourage an assessment of the institutional designs themselves in the sense of making it possible to analyze how effectively the designers achieved their goals. Of the alternative hypotheses, a principal-agent explanation is the most static in the sense that it rests on three snapshots in time: one, of the principal-agent problems created by the old institutions; a second, of the rationally designed plans for the new institution; and a third, of the resulting effectiveness of the new institutions in resolving the problems identified in the first snapshot.

A comparative institutionalist assessing the consequences of the creation of new institutions would explore a more dynamic hypothesis about change. The approach, having explained how a new institution came into being as a result of conflict that played out within the constraints and opportunities provided by historically derived institutions and the interaction among them, would anticipate that the new institution would encourage the emergence of new conflicts, new claims for resources, new spaces for contestation, or efforts by various collectivities to undo the impact of the new institutions on their claims to power and influence. In distinction to the new equilibrium in the rational choice and institutional design explanations, a comparative institutionalist approach would hypothesize that change creates new sources of conflict or the potential to reassert old ones. It would also encourage research on new political actors—whether these are collectivities, their leaders, or those who benefited or lost from the redistribution of power and access to benefits—and new ways of organizing for political contestation. In the cases of Venezuela, Bolivia, and Argentina, for example, new institutions would be arenas in which political parties, interest- and community-based groups, and other political actors would reorganize, recombine, or reassert themselves to take advantage of new resources or reclaim lost ones; they would reconnect in conflict, coalition building, and bargaining over the distributional consequences of change, probably with reconfigured access to political, economic, and leadership resources.

Traditions of political analysis that draw on economics and sociology thus suggest at least four hypotheses about the consequences of institutional choice (see Box 3). They differ primarily in terms of the predicted stability of the new rules of the game (a new equilibrium vs. continued evolution) and the impact on political interaction (predictable choices, reduced costs, increased accountability, or renewed conflict).

## Hypotheses and Cases

In the following chapters, the analysis of democratizing reforms in Venezuela, Bolivia, and Argentina also provides a means of exploring the utility of alter-

**What Are the Political Consequences of the Creation of New Institutions?**

*Hypotheses about the impact of new institutions:*

*Rational Choice*
• Institutional change creates a new equilibrium in the strategic context of politics that consequently shapes rational political behavior by individual actors.

*New Institutionalism—Transaction Costs*
• New institutions lower the transaction costs of doing politics and introduce formal and informal rules that shape subsequent political interactions and institutional evolution along particular paths.

*New Institutionalism—Institutional Design*
• New institutions resolve the principal-agent problems by increasing the capacity of principals to influence or monitor the behavior of agents.

*Comparative Institutionalism*
• New institutions create altered contexts for the emergence or reemergence of conflict, political actors, claims for resources, or efforts by various collectivities to contest the distributional consequences of institutional change.

BOX 3

native hypotheses to explain motivations, institutional creation, and political consequences. But the cases of institutional innovation in these three countries are stories that also need to be told in their own right, because they are stories about political creativity. Moreover, they are about institutions that are widely advocated as producing public good in the sense of bringing greater public participation, enhanced democratic control of government, and more accountability of public officials into political systems. Thus, chapters 3–8 present these stories, each one organized in terms of the three questions posed in this chapter.

# Institutional Invention in Venezuela

## Legitimizing the System

A new political era in Venezuela began in 1989. On December 3 of that year, 4.15 million citizens went to the polls and elected governors for each of the twenty-two states making up the republic. It was the first time in Venezuelan history that they had done so. The first elections for 269 mayors were also held that day. Again, this was a historic first for Venezuelan citizens. Later that same month, the "Basic Law for Decentralization, Delineation, and Transfer of Public Functions" established the foundation for states to take responsibility for a wide variety of public services, including, among other functions, education, public health, civil defense, development investment, public housing, agriculture, and public works.[1] This law also specified an increase in the block grants that states and municipalities would receive from the national government and set in place the structure of state-level development committees and planning processes.[2]

Further innovation in the political system was introduced through yet another reform to institute open and unblocked lists of candidates for election to legislative positions. In practice, this meant that when they went to the polls, Venezuelans would be given a choice between voting for individuals listed by name or using the traditional method, by which they voted for a party-determined list of candidates represented only by a party name, color, and symbol on the ballot. In Venezuelan terms, this meant that the vote became personalized, in the sense that citizens would be able to identify their votes with particular individuals. In the 1989 elections for municipal council-lors, 24.1 percent were elected by name, the remainder by list.

These reforms are noncontroversial from the perspective of democratic institution building. They are also consistent with democratic principles of allowing for meaningful citizen participation and the capacity of voters to hold public officials accountable for their actions. But from the perspective of Venezuelan history and institutional development, the magnitude of the change they represent is hard to escape.

Venezuelan presidents had had the constitutional right to appoint state governors since 1864. Many of the country's twenty-six constitutions had been explicit in stating that the task of the governor was to represent national authority at the state level. The 1961 constitution, in effect at the time of the 1989 reforms, had given state governments only residual functions and de-nied states the ability to raise their own revenues.[3] During the democratic regime that was installed in 1958, presidents had appointed governors in con-sultation with the core leadership of their parties in Caracas. The positions were distributed as patronage to those who had worked long and hard for the party in power and who had demonstrated deep loyalty to the party leaders. In return, the appointees were expected to represent the central administra-tion's objectives at the state level and the party bosses' bidding in distributing patronage jobs and contracts. They were also expected to mobilize votes for the party's presidential candidates and lists in national elections. Providing opportunities for state-level leaders to generate local bases of support that could be independent of politicians in Caracas was a major step toward dis-mantling a system of centralized party control and clientelism that had grown more powerful as each decade of democratic government unfolded after 1958. Central policy direction, thousands of patronage jobs and contracts, and an entire incentive system for gaining and retaining office were the most obvious costs of change for political leaders in the center.

Moreover, in the traditional system, state governors had little to do other than perform political functions in the service of the highly centralized cli-entele system because the same system had, over the years, systematically assumed power over public works and service provision from the states. Al-though municipal governments had traditionally had some autonomous re-sponsibilities and functions, states had become empty shells in terms of the provision of public goods. During much of the country's history, "successive federal governments cynically exalted the importance of municipal autonomy simply in order to justify their assault on the rights of the states."[4] As one minister of the interior remarked, even after direct election was instituted but before the decentralization law was passed, "Once the governors were elected, they really had nothing to do because all the services were provided by the central government."[5] The new law for administrative decentralization reversed the historical trajectory of usurpation of local functions and reinforced the potential political autonomy of state governors by giving them control over development-related and social service activities.

The creation of the position of mayor was also significant in democratizing government in the country. Prior to the 1989 elections, municipal councils, which were directly elected using the blocked and closed party-list system, elected one of their members to serve as council president, fusing the executive and legislative powers of local government and ensuring that the president of the council was almost always a member of the party with the largest representation in the council. In the capital city, Caracas, the president appointed the mayor. Beginning in 1989, citizens had direct input into naming the person to be held responsible for the performance of local government. Like the governors, the mayors could also develop independent bases of political support and dispense local jobs and contracts with their own political ambitions in mind. Their terms of office were shortened, as were those of the governors, from five years to three, thus increasing the potential for democratic accountability and the development of campaigns around local rather than national issues that dominated when presidents were elected every five years.

The capstone of the reform initiatives was set by the change in the electoral law. As indicated, throughout the period since 1958, Venezuelans had gone to the polls to vote for president and to cast a ballot for the party of their choice for all other positions. After the votes were tallied, positions for state and national legislatures and municipal councils were distributed on the basis of proportional representation to specific individuals whose names were "hidden" on the ballots by the party banner. This system centralized enormous power in the hands of party leaders who controlled the lists and ranked the candidates according to the criteria of party loyalty and service.[6] Once elected, officials owed their positions to the party bosses who placed and ranked them on the list rather than to those who voted for them. Aspiring politicians courted the favor of party leaders for a position on the list rather than the voters at the local level.[7] Lists were controlled from the center, not only for candidates for national office but also for state- and, in some cases, local-level positions.

Because the reforms implemented in 1989 are so significant in terms of the changes they introduced, they require explanation. In this chapter, I explore the origins of these institutional inventions in terms of their relationship to the history of a dominant institution in Venezuelan politics—centralism—and how it functioned in terms of political parties and the presidency. The trajectory of that history was altered significantly in the 1980s, when a series of events caused political leaders to be seriously concerned about the ongoing legitimacy of the political system. These concerns led eventually to a direct challenge to the accumulated institutional history of the country. These events are important in explaining how reformist initiatives gained credibility and eventual acceptance by political leaders; they provide some insight into why rational politicians would decide to cede power. In addition, it is important to track the progress of the reform initiatives to explain why these particular changes were the ones chosen to solve the problems perceived by politicians in the country. This chapter traces the activities of a group of reform entrepreneurs and the way in which political decentralization became "the solution" to a set of concerns shared among the country's political class. Chapter 4 explores how the new institutions played out the challenge to central power in terms of the political consequences of the democratizing reforms.

## The Way Things Were: Centralism as a Way of Life

History presents a stark picture of the tradeoff between anarchy and centralization in Venezuela. Although it was one of the first regions of Spanish America to declare independence—on July 5, 1810—eleven years passed before the Spanish departed in defeat, and more than a century passed before the country established a legitimate national government. The years of the war for independence, 1810–21, were a period of bloodletting, intrigue, and internal disorder. The aftermath of independence was equally scarred by bloodletting, intrigue, and internal disorder. In fact, after the failure of an ambitious initiative by Simón Bolívar to create a union of Gran Colombia in the Andean region, a country of Venezuela could hardly be said to exist between 1830 and the early twentieth century.[8] It was, instead, a site for ongoing conflict among regionally based warlords, known as *caudillos*, who fought for local autonomy and, from time to time, national dominance.

When these regional caudillos managed to fight their way to temporary national power, they would assert loyalty to Conservative or Liberal Party ideals, but in fact, their rule was based on force, their actions were motivated by greed, and their claims to power were generally precarious.[9] Indeed, military force put an end to thirteen governments between 1830 and 1935, a fairly low success rate considering there were, during this same period, at least "thirty-two major attempts at revolution and 138 minor uprisings," according to one count.[10] Some governments endured over several consecutive years, and the first of the "national *caudillos*," Antonio Guzmán Blanco, managed to dominate the country between 1870 and 1888. He put in place the beginnings of a national infrastructure, a market system, national records, and taxation, but his death set off another period of chaos and regional warfare.[11] Political parties ceased to exist, and political life revolved around personalism and regionalism. Anarchy was thus the standard throughout most of the nineteenth century; life was precarious at best. The Federal War, fought between 1859 and 1863, for example, claimed forty thousand lives and left the country even more economically backward than it had been prior to the conflict.

So difficult was the task of national unification that the country had no national currency until 1879. It was not until after dictator Juan Vicente Gómez took power in 1908 that the country had a national army that was more than a coalition of regional armies that continued to owe primary allegiance to regional *caudillos*.[12] Until his death in 1935, Gómez worked to create a centralized and stable Venezuelan state by repressing all competing centers of power, proscribing political parties, and simultaneously developing a national state bureaucracy. His army was provisioned with modern weapons, instructed in modern military discipline, and well paid with the revenues from the petroleum that was increasingly exported during the 1920s.[13] Again, however, instability followed his demise, as dictators came to power through violence in 1936 and 1948 and even democrats achieved power through similar means in 1945 and again in 1958. Each of these regime changes occasioned a new constitution. Only in 1961 was a democratic constitution put in place that would endure for more than a few years.

For Venezuela, then, the work of developing stability and national integration was an arduous task of centralizing power and overcoming regional forces that personified anarchy and violence. Centralization of power was historically cast as an alternative to anarchy and instability. In fact, the issue of decentralization, which the vast majority of development professionals, academics, and democracy advocates believe to be essential to effective, efficient, and accountable government, was viewed through historical lenses by many in Venezuela in the late 1980s as bearing the real imprint of national disintegration and a return to chaos, even after thirty years of a relatively stable regime. Concerns about such a fate affected decision making about the nature of the country's political system. In the debates that surrounded the drafting of the 1947 constitution, for example, fear of the potential consequences of direct election of governors resulted in an agreement to delay a decision until a plebiscite four years later; the constitution of 1961 included a provision recognizing direct election of governors but conditioned it on the need to pass a law to put this provision into effect. In the first case, the democratic regime was overthrown before the plebiscite could be held; in the case of the 1961 constitution, no laws to enable the direct election of governors were considered until 1989. For opponents of direct election, "What federalism has meant is competition for power and power rivalry throughout the country. . . . It is not a practical condition for this country."[14] From a historical perspective, the reforms of 1989 were indeed audacious, if not outright threatening to a nation that took so many years and so many lives to construct.

In addition to the benefits that centralism brought to the country in terms of stability, it was also an institution identified with the benefits of economic growth and abundance. The petroleum wealth of the country created a rich central government, able to provide a wide range of benefits and subsidies to virtually all classes in the society. Indeed, the oil wealth of the country has been credited with a style of development in which social conflict was minimized because it sustained long-term, "expanding pie" politics of accommodation to diverse demands.[15] The identification of abundance with the activities of central government was particularly strong in the 1970s, when the first administration of Carlos Andrés Pérez (1974–79) set out to create a "Great Venezuela" with the petroleum windfall. Extensive public investment in infrastructure, housing, social welfare programs, and state-led industrial development sustained extensive growth in the size and responsibilities of the state, which came to be identified as the *piñata* of national development (see Table 3.1).[16] By the late 1970s, public investment accounted for more than two fifths of all investment and reached more than 18 percent of GDP in 1978. In 1980, Venezuelans had a per capita income of U.S.$4,410—by far the highest in Latin America. Centralism, in terms of the power and wealth of the national state and its presence in the daily lives of millions of citizens who worked for the government or benefited directly from government policies, brought not only stability but also prosperity. Centralism embodied the good life for many Venezuelans.

*Political Parties: Legacies of Birth and the Fruits of Power*

In consequence, political institutions in Venezuela were structured to ensure national coherence and orderly transfer of national power rather than re-

**TABLE 3.1**

**ECONOMIC INDICATORS IN VENEZUELA, 1960–1980**

| Indicator | 1960 | 1961 | 1962 | 1963 | 1964 | 1965 | 1966 | 1967 | 1968 | 1969 | 1970 | 1971 | 1972 | 1973 | 1974 | 1975 | 1976 | 1977 | 1978 | 1979 | 1980 |
|---|---|---|---|---|---|---|---|---|---|---|---|---|---|---|---|---|---|---|---|---|---|
| GNP per capita[a] | | | | | | | | | | | 1,250 | | | | | 2,600 | | | | | 4,410 |
| GNP growth rate (%) | -4.0 | 5.1 | 9.0 | 6.9 | 9.7 | 5.9 | 2.5 | 4.0 | 5.2 | 4.2 | 7.6 | 3.1 | 3.3 | 6.3 | 6.1 | 6.1 | 8.8 | 6.7 | 2.1 | 1.3 | -2.0 |
| GNP from oil and nat. gas as % of total GDP | — | — | — | — | — | — | — | — | — | — | 16.1 | 22.6 | 22.9 | 24.4 | 39.7 | 29.7 | 27.0 | 24.7 | 20.7 | 26.7 | 29.0 |
| Public investment as % of total investment | 27.9 | 30.4 | 21.6 | 23.1 | 29.0 | 28.7 | 33.2 | 40.7 | 33.6 | 29.4 | 23.3 | 23.3 | 37.9 | 35.4 | 32.4 | 35.0 | 41.1 | 39.1 | 42.4 | 42.6 | 48.6 |
| Public investment as % of GDP | 4.9 | 4.3 | 2.9 | 3.0 | 4.1 | 4.1 | 4.8 | 5.8 | 7.7 | 7.0 | 5.0 | 5.5 | 9.9 | 9.5 | 8.0 | 10.3 | 14.3 | 16.4 | 18.1 | 14.3 | 14.3 |

*Sources:* Lines 1–2, World Bank (1997); line 3, Ministerio de Energía y Minas (1970 through 1985, various years); lines 4–5, Banco Central de Venezuela (1995: 155–56).

[a] Current U.S.$.

gional or local autonomy, representation, or democratic responsiveness. Among these institutions, the emergence and consolidation of political parties clearly demonstrate the pull of centralism on the structure of power in the country. Modern political parties in Venezuela trace their origins to the 1930s and their structural identity to their role in opposing the dictatorship of Juan Vicente Gómez. The parties were born in clandestine movements of university students whose activities were met with persecution, imprisonment, and forced exile.[17] The structure of the parties reflected the secret and illegal nature of opposition movements—cells of dissidents who knew little about other cells or the identity of their leaders, acting out of loyalty to a cause and obedient to calls for sacrifice and perseverance in the face of adversity. These parties, and associated movements of workers and students, were predominantly leftist and centrally concerned with achieving the political and social rights of citizens in a modern democracy. Their work as sites of opposition to dictatorship was not easy, even after the death of Gómez in 1935. Acción Democrática (AD), which became the dominant party in the democratic regime installed in 1958, was outlawed between 1936 and 1941. Its leaders were forced into exile or prison in the aftermath of its first period in office, from 1945 to 1948.

The parties that emerged from opposition to dictatorship became centralized, mass-based organizations with multiclass constituencies in the 1940s. AD was formally organized in 1941 and became the leading example of how to build a mass base of support that extended to virtually every village in the country. The party also set the standard for other parties by organizing functional groups—unions, women's federations, professional organizations, and student movements—identified with the party label. Despite the more open political environment of the early 1940s, AD maintained its heritage of cell organizations and strict discipline that had ensured its survival under the dictatorships of Gómez and his military successors. Other parties also emerged in the 1940s from clandestine origins, and they emulated AD's organizational structure and appeal to mass followings. The Comité de Organización Política Electoral Independiente (COPEI), which was to become the principal rival to AD, was formally organized in 1946 but had antecedents in a movement of Catholic students in the 1930s and political parties formed in 1941 and 1942 to embody the social teachings of the Catholic Church. The Unión Republicana Democrática (URD), with a strongly leftist—but non-Communist—program and support base, was organized in 1945. The national Partido Comunista de Venezuela (PCV) resulted from the union of various leftist factions in 1947.

As the most prominent and national of the political parties by the mid-1940s, AD was excluded from power by the continued presence of military dictators. In October 1945, however, AD joined dissident officers in a conspiracy to overthrow the military government. The mixed civilian and military *junta* that was established initiated elections for a constitutional congress that then drafted a constitution. Through this nondemocratic route to power, Venezuela experienced its first period of democratic government between 1945 and 1948, a period known as the *trienio*. Among other reforms, the AD government instituted universal adult suffrage, the direct election of the president, senators, and deputies, as well as far-reaching agrarian reform.[18]

The pace of political mobilization during this period was dramatic: new political parties and other mass organizations, such as unions of workers and peasants, proliferated. The growth of competition among these groups was rapid and often acrimonious, however. Among the most bitter rivalries that emerged during this period was that between AD, with its anticlericalist and leftist orientation, and COPEI, with its pro-church and center-right orientation.[19] The reforms, the pace of political mobilization, and the arrogance with which AD used its power contributed to the short life of this experiment with democracy. On November 24, 1948, a military coup brought a *junta* to power that was the vehicle through which Colonel Marcos Pérez Jiménez emerged as national strongman in 1950. The military dictatorship, which lasted until 1958, repressed political organizations and reintroduced the persecution of party leaders and members, particularly those of AD, which was outlawed again, along with its affiliated peasant and worker organizations. The parties were forced back to their clandestine roots.

The democratic regime that approved political and administrative decentralization in Venezuela in 1989 was a "pacted democracy," called into being by opposition to Pérez Jiménez and a concerted effort among political elites to overcome the partisan acrimony and hostility that had characterized the *trienio*. In December 1957, the principal leaders of the three main political parties (AD, COPEI, and URD) and two prominent businessmen met in a hotel room in New York City to establish the basis of the Pacto de Punto Fijo. The pact was an agreement among political and economic elites that they would observe democratic rules of the game, including national elections for president and legislators, state-level elections for legislators, and local elections for municipal councillors. They agreed to a power-sharing formula involving proportional representation in all elected positions and division of appointed government positions on a proportional basis among the parties. Further, they committed to a basic agreement on the principles for national economic development, including assurances to the business sector to respect private property.[20]

Shortly after the pact was agreed to, a national strike drove Pérez Jiménez into exile and ushered in national elections for president and a new effort at democratic governance based on the principles of the pact. A constitutional convention devised the 1961 constitution. Central to the founding of the new regime, and consistent with the motivations behind the pact, was a concerted effort by the country's political elite to moderate conflicts among competing political parties and to manage the process of mass mobilization so that instability could be averted. Thus, the pact was a significant event in the development and duration of democratic government in the country. Indeed, over the years, political elites in the country became accustomed to consultation and consensus building as the principal means for resolving conflict and maintaining political stability.[21] Just as important, the pact was the result of a broad agreement among elites to exclude "threatening" elements, such as the Communist Party.[22]

The parties that agreed to the pact continued to evolve as highly disciplined and centralized organizations, responsive to the political objectives of their leaders, and increasingly centered around patronage rather than issues or ideology. They continued to be based in cells, with members who demonstrated obedience to national leadership and with local leaders whose job it was to enforce party discipline. In the Leninist tradition, while debate on issues was permitted prior to policy decisions by the national leadership, after such decisions were made, rank and file were obligated to support them. In congress, party discipline was strict; any members voting against the party could be dismissed from it, thereby losing any opportunity for elected or appointive office in the future. As a result of such discipline, voting on legislation was a mere formality, its outcome foreseen by the relative strength of the parties represented in the legislature.[23]

Strong discipline was maintained by a very small group of party leaders, who, when in the majority and in possession of the executive branch, worked with the president and in consultation wih local and regional party bosses to distribute patronage: appointment of candidates in legislative elections at national, state, and local elections; non-elected positions in government; contracts for provisioning government and constructing public works; freedom to collect rents from the variety of supplicants for government favor in an increasingly regulated economy; access to basic services; and the allocation of development projects. The parties also sponsored or co-opted non-party organizations throughout society and elections for leadership positions in groups as diverse as mothers' clubs, professional associations, unions, and community betterment organizations that were constituted along party lines.[24] Rewards for party obedience were carefully apportioned and based on the extensive information about member behavior that the cells and sub-national party operatives made available for the party bosses at the center.[25] As Michael Coppedge points out, the parties had the ability to mobilize mass bases of support, but they also had the capacity to constrain the use of power and the activities of their supporters when necessary, factors that helped maintain political stability by reining in competitive passions and allowing party leaders to negotiate with business elites and the military on the basis of "credible" control of their followers.[26] In addition, of course, the parties made many positions available outside of government in the parties themselves. They continued to incorporate a wide range of social classes and interests, reinforcing cleavages based on party identification rather than class or interest. By the mid-1980s, AD was the largest social democratic party in the world, with more than two million members.[27]

The cost of party obedience was an extensive clientele system that permeated the parties and the government, but that cost was minimal until the 1980s because of a rapidly expanding economy and an even more rapidly expanding state. Oil wealth had a significant impact on the formation of stable democracy in Venezuela in that it was "the lubricant that eases the social frictions that arise in a democracy. It lessens the need for hard choices."[28] Equally important, oil evolved into part of Venezuelan political culture as an explanation for the country's "exceptionalism." Aníbal Romero refers to the consequence of great oil wealth as the "myth of unlimited resources" that many Venezuelans believed to be true.[29] The origin of this myth was not misplaced propaganda or nationalism, however. It was based on the prolonged experience of growth and increasing wealth that was widely shared.

The centralism of the political parties, at least until the 1980s, was concomitant with the expansion of good things for Venezuelans—an end to military rule, the maintenance of political peace, and the expansion of the economy. As long as these good things continued to go together, there was little reason for widespread concern that democracy had a very undemocratic structure in Venezuela.

*Presidential Power: The Apogee of Centralism*

While Venezuela's political parties developed as highly centralized organizations, the centralization of political power in the office of the presidency was even more notable after the 1958 democratic regime was installed. As the office evolved, presidents were the initiators of legislation and the principal actors in national politics, tendencies reinforced by the closed- and blocked-list method used to elect all other officials. Presidents were leaders of their parties, the boss among the bosses, and when their parties had the majority in congress, they feared no effective opposition to their mandate; when their parties did not have the majority, they had the ability to govern through the use of decree laws, which required no legislative approval.[30] Where presidents were at odds with their party's leadership, a tradition of consultation and compromise on policy issues generally prevailed.[31] Their patronage was extensive, reaching so far as to lead one observer of national politics to explain it as the defining characteristic of presidential power: "Presidentialism in Venezuela . . . is based on the control of positions and the ability to distribute these positions."[32] Not only did the president dominate executive-legislative relationships, he also dominated the judicial branch through mechanisms of appointment and patronage. Indeed, it is not hard to confuse the modern Venezuelan presidency with the traditional *caudillos* who populated the history of the country.

Venezuela's presidents had extensive benefits to distribute and institutional resources that allowed them to dominate other branches of government. They also generally had extensive mandates to govern. Voting (obligatory for all citizens) generally rewarded the winner with significant majorities. In the first six presidential elections of the democratic regime, from 1958 to 1983, the winning candidate generally won by sizable majorities in multiparty elections in which as few as eight and as many as forty-nine parties contested. In four of the six elections, AD won by 12 to 34 percentage point margins (see Table 3.2). Moreover, AD was always voted into the majority position in the house of deputies and performed almost as well for the senate, with the exception of 1978, when AD and COPEI were equally represented in the senate (see Table 3.3). This allowed AD presidents to govern without relevant constraints from the legislative branch. Many have described the system as hyperpresidentialist in terms of the extent to which the president had the capacity to claim the position of maximum policy leader in the country.

This centralized formula for governing went hand in hand with an impressive national income based on petroleum: it limited the extent to which government needed to tax its citizens (and the extent to which citizens believed they *needed* to pay taxes) and expanded the extent to which subsidies on capital, labor, energy, infrastructure, and social services could be provided

**TABLE 3.2**
PRESIDENTIAL ELECTIONS IN VENEZUELA, 1958–1983
(Percentage of Total Votes by Party)

| Party | 1958 | 1963 | 1968 | 1973 | 1978 | 1983 |
|---|---|---|---|---|---|---|
| AD | 50.05% | 32.81% | 28.24% | 48.79% | 43.43% | 57.67% |
| COPEI | 15.45 | 20.19 | 29.13 | 36.75 | 46.77 | 35.10 |
| URD | 34.50 | 18.89 | 22.22 | 3.07 | — | — |
| MAS | — | — | — | 4.26 | 5.19 | 2.71 |
| MEP | — | — | 19.34 | 5.07 | 1.12 | 3.39 |
| Others | — | 28.12 | 1.07 | 2.20 | 3.49 | 1.13 |

*Source:* http://www.georgetown.edu/LatAmerPolitical/Electoral/Venezuela/venezuela_nat.html, and author's calculations.

broadly to the population and per capita income could grow. By the 1960s, oil wealth flowing directly into government coffers was the gold that made it possible to expand the size and the role of the state dramatically. This expansion could be measured in terms of positions, contracts, and projects to distribute; of numerous subsidies available for those considered worthy of them; of the creation of state-owned enterprises in basic industry and infrastructure; and of a rapidly expanding number of permits, licenses, and registrations required for economic activities of any kind. Table 3.1 provides an indication of the growth in public-sector investment that also hints at the extent of government largesse and patronage.

Table 3.4 indicates the extent to which oil fueled the bonanza of public investment. Indeed, "balancing political needs with economic constraints had no place on the agendas of Venezuelan politicians and government officials."[33] This system worked well for the private sector, workers, and the agricultural sector: "Concretely, each government granted extensive subsidies, contracts, and infrastructure to entrepreneurs while charging the lowest taxes on the continent and allowing some of the highest profits. At the same time, democratic governments could afford to support collective bargaining for the highest wages on the continent, price controls, huge food subsidies, and an agrarian reform."[34]

As many Venezuelans recognize, "Petroleum made the Venezuelan state. It made the *state* rich. The state became the only employer, the only investor, the only producer."[35] The wealth of the country, then, and its ability to provide benefits to the population and to specific groups within the population, was a resource that became concentrated in presidential hands.

**TABLE 3.3**

CONGRESSIONAL ELECTIONS IN VENEZUELA, 1958–1983

(Percentage of Total Deputies and Senators by Party)

| Party | 1958 Deputies | 1958 Senators | 1963 Deputies | 1963 Senators | 1968 Deputies | 1968 Senators | 1973 Deputies | 1973 Senators | 1978 Deputies | 1978 Senators | 1983 Deputies | 1983 Senators |
|---|---|---|---|---|---|---|---|---|---|---|---|---|
| AD | 54.9% | 62.8% | 34.7% | 46.8% | 25.6% | 36.5% | 51.0% | 59.6% | 44.22% | 47.7% | 56.5% | 63.6% |
| COPEI | 14.3 | 11.8 | 20.8 | 17.0 | 24.0 | 30.8 | 32.0 | 27.7 | 42.21 | 47.7 | 30.0 | 31.8 |
| URD | 25.6 | 21.6 | 17.4 | 14.9 | 9.3 | 5.8 | 2.5 | 2.1 | 1.51 | — | 1.5 | — |
| MAS | — | — | — | — | — | — | 4.5 | 4.3 | 5.53 | 4.6 | 5.0 | 4.6 |
| MEP | — | — | — | — | 12.9 | 9.6 | 4.0 | 4.3 | 2.01 | — | 1.5 | — |
| CCN | — | — | — | — | 12.0 | 7.7 | — | 2.1 | — | — | — | — |
| Others | 5.3 | — | 29.1 | 21.3 | 26.5 | 9.6 | 6.0 | — | 4.52 | — | 5.5 | — |

*Source:* http://www.georgetown.edu/LatAmerPolitical/Electoral/Venezuela/venezuela_nat.html, and author's calculations.

## TABLE 3.4
### OIL AND DEVELOPMENT IN VENEZUELA, 1970–1991

| Year | Oil GDP as % of GDP | Fiscal Income from Oil as % of Total Fiscal Income | Oil Exports as % of Total Exports |
|------|------|------|------|
| 1970 | 16.1 | 60.5 | 91.3 |
| 1971 | 22.6 | 66.0 | 92.6 |
| 1972 | 22.9 | 65.1 | 92.7 |
| 1973 | 24.4 | 69.7 | 87.7 |
| 1974 | 39.7 | 85.6 | 91.4 |
| 1975 | 29.7 | 77.4 | 90.5 |
| 1976 | 27.0 | 73.5 | 90.9 |
| 1977 | 24.7 | 72.7 | 94.8 |
| 1978 | 20.7 | 64.3 | 94.2 |
| 1979 | 26.7 | 68.9 | 94.5 |
| 1980 | 29.0 | 72.3 | 94.3 |
| 1981 | 27.1 | 76.5 | 96.5 |
| 1982 | 22.2 | 62.9 | 94.2 |
| 1983 | 20.1 | 56.5 | 92.0 |
| 1984 | 21.2 | 61.0 | 87.1 |
| 1985 | 17.5 | 57.8 | 81.8 |
| 1986 | 11.9 | 42.5 | 68.3 |
| 1987 | 14.0 | 44.0 | 81.8 |
| 1988 | 12.7 | 57.2 | 76.4 |
| 1989 | 21.7 | 76.7 | 74.9 |
| 1990 | 28.2 | 83.0 | 80.1 |
| 1991 | 22.2 | 80.1 | 81.6 |

*Source:* Ministerio de Energía y Minas (1970 through 1991, various years).

In summary, in the development of Venezuela's modern political institutions, centralism was a "civilized" alternative to regionalism. Throughout much of its history, the country was officially proclaimed a unitary state as a way of emphasizing the importance of national integration and the threat embodied in federalism. Even the constitution of 1961, which declared the country to be a federal republic, postponed the implementation of this declaration by adding that governors would be placed and removed by the president until such time as the legislature enacted an alternative way to seat and unseat these officials.[36] Moreover, the prologue to the constitution stated that among its goals of maintaining independence and assuring liberty, peace, and institutional stability, were those of maintaining its territorial integrity and strengthening its unity. Such concern for national unity hints at the conflict-ridden history of the country. Similarly, the country's major political parties emerged as highly centralized and disciplined entities. After 1958, moreover, the pattern of a strong presidency found in most countries in Latin America was embedded in an extreme form in the development of the democratic system. This clear pattern of centralization and the historical experience behind it was challenged by the 1989 reforms. What happened to make an alternative to centralism an attractive choice for the country's political leaders?

## Reinventing Democracy, 1988–1989

Venezuela's democratizing reforms were a clear reversal of decades of increasing centralization, party control of government, and presidential dominance of politics, and they were a clear invitation to Venezuelan citizens to claim more control over elected officials and to diminish the power of the party bosses in Caracas. As such, it is difficult to view the reforms as the products of institutional evolution. From a comparative perspective, the reforms were also interesting. Much experience with decentralization in Latin America and many other developing countries has begun with *administrative* decentralization.[37] *Political* decentralization in terms of devolving autonomy to lower levels of government, in contrast, has rarely been undertaken prior to administrative decentralization. When political decentralization precedes administrative decentralization, the likelihood that responsibility will be assumed when there is very little, if any, capacity to manage it increases considerably.[38] Certainly this was very true in Venezuela, as we will see in chapter 4. From this comparative perspective, then, there is all the more reason for asking how the reforms happened.

*Worrying about Legitimacy: COPRE, Presidents, and Party Elites*

On December 17, 1984, President Jaime Lusinchi established by decree a national task force, the Presidential Commission for the Reform of the State, to study problems being experienced by the country and to make recommendations to the president about what should be done. As was specified in the decree, the commission's mandate was to focus on the creation of a modern state in Venezuela.[39] The commission was to "carry out the studies necessary for determining the objectives, policies, and actions that have to be followed for the establishment of a modern state that is responsive to the needs and requirements of Venezuelan society."[40] It was to develop a plan for an "integrated" reform of the state, propose appropriate measures to the president, and work with him to carry out activities in pursuit of the reform.[41] COPRE, as it soon became known, was the nest in which the reforms were hatched.

The creation of COPRE was not a response by the president to direct public pressure to reform the state, although there was certainly widespread disenchantment with politics and government in the country at the time. Nor was it an important part of his own agenda, even though during the campaign he had promised to initiate a reform of the state apparatus as well as deal with the country's difficult economic situation. In reality, this promise contained little in terms of concrete actions or objectives to be pursued.[42] COPRE was instead the brainchild of the then minister of the presidency, Simón Alberto Consalvi, and a small group of people who met with him during the course of 1984 to discuss issues that had to do with the way government worked and its capacity to deal with the problems of national development. The group, consisting of Consalvi, Ramón Velásquez, a historian and AD loyalist, and Carlos Blanco, an academic with political ties to a left opposition party but personal connections to AD, had actually begun talking with a variety of people in 1983, even before the Lusinchi administration took office, about the problems that the country faced. Then, after Lusinchi took over the presidency, Consalvi, Velásquez, Blanco, and others held a series of consultations with influential politicians, businesspeople, and academicians to explore the range of factors that seemed to need fixing in the country's political and economic development.[13]

The minister, who was an influential and trusted presidential adviser, together with Velásquez and Blanco, managed to convince a reluctant Lusinchi to establish COPRE as a mechanism for bringing representatives of various groups and interests together with intellectuals and government officials to discuss the problems and outline recommendations for policy and action for the administration. The commission was placed under the wing of the Ministry of the Presidency, with Velásquez as its president and Blanco as its executive secretary. When Consalvi was tapped to head the Ministry of Foreign Affairs, other reformist politicians took over the leadership of the Ministry of the Presidency and, later, of COPRE. In addition, reformists from both AD and COPEI were involved in the work of the commission, even while the party traditionalists were skeptical about its activities. Over time, the executive secretary, Carlos Blanco, provided leadership for the reform group, in part because he was not involved with either AD or COPEI politics.[44]

While Lusinchi was persuaded to establish COPRE, there is little indication that its existence was an important part of his administration. In retrospect, one of the commission's members argued, "Lusinchi didn't care one bit about decentralization. He created COPRE in order not to do anything. I repeat: he did something in order not to do anything—he named a commission."[45] Nevertheless, the title of the new commission, Presidential Commission for the Reform of the State, seemed to signal that it had high-level support and that the purview of the commission was to go beyond the routine types of public-sector reform commissions that had been set up periodically in the modern history of the country.[46] The commission would focus its attention on the reform of the state rather than on a more narrow set of issues related to public administration and civil service reform. Moreover, the Seventh National Plan that the Lusinchi administration submitted to the legislature in 1984 placed emphasis on a reform of the state that would deal particularly with the decline in public services and inadequate and inefficient institutional structures.[47] Thus, those who agreed to join the commission believed that they had both high-level support and large public purposes to achieve in terms of the mandate to assess and recommend a very wide array of reform measures.

Behind the creation of COPRE were a number of concerns that had percolated among intellectuals and observers of Venezuelan politics, as well as among some of the more thoughtful politicians and public officials, since the mid-1970s. Among those who shared a growing sense of unease about the trajectory of national economic and political development were representatives of younger, more technically and internationally oriented elites from government and business as well as leaders of emergent social movements, such as the neighborhood association movement.[48] Intellectuals, leaders of "modernist" organizations, and some reformist politicians had begun to argue that the political system was in crisis, that the party system was boss-driven and centralized, and that political decision making did not represent the large majority of Venezuelans, even though they routinely voted for the two main political parties, AD and COPEI.[49] Similarly, there were those who were convinced that a principal problem plaguing the state was inefficiency and ineffectiveness in delivering services and managing routine functions of government. They were concerned about the weakness of the state that was revealed in this incapacity, while others were more concerned that the state was playing too strong a role in the economy. Many were suspicious that government was not effectively managing the economy and that the statist model of development being pursued had reached "exhaustion" and had to be altered.[50] A further factor was the incipient organization of civil society into new groupings, such as independent unions and neighborhood associations that were not incorporated into the party system. These conditions, some observers began to assert, amounted to a crisis of legitimacy for the government and a crisis of effectiveness for the country's development model. In the two and a half decades since the historic Pact of Punto Fijo in 1958 and the reestablishment of democracy, they argued, the government had taken on far too many functions and the political system was no longer relevant to a diverse, urban, and mobilized society.[51]

Moreover, the economic wonder of Venezuela's rapid growth had stopped. Beginning with the sharp decline in the prices of petroleum in the early 1980s, government revenues fell and international creditors began to demand repayment of the foreign debt the country had accumulated during its years of rapid growth. During this period, the government continued to adopt policies that increased the extent of the economic crisis and the difficulty of dealing with it and encouraged a massive flight of capital from the country. Inevitably, the economy began to slow and then to stall, unemployment rose, and per capita income fell steadily, from U.S.$4,940 in 1981 to $3,760 in 1985. In 1981, the economy did not grow at all; in both 1982 and 1983, it declined by more than 4 percent (see Table 3.5). While these trends gathered speed, many Venezuelans, convinced of the unlimited wealth of their country, turned their anger and resentment on politicians, blaming them for robbing the country.[52] The days of ebullience about the present and future of the country were clearly over, and some politicians were concerned about the increased hostility directed toward them.

Although these arguments were important in convincing the president to establish COPRE and in bringing elites together within the commission to discuss important national problems, it was not the case that these issues were broadly debated in politics, nor were they the basis around which social conflict was organized. Complaints about government inefficiency, yes; complaints about declining wages and standards of living, yes; complaints about the centralization of the parties and the rule of the bosses, yes; but widespread social mobilization and public conflict over these issues were not important factors in the creation of COPRE. Nor were issues of state reform being widely pressed on government by mobilized groups in society. Rather, there was a generalized sense of malaise with the political system and the economy, felt most strongly among the country's political and economic elites. At the level of elites in the system—the leadership of the private sector, the church, the armed forces, the labor unions, the parties, and intellectuals—there was enough unease to bring them to the table to begin the work of COPRE but little in the way of particular ideas or reforms to change current conditions.

**TABLE 3.5**

**ECONOMIC INDICATORS IN VENEZUELA, 1980–1990**

| Indicator | 1980 | 1981 | 1982 | 1983 | 1984 | 1985 | 1986 | 1987 | 1988 | 1989 | 1990 |
|---|---|---|---|---|---|---|---|---|---|---|---|
| GNP per capita[a] | 4,410 | 4,940 | 4,850 | 4,570 | 4,110 | 3,760 | 3,650 | 3,430 | 3,460 | 2,630 | 2,670 |
| GNP per capita growth rate (%) | — | 12.0 | −1.8 | −5.8 | −10.1 | −8.5 | −3.0 | −6.0 | 0.9 | −24.0 | 1.5 |
| GNP growth rate (%) | — | −0.1 | −4.6 | −4.4 | 0.5 | 0.2 | 7.4 | 3.8 | 5.7 | −10.1 | 7.7 |
| Annual inflation | — | 16.1 | 9.7 | 6.3 | 11.3 | 11.2 | 11.5 | 28.5 | 29.2 | 84.7 | 40.6 |
| Govt. deficit (−) or surplus as % of GNP | 0.1 | −3.9 | −12.7 | −4.4 | 13.5 | 23.6 | −10.0 | −39.5 | −41.8 | −1.2 | 19.6 |
| Inc. from oil as % of total income | 72.3 | 76.5 | 62.9 | 56.5 | 61.0 | 57.8 | 42.5 | 44.0 | 57.2 | 76.7 | 83.0 |
| Total external debt[b] | 29,345 | 32,162 | 32,158 | 38,303 | 36,886 | 35,334 | 34,340 | 34,570 | 34,738 | 32,377 | 33,170 |
| Public debt as % of total external debt | 10.8 | 11.2 | 15.5 | 23.4 | 23.6 | 24.5 | 21.6 | 72.3 | 72.5 | 77.7 | 75.7 |

*Sources:* Lines 1–5, 7–8: World Bank (1997); line 6: Ministerio de Energía y Minas (1970 through 1991, various years).

[a]Current U.S.$.

[b]Millions of current U.S.$.

The commission gave voice and focus to the incipient independent organizations of civil society but did not emerge as a response to clear societal demand.[53] In fact, according to one close observer of the process, "[Political] decentralization was the idea of five or six people without an audience before 1989."[54]

Based on a list of names drawn up by Consalvi, Velásquez, and Blanco, the president named thirty-five well-known individuals from various sectors to serve on the commission.[55] Then, its leaders got to work, focusing their efforts through a set of strategic principles. According to Blanco,

> Our strategy for COPRE, which I think was a very good strategy, had several important parts. First, we consulted broadly. We consulted all the former presidents, leaders of the political parties, the military, the private sector, the union leaders; we went to the interior of the country. And we listened. Bit by bit people began to realize that we were listening, that we hadn't come to impose something but were really interested in hearing what people had to say. This was important for the legitimacy that we had when we finally made our report. Second, we put together a team of very good people who came from a variety of different sectors, but they came as individuals, not as representatives of particular interests. Third, we worked on tangible problems in order to avoid ideological divisions. . . . Fourth, we were very conscious of the need to focus on the immediacy of problems and not get lost in philosophical discussions. Fifth, we realized that we couldn't reform everything and tackle all problems at the same time. So we looked for strategic points in the sense of focusing on finding changes that would produce a much wider dynamic of change as a consequence. Sixth, we insisted that COPRE was a commission of the state, not of a particular administration . . . Seventh, we were aware that it was important to have public opinion on our side; we couldn't make ours a set of reforms that would be imposed from the top because the top was going to be part of the resistance to change.[56]

The strategy focused centrally on a search for consensus among the various interests in the country.[57]

The reform team leading COPRE decided on three major foci of activity and set up committees to study and discuss each one. One group would focus on the broad outlines of the reform of the state, another would focus on the reform of public administration, and the third would be concerned with the most pressing immediate problems of government in the country. Then, with the assistance of full-time technical teams responsible for research on the various issues, the commission began a series of committee meetings, delegating particular issues to working groups.[58] The leadership continued to encourage broad consultation and then discussion of the findings that came from "taking the pulse" of the country. The committees and working groups were given freedom to tackle a very wide range of issues. Again, according to Blanco, "In the end . . . what we managed to create was a vigorous intellectual environment, the only place in the country where real thinking and grappling with problems was going on. It was a place for real reflection."[59] Perhaps inevitably, given the impetus to consult and the ongoing discussions, the number of reform projects identified far exceeded the capacity of the commission—or the government—to study and make the subject of concrete proposals for change. The projects identified often responded to the particular interests of the most active commission members, given the broad scope for setting committee and working-group agendas.[60] At the end of its first full year of activities, COPRE reported having held ninety formal meetings and 250 consultations with organized groups and seven hundred individuals.[61]

Central to the focus of many of the reform projects and consultations was a general consensus that the state in Venezuela was broken. It was, "broad, but weak; large, but flabby; omnipresent, but useless."[62] In addition, commission members were generally agreed that the country's political parties were far removed from being effective mediators between state and society because of their high degree of centralization and their control of organizations in civil society.[63] And in considering ways to respond to this central concern, the choice of promoting political decentralization, as opposed to administrative decentralization, appeared to have been deliberate. According to a close observer and participant in the process, "The decision to start off with political changes was premeditated. It was based on the conviction that the resistance to decentralization manifested by the majority of the party leaders would have prevented the process from developing if the first step had been to improve the organizational conditions of local governments and municipalities, as some were proposing. The sequence favored by any planner . . . would have ended the process before it had begun."[64]

On April 10, 1986, the commission approved and then presented to the president a set of proposals for political reforms. Among these proposals were the direct election of governors, primary elections for party candidates, changes in political party financing, and a modification of the proportional representation system that would weaken the control of the parties. The reformers also recommended that the executive and legislative branches be separated in municipal government, creating the position of mayor, which would be popularly elected by the citizens in periodic elections. Although widely discussed in the news media, these recommendations were not welcomed by the president or by some members of AD who were part of the commission, even while other members of the party were more supportive.[65] Carlos Blanco recalled this period in an interview, specifically with reference to the president's reaction to the direct election of governors: "This was the beginning of our rupture with the president. He saw the direct election of governors as the creation of twenty little presidents, competing with him.[66] So he started pulling back from supporting us and making it very clear that our mission was only advisory and that it had no real mandate to do anything. He understood *perfectly* what direct election meant for the political system, and he was having none of it."[67]

A second meeting with the president, this one in January 1987, produced even more hostility. "After that," according to Blanco, Lusinchi "began to make statements in his public addresses about COPRE that were negative and that the plans we had come up with were not good ones."[68] The commission was moved from its offices in the presidential palace. Official statements by AD leaders in the spring of 1987 indicated that the reforms were "too advanced" and that the party needed time to study them more fully.[69] Some party officials rejected the COPRE recommendations outright. Because AD had an absolute majority in congress, its reception of the report signaled a dim future for COPRE's recommendations under Lusinchi's leadership. The presidential commission had generated important ideas and had engaged a broad discussion among elite sectors of the population, but it could report little success in influencing political or policy change, at least in the immediate aftermath of its report. Nevertheless, representatives of the major opposition political parties— COPEI, Movimiento al Socialismo (MAS), Movimiento Electoral del Pueblo (MEP)—as well as representatives of the neighborhood association and the national chambers of commerce began to lobby in favor of greater local autonomy and the direct election of mayors and governors. AD was largely silent on these issues.[70]

Despite this failure to interest the majority party or the president, the work of COPRE, which by 1987 had generated a deep commitment among many of its participants about the importance of far-reaching reforms, became more urgent as concern about the political system continued to mount and as a wider range of the political elite and party leadership became increasingly worried. By this time, criticism of "partyarchy" had become commonplace in political discussions. The rate of abstention in national elections was a factor that focused great attention on the question of system legitimacy. Mounting abstention—not great in comparison with those of many other countries— were alarming to political elites in a country in which voting was compulsory. In 1973, 3.5 percent of eligible voters stayed away from the polls; in 1978, the abstention rate was 12.4 percent; it was 12.2 percent in 1983. Regional and local elections in 1984 produced a record high of 40.7 percent abstention. With the approach of presidential elections in December 1988, party leaders were deeply concerned about the possibility of not being able to mobilize even the party faithful, and the issue of the legitimacy of the political system was more broadly debated in the press and among citizens.

For the reform team in COPRE, the approach of national elections offered a respite from the treatment they had received from Lusinchi. In fact, the cold shoulder that Lusinchi had turned to the commission encouraged those opposed to him to look seriously at its work. As early as 1986, opposition parties began to attack the president for his lack of response to the need for political reform. In particular, the direct election of mayors was publicly supported by opposition parties. In March 1987, neighborhood associations and other organizations declared "neighborhood day" as a way of raising public awareness of the need for municipal reform. In May and June, the associations collected ten thousand signatures on a petition for reform and presented it to congress. Initiatives for muncipal reform and the election of governors were debated in congress.[71] Public opinion also mounted in favor of the reforms.

Among those who began looking at the COPRE reforms at this time was Carlos Andrés Pérez, an Adeco (member of AD) like Lusinchi, but one who had begun to break with the traditional leadership of the party, represented by the president and the party bosses in Caracas. Pérez, who had initiated the effort to create a Great Venezuela during his first presidency from 1974 to 1979, had traveled widely during the 1980s and had become aware of the limits to the Venezuelan model of economic development, with its extensive reliance on petroleum revenues, its highly regulated markets, and its widespread state subsidies. Gradually, he became more convinced that international conditions would force Venezuela to join other Latin American countries in modernizing their economies—deregulating, privatizing state-owned industries, opening up to internal and international trade, and cutting back on the size and responsibilities of the state. Similarly, he became more sensitive to the ossified nature of the political system. This new vision of what the country *ought* to be was not fully developed in 1987, but during that period, his "reformed" ideas increasingly placed him at odds with the ideology and leadership of AD. The pre-electoral campaign, focused on determining who would be the standard bearers for the parties, gave Pérez an opportunity to stake out a position in favor of the reform. Although he was not the candidate that the leadership wanted to head the ticket in 1988 and he was not the choice of President Lusinchi, he won the pre-electoral battle by mobilizing reformist elements within AD.[72]

Several of the members of the commission had close relationships with Pérez and discussed COPRE's reform proposals with him. Pérez began to pick up on some of these ideas. Again, according to Carlos Blanco, "He had a series of meetings with us and he announced to us that he was going to take up the flag of political reform, particularly with regard to direct election."[73] On January 22, 1988, the day before Venezuelans celebrated the thirtieth anniversary of the fall of the dictatorship of Pérez Jimenez, Carlos Andrés Pérez announced his commitment to the direct election of governors in a speech in the 23 of January ward of Caracas and called on other political leaders to form a pact in favor of political reforms.[74] Eduardo Fernández, the candidate who emerged to lead COPEI's presidential ticket and who had long spoken out in favor of political reform, was also well known to COPRE's core team. In fact, Fernández challenged Pérez to back COPRE's recommendations prior to the AD candidate's announcement on January 22. At this point, COPRE's leaders invited the presidential candidates to their offices and, in a public event on January 27, a commitment to the political reforms was signed. That day, apparently influenced by the rising tide of interest in political reform, President Lusinchi called a meeting to begin interparty discussions of COPRE's recommendations.

Supporting political reform was not an easy choice for Pérez. On the one hand, becoming an advocate of decentralization might garner a few votes in the election. Nevertheless, these reforms were in direct conflict with the interest of the party bosses in maintaining control of patronage and in holding the party together in its centralized form through the use of the appointment powers of the president. Championing the COPRE recommendations further increased the rift between the core of the party and its presidential candidate. But, as the candidate, he determined formal leadership positions within the party, and although Lusinchi was still president, the discussion of reform began to move forward in congress, pushed along by the Pérez faction.

Despite the volatility of the issue in terms of the relationship between the candidate and the traditional leadership of AD and despite Pérez's public announcement in favor of reform in January, the campaign itself was not notable for the discussion of major reform themes. Instead, the campaign was fought on the basis of party identification and the personalities of the major contenders: "The Pérez campaign, for all practical purposes, replicated the same campaign that produced his victory in 1974; optimism and veiled messianism were its chief elements. . . . The truth is that nothing was known with any reasonable certainty about the intentions of Carlos Andrés Pérez or of his principal opponent with regard to their proposed formula of government."[75] Both AD and COPEI had produced written programs providing the outlines of a number of economic and political reforms, broadly in line with the neoliberal ideology that had become characteristic of most governments in Latin America by the late 1980s; they provided little detail and were not the focus of campaign rhetoric or issues, however.[76] Nevertheless, as the campaign unfolded, the readiness of COPEI to embrace reforms as well as Pérez's control over the machinery of AD led to more congressional discussion of the direct election of governors and mayors. In August 1988, laws to create the position of a directly elected mayor and to allow for the direct election of the governor were passed.[77] In neither case, however, did the legislation go as far as COPRE had recommended. This was especially true for the direct election of governors, whose functions were significantly curtailed because the reform limited their autonomy and did not provide them with resources to carry out any activities. Indeed, it was not clear if these new laws would actually be implemented. Some believed they were passed to provide the parties with "political respectability" but with little intention of putting them into practice.[78]

The campaign proceeded through the fall of 1988 and resulted in a clear victory for the AD candidate. Many Venezuelans, in fact, voted for Carlos Andrés Pérez because they expected him to reintroduce the days of rapid economic growth and of increased state-provided services and subsidies that had marked his first presidential period.[79] Hopeful to see these days again, 52.8 percent of the voters cast their ballots for Pérez, even while delivering AD a blow in the loss of its absolute majority in congress (see Table 3.6). The vote was not a mandate for reforms of the kind that COPRE recommended but rather a vote for a return to the past. The country's political class was gravely concerned, however, when the abstention rate reached 18.1 percent of the eligible voters, and public discussion about the delegitimation of the political system seemed to grow more insistent.

When the Pérez administration took office on February 2, 1989, it was difficult to sustain the belief that the good old days of petroleum abundance would return; in any event, Pérez entered his presidency convinced of the

**TABLE 3.6**
VOTING FOR PRESIDENT AND CONGRESS IN VENEZUELA, 1988

| Party | President (% of votes) | Chamber of Deputies (% of votes) | Deputies (no. of seats) | Senators (no. of seats) |
|---|---|---|---|---|
| AD | 52.76 | 43.24 | 97 | 22 |
| COPEI | 40.09 | 31.06 | 67 | 20 |
| Convergencia | 0.39 | 3.30 | — | — |
| La Causa Radical | 0.37 | 1.65 | 3 | — |
| MAS | 2.71 | 10.15 | 18 | 3 |
| Others | 3.68 | 10.60 | 16 | — |

*Source:* http://www.georgetown.edu/LatAmerPolitical/Electoral/Venezuela/venezuela_nat.html, and author's calculations.

need for economic reforms of the type promoted by international financial agencies, such as the International Monetary Fund and the World Bank, and followed by countries from Mexico in the north to Argentina in the south of Latin America. The Lusinchi administration, distant from the tide of reform that was affecting most of the governments in Latin America and bringing with it major changes in national development strategies and economic policies, had continued to manage the economy as in the days of petroleum abundance. As a result, the national debt had increased, inflation was rising, and the government deficit had escalated precipitously (see Table 3.5). Significantly, the number of Venezuelans living in poverty also grew from slightly more than half a million in 1980 to two and a half million in 1989.[80]

These problems combined with Pérez's new awareness of the ideas surrounding market-oriented development strategies to focus the attention of the administration on the economic problems facing the country. In doing so, however, the president reaped a sizable number of political problems. First, he appointed a cabinet that offended the traditional bosses of the AD and destroyed their expectation of a government that would fully reward loyalists with control over public positions. With the exception of some of the traditional ministries, he filled his cabinet with young, well-educated technocrats who would dominate economic policy making.[81] These technocrats had no experience in the party or in government, and they were convinced of the need to change the country's national development strategy by imposing austerity and undertaking the structural adjustment of the economy. Second, he disappointed the voters, who had anticipated a return to the years of abundance. Instead, they found a government that was intent on neoliberal reforms, beginning with harsh stabilization measures. Third, he added to concern about government's legitimacy by failing to consult broadly or communicate the purpose of the economic reforms that he now championed.[82] The special legislative sessions convoked with the intention of dealing with both the economic and political reforms produced little action or consensus. This was not a propitious beginning for an administration committed to bringing about significant change in the economic and political development of the country. Worse was to come.

## Politicians and New Institutions

Three weeks after the February 2 inauguration, Caracas erupted in violence. On February 27, citizens streamed out of its many neighborhoods, particularly the poor ones, looting and destroying property in the central areas of the city. The riots left some three hundred people dead and countless more injured. During those days, the national police demonstrated its incapacity to manage the situation, and the army was called out to quell the rioters. The immediate cause of the spontaneous outbreak of violence was a significant increase in bus fares that the government had failed to prepare riders for; when boarding buses on Monday morning, workers discovered that they were asked for twice what they had been accustomed to pay.[83] But deeper causes were at work. The economic situation of the country was dire, and the population had experienced eight years of declining wages. Per capita income had declined by one third since 1981 and was continuing to fall. Moreover, the inefficiency and ineffectiveness of many public services undermined further the basis of legitimacy and authoritativeness of national and local authorities. The failure of the police to control the situation only added to the evidence that government had failed. And some argued that violent protest was a reaction to a political system so controlled by political parties and their bosses that citizens had no other way to make their voices known.[84]

These riots, known as the *caracazo*, shocked the country's political class. Combined with the mounting concern over the abstention rate in elections, political upheaval created a clear perception among the party leaders and most political observers that the system was in deep crisis and that a response from the political leadership was essential. On April 13, 1989, the congress passed a revised law for the direct election of governors; the law set December for the first elections.[85] A revised law and date for electing mayors followed on June 15.[86] In December, the law that actually transferred resources and responsibilities to state and local officials was passed, indicating a serious intent to put the reforms into practice.

The momentum behind the desire to "do something" about the distance between citizens and the parties and the government was clear to those who spearheaded these initiatives through congress in April, June, and December of 1989. They linked their alarm about the threat to the political system to the action taken. One politician, for example, recalled the sense of urgency prevailing at the time: "Why did politicians decide to give up power? It's easy! It was fear! . . . I was in congress at the time and I can assure you that it was fear that motivated the congress."[87] A legislator made a similar point: "The 'national commotion' at the end of February was perhaps one of the most important events of the century in Venezuela. . . . It wasn't really about economic problems or reforms. It was a political statement."[88] Another politician reported simply, "Decentralization was the child of the *caracazo*."[89] The sense of urgency appeared to override concern about the implications of change. According to one legislator, "Direct elections were offered to the people as a way of dealing with their disillusion and alienation from the political system without really much sense of it being something that could actually be accomplished and without much concern for what it might lead to."[90] An observer of the process made the same point: "Congress didn't *want* to sign, but I think they thought they had no alternative because of the issue of the delegitimation of the state and the parties. They knew they were voting against their self interest, but they did it anyway."[91] The concern about the legitimacy of the political system, about the depth of commitment to democracy, and about the ability of the political parties and their machines to survive were important factors in accounting for these laws.

President Pérez credited his support of reform to lofty motives, including his desire to be well remembered in the history books, in terms of his role in modernizing the country:

> I have said many times I am a man with only one ambition—history. I want to go down in history as a man who was capable of overcoming the worst [economic and political] crisis in Venezuela's contemporary history. I want to go down in history as the man who left a legacy and adopted the appropriate actions for Venezuela's modernization and decentralization process. I want history to state that the irreversible changes currently taking place in our country were the result of the courage—with due modesty—with which I handled

this phase of our national life. . . . During my administration, the country was decentralized, the presidency's omnipotent power was broken, the state discretionary power was eliminated, provincial posts and state governorships were opened to popular elections, and mayors of cities, towns, and municipalities were chosen through direct elections.[92]

On another occasion, he explained political decentralization as a response to globalization: "It does seem irrational that a president would champion a political decentralization. . . . It amounts to giving up power. But it is responding to irreversible changes taking place in the world. There is no other option."[93]

## Conclusions: The Dynamics of Change

Venezuela provides a first lens through which to view the two sets of contending hypotheses set out in chapter 2. First, why did politicians there adopt political reform? As we have seen, Carlos Andrés Pérez adopted the reforms as part of a political platform while he was running for president. But interestingly, in doing so, he had only partial support within his own party and did not focus his campaign on commitment to these reforms. Moreover, he entered into a pact with other candidates in support of the same reforms. Thus, it is hard to argue that he saw them as a way to win the election. While they may have garnered him some support among the electorate, votes were much more influenced by the extent to which he represented an earlier and more abundant period in Venezuelan history. Ideologically, he had become more of a reformer, as his actions after taking power indicated, but to the extent that he was identified then as a modernizer, his attention was much more on the economic policy reforms than on political reforms. Short-term electoral advantage is not a good way to understand his support of reform.

Nor does it appear that the reforms were championed by one side in an ongoing conflict among interests or classes. While there were certainly many in Venezuela who supported them, remarkably little conflict about the merits of the reforms can be found in the public record, nor is there an indication that interest was pitted against interest in supporting and opposing change. Prior to the *caracazo,* many politicians found the reforms "inconvenient," but they sought to delay and undermine the reforms rather than oppose them publicly. The reforms had been vetted by a fairly broad spectrum of elite opinion in the country, they had been worked out in terms of their technical details by COPRE; they were endorsed by the major presidential candidates; and they were available at a time of deep crisis and concern about the legitimacy of the political system, ready to be picked up as a response to this particular concern. These were elite projects, driven by concern of the political class about the future of the parties and the political system. In supporting them, politicians *were* concerned about their survival, but their concerns were not of the normal "how to survive the next election" kind. In 1989, at the outset of a new presidential administration, elections were in the distant future. Instead, those who supported change subsumed concern about their own political survival in a broader concern about the collective survival of the political system. Neither societal conflict over the terms of reform nor concern for immediate electoral consequences provides a satisfactory response as to why politicians would vote to give up power in Venezuela.

A second set of hypotheses raises the issues of why these reforms emerged rather than other, equally plausible changes that could have been championed as a way to shore up the legitimacy of the political system and the parties. The parties, for example, might have decided to reorganize themselves in an effort to become more responsive and representative of their bases. The Pérez administration might have introduced public consultations about the state of the country or about the purpose of the economic reforms (as had been done in a number of other Latin American countries), or it might have initiated a well-publicized drive against corruption, or poured emergency public resources into special projects to generate employment and respond to social needs. A variety of other possibilities might have been undertaken to achieve the same result. Why this set of reforms? This is a particularly important question, given the history of Venezuela and the belief shared by many that political decentralization had the potential to tear the country apart. In 1988 and 1989, though, political decentralization became a reform that many championed as the only way to hold the country together.

Part of the response to why these particular solutions were promoted and then approved as a way to shore up the legitimacy of the political system has to do with the fact that the proposals for direct election of governors and mayors had been around for some time; these were not new ideas. Indeed, the constitution of 1961 declared the country to be a federal one, although stopping short of putting that statement into effect. In addition, the input of intellectuals and elite networks that emerge around reform initiatives was important. That COPRE had consulted widely among the politically relevant elites and had generated a particular set of recommendations, bringing with them the stamp of elite tolerance if not always approval, helped signal which

among a variety of actions the government might adopt. Thus, the direct election of state and local officials was a proposal that was familiar and that suffered from little or no mobilized opposition, other than the reluctance of
party leaders to carry through with them prior to the *caracazo*. Political and
economic elites were not taken by surprise when they were put forth. Indeed,
it appears that the direct election of governors and mayors was picked up as a
ready solution to a widely perceived problem that had, other than the COPRE
proposals, few other ready solutions worked out. Conflict emerged over the
reforms, but not until after they were put in place.

# New Rules of the Game

## Consequences of Change in Venezuela

*Decentralization is about the redistribution of power*
*in a country with a centralist mentality.*

—Ramón Guillermo Aveledo,

President of the Chamber of Deputies, 1997

The institutional reforms altered the practice of politics in Venezuela— but not easily. In the years following the introduction of the direct election of governors and mayors and changes in the electoral laws, major economic reforms were enacted and then rejected, two coup attempts occurred, the crisis of faith in the capacity of democracy to resolve the country's development problems continued to deepen, and the electorate firmly rejected the traditional political parties in the presidential elections of 1998. Party leaders at the center of power resisted institutional reform and sought to halt changes that diminished their control over the direction of national and local politics. Elected officials at state and local levels were at times reluctant to take on responsibilities for the management of services traditionally provided by the central government. Some sought to use their new powers to create local political machines through clientelism and patronage. At the same time, however, locally elected officials and party activists gained increased autonomy, electoral campaigns began to feature concern about local problems and to provide opportunities for political alliances that were unexpected by central party leaders, and political careers developed in novel ways. Politics in Venezuela became more pluralistic.

Indeed, the first generation of governors and mayors, elected in 1989, provided significant evidence of the positive consequences of democratizing reform. Within the context of supportive national governments from 1989 to early 1994, state and local governments instituted new initiatives to promote economic development and improve services within their jurisdictions. By the end of 1993, twenty-seven agreements had been reached between individual states and the national government to transfer services, such as for health, education, agricultural development, airports, roads, and water, to the states and municipalities.[1] A large number of petitions to transfer services were initiated but not completed during this time also. In 1993, some $1.6 billion in national investment funds were transferred to states, an amount that rose to $1.85 billion in 1994 and $2.86 billion in 1995. Municipal governments received $219 million in 1993, $268 million in 1994, and $433 million in 1994.[2] National attention was drawn to the activities of particularly innovative governors and mayors, and new associations of governors and mayors were formed to lobby for state and local interests in national and regional politics. With the election of a new president, who took office in early 1994, however, those who had lost power through institutional change demonstrated increased capacity to mobilize resistance and to find opportunities to reassert their control over the political process at state and local level. New rules of the game were successfully institutionalized during this period and produced major changes in political dynamics, but the game was by no means over as the end of the decade approached.

The impact of change—and of resistance to it—is the topic of this chapter. In it, I explore the trajectory of democratizing reforms in the period after 1989 and the impact of institutional change on political parties, political campaigns, and political careers in Venezuela. At least in the first nine years of the new institutional order, the dynamics of day-to-day politics suggests ongoing conflict over the distribution of power in the political system and ongoing efforts to adapt the new institutions to individual and party advantage. Thus, reform encouraged revised strategic behavior on the part of politicians and party organizations. More generally, the democratizing reforms of 1989 did not solve the problem of political legitimacy, but they may well have prolonged the life of the regime, allowing it additional time to strengthen its legitimacy.

## Political Legitimacy and Economic Reform, 1989–1997

The *caracazo* of February 27, 1989, was an emphatic warning that faith in Venezuela's democratic institutions was severely eroded.[3] Although the trigger factor was an unexpected increase in the cost of transportation for urban workers, the riots not only captured public anger over years of economic stagnation and decline but also deep public frustration about powerlessness and corruption in government. As indicated in chapter 3, the combination of politics controlled from the center by clientelistic and boss-ridden political parties and a strong presidency but a weak public administration left the majority of Venezuelans with little capacity to influence policy and political decision making and deeply dissatisfied with the long-term decline in public services. Individual citizens could benefit from clientelistic links to party and government machineries, and much of the population had free access to subsidized goods and services provided by government. But the utility of these benefits was clouded by the impossibility of turning clientelism into more generalized influence over policy or the conduct of politics and the increasing incapacity of government to provide the quantity or basic quality of goods and services that were needed by the population. Health and education services virtually collapsed, and even the most basic of government functions, such as police protection and traffic management, were provided only intermittently and poorly.[4]

Indeed, political elites in Venezuela interpreted the *caracazo* primarily in political rather than economic terms. As I indicated in chapter 3, this interpretation was important in spurring action on the political reforms in 1989.[5] But this year was also notable for the introduction of a major economic reform program, announced by Carlos Andrés Pérez on February 16. Called the "Great Turnaround" by the government and known universally as "the package," the program conformed to an orthodox shock program. It emphasized macroeconomic stabilization through devaluation, restraint of public spending, deregulation of interest rates and most prices for private goods and services, along with increased prices for publicly provided goods and services, a restructuring of the foreign debt, introduction of a value-added tax, and a more effective tax system.[6] Privatization and restructuring of public administration were expected to improve government performance. A new foreign investment code eliminated almost all restrictions on foreign investment, and a sweeping program of privatization affected commercial banks, the national airline, telephones, ports, and several of the government's commercial activities.[7] The speed of the reform program was significant as the president decreed change after change in the years between 1989 and 1992.

The economic policy changes were draconian, but they appeared to bring positive results. In 1990, the economy recovered growth, and inflation was reduced from 84.7 percent in 1989 to 40.6 percent. The fiscal deficit was reduced significantly. Unemployment figures showed some decline and wages stabilized. From a technical perspective, the reforms were well designed and

**TABLE 4.1**

ECONOMIC INDICATORS IN VENEZUELA, 1989–1995

| Indicator | 1989 | 1990 | 1991 | 1992 | 1993 | 1994 | 1995 |
|---|---|---|---|---|---|---|---|
| GNP per capita[a] | 2,630 | 2,670 | 2,720 | 2,920 | 2,890 | 2,770 | 3,020 |
| GNP per capita growth rate (%) | −24.0 | 1.5 | 1.9 | 7.4 | −1.0 | −4.2 | 9.0 |
| GNP growth rate (%) | −10.1 | 7.7 | 11.2 | 5.0 | 0.4 | −3.0 | 2.9 |
| Annual inflation | 84.7 | 40.6 | 34.0 | 31.3 | 38.6 | 60.7 | 59.9 |
| Govt. deficit (−) or surplus as % of GNP | −1.2 | 19.6 | 34.2 | 31.4 | 38.1 | — | — |
| Inc. from oil as % of total income | 76.7 | 75.4 | — | — | — | — | — |
| Total external debt[b] | 32,377 | 33,170 | 34,122 | 37,848 | 37,539 | 36,853 | 35,842 |
| Public debt as % of total external debt | 77.7 | 75.7 | 75.2 | 75.7 | 71.0 | 74.7 | 77.3 |

*Sources:* Lines 1–5, 7–8: World Bank (1997); line 6: Ministerio de Energía y Minas (1991:1).
[a] Current U.S.$.
[b] Millions of current U.S.$.

were achieving the expected goals. In fact, by the beginning of 1992, the economic reform program of the Pérez government appeared to be a textbook case of good technical work in designing stabilization and structural adjustment measures that paid off as anticipated in terms of improved economic performance and renewed growth for the country (see Table 4.1). Moreover, even though there were protests against the measures—strikes, marches, and public pronouncements by large numbers of organized groups—there was no repeat of the kind of violence demonstrated by the *caracazo*.[8] This relative political calm was not to last, however.

In early 1992, a coup attempt led by mid-ranking officers in the army caught the entire political elite off-guard and rapidly became a symbolic statement of the political system's loss of legitimacy, even in the eyes of that elite.[9] The coup attempt, beginning in the early hours of February 4, featured the bombing of the presidential palace and residence, an early-morning escape from the palace by the president, and his rush to a television station to declare the coup attempt routed.[10] The coupmakers intended to kidnap or kill the president and take command of television stations in order to outflank their opposition within the military.[11] Poor logistics and tactical blunders, as well as the failure of the coup leaders to generate wider support from the military and the civilian population, brought the attempt to an end within a few hours, however.

The coupmakers were motivated by deep antipathy to the Pérez government and to the economic decline and political corruption they laid at the door of the traditional political system as well as by the failure of the political parties and their leaders to take the country's problems seriously. They were also concerned about the politicization of promotions within the higher ranks of the military and were convinced the country could be made prosperous again if it had good leadership and if the policies of the current government were abandoned. A leader of the coup, acknowledging on television that the attempt had failed, promised that there would be future opportunities to "embark on the road to a better destiny."[12] Similarly, a leaflet circulated after the failure of the coup claimed that those who supported it did so because "we are fed up with so much misery, with so many lies, with so few people benefiting from the immense wealth of our country. . . . The opportunity to be free of the obstacles imposed by bureaucracy, party rule, and corruption is in our hands. . . . We shall return."[13]

Although a failure, the coup initiative had a much deeper impact than its short duration implied. In a country with democratic institutions dating from the late 1950s and with no history of military involvement in politics since the early 1960s, a coup attempt might be expected to rally members of the political elite and the population in defense of those institutions. Instead, the attempt was met with considerable popular sympathy and resonated with the widespread belief among many Venezuelans about the distorted nature of the country's democratic development. And, perhaps more important in this centralized system, ambiguous messages from some political leaders appeared to support the views of the coupmakers and distrustful citizens. Among these was the public response of ex-president Rafael Caldera, one of the original signers of the Pacto de Punto Fijo and the venerable leader of COPEI. In a televised speech to congress, he spoke out against the use of force but then supported the coup makers' views about the disastrous state of the country's affairs and attacked "the package" in virulent terms. Essentially, he implied, the government had only itself to blame for the coup attempt. Caldera demanded that the president abandon the economic reforms and resign. To many citizens listening to the speech, it appeared that one of the leaders and creators of the political system was endorsing their own belief that the political system was at fault for the country's problems.

Following on the coup attempt, protest against the economic program and demands for the resignation of Pérez increased rapidly and broadly; they came from all major groups in the country.[14] The leadership of the president's party, AD, long angered over his decision to fill his cabinet with independent technocrats rather than the party faithful and the impact of austerity on their capacity to distribute government resources as patronage, provided little support.[15] In a May 1992 public opinion poll, 64 percent of respondents ranked Pérez's performance as bad, and 56 percent believed a military coup would occur if the economic and social situation did not improve.[16] Oddly, through-out 1992, the economy continued to perform well, growing at 5 percent, even while political disarray increased.

In the midst of this situation, a second coup attempt occurred on November 27, 1992, this one organized by high-level air force and navy officers. Their statement of grievances focused attention on the same problems of lack of legitimacy of the political system, committing themselves to the need "to reclaim democracy and our unfaltering decision . . . to eradicate corruption in a nation of obscene privileges and nightmarish poverty."[17] The coup attempt was crushed within a few hours, and it left behind a population still cynical about the political system and opposed to the Pérez government but sobered by the prospect of authoritarian and possibly incompetent military officers in power. Despite increased caution about the implications of military intervention, it was the civilian politicians, and particularly AD, that took much of the brunt of the public dissatisfaction. In January 1993, just two months after the second coup effort, a national poll found that only 13 percent of respondents were willing to state that they were Adecos, down considerably from the same poll in 1989, which revealed 27 percent of respondents affirming their loyalty to that party.[18]

The first coup left some seventy people dead, the second one, hundreds. Together, these events underscored the extent to which the country's political system was considered weak and ineffective, corrupt, and elitist by many citizens and even by the creators and beneficiaries of that same system. The economic program of the Pérez government was a focus of much of the protest, but it was also clear that animosities went far deeper than dislike of neoliberal economic reforms. Given the deep disillusion with the political system and the evident failure of even many elites in that system to support democratic processes for altering policies and personnel in government, the December 1992 elections for governors and mayors were an important milestone. According to public opinion, state and local governments were bright spots in otherwise dismal evaluations of government in the country. In a national poll conducted in May 1992, in the period between the two coup attempts, 29 percent believed that their state government functioned best among the three levels of government; 23 percent gave this place to local government; and only 8 percent ranked national government first.[19] When asked which level of government functioned worse, fully 46 percent of respondents replied that it was the national government.[20] Fifty-three percent believed their mayor was doing a good job and 61 percent responded that their governor was doing a good job, but only 31 percent believed Carlos Andrés Pérez was doing a good job.[21] By January 1993, 61 percent of respondents to a national poll affirmed that future presidents needed to have served as governors in order to show that they knew how to govern; 61 percent also replied positively to a statement that electoral reform had improved things in the respondent's community.[22]

Not only was the legitimacy of the state and local governments considerably stronger than that of the national level, the association of governors was outspoken in its condemnation of the coups and its demands that the military retreat to the barracks.[23] Advocates of political decentralization argued that the elected state governments were a long-term insurance policy against military intervention in politics because, as stated by one such advocate, "You can only have a successful coup when you have one center of power and by taking that over, you take over everything. This cannot happen now, as there are now 22 centers of power in the country."[24]

The problems of the Pérez administration did not disappear in the wake of the coup attempts and the cautious support given to democratic institutions by the December elections. In early 1993, AD leaders, displeased with the activities and reforms of Carlos Andrés Pérez and personally angry with him for his failure to recognize the traditional claims of the party for cabinet positions and access to decision-making councils, joined with opposition politicians to seek his impeachment by the senate on charges of fraud and corruption. The president had lost meaningful support, even within his own party. The attorney general investigated a reported slush fund in the Interior Ministry that, it was charged, was used to reap benefits of a devaluation on the basis of insider information. According to his report, the profits from this activity, traced to the office of the president, could not be found. The Supreme Court indicated that sufficient evidence existed to authorize a trial of Pérez and two of his ministers. In May 1993, charges were brought against him in the senate for misuse of funds, causing Pérez to step down until a trial was held.[25] He was convicted and imprisoned, through a judgment that was upheld in May 1996, after an appeal to the Supreme Court. Pérez was placed under house arrest to serve out the remainder of his sentence. He also was deprived of his membership in AD, although the ministers charged with him were not.

The former president continued to argue publicly that the report, the charges, and the trial were the result of a conspiracy by the general secretary and long-time boss of AD, Luis Alfaro Ucero, and by the father of COPEI,

Rafael Caldera, to destroy him.[26] Subsequently, Pérez organized a movement, Apertura y Participación Nacional (Opening and National Participation), that he believed would tap regional and local adherents of Acción Democrática who felt shut out by the party's centralized management and who would support his bid for the national senate.[27]

## Presidents, Governors, Mayors: Innovations and Retreat

The president of the senate assumed the presidency when Pérez stepped down and then an interim president was elected by congress on June 5, 1993, to finish the final eight months of the Pérez presidency. The new president, Ramón J. Velásquez, who had been central to the creation and subsequent activities of COPRE, having served as its president from late 1984 to early 1986, continued to be a committed advocate of political and administrative decentralization in the country. Among his first activities as president was the creation of the Ministry of State for Decentralization, on June 7, 1993. He named as minister a respected lawyer and COPRE member, Alan Brewer-Carías, and installed the ministry in the presidential palace of Miraflores. In the eight months of the Velásquez presidency, no effort of government received more attention than did that of decentralization.[28] During this period, the president signed numerous decrees facilitating political and administrative decentralization and fourteen new or revised laws. He encouraged the transfer of functions to states and municipalities in unprecedented numbers. The scope of the powers of the governors was expanded and clarified, and each ministry of the national government was directed to name a high-level official who would be responsible for an office of decentralization and whose task it was to establish and maintain contact with state and local governments. Together, these officials formed the National Decentralization Commission, which was to help negotiate the transfer of functions to the states and localities. The National Council of Mayors was also created to increase intergovernmental coordination.

Among the important contributions of this interim presidency was the creation of the Intergovernmental Fund for Decentralization (FIDES). FIDES was established on November 25, 1993, as a response to the paucity of funds and technical assistance available for state and local governments. As indicated in chapter 3, the direct election of state and local executives was mandated prior to any form of administrative decentralization that would have allocated specific functions to local governments. While municipalities had some functions assigned to them by the constitution, states had virtually none. The decentralization law of December 1989 designated an extensive list of functions that could be transferred to the states. FIDES complemented these actions by providing funds for investment purposes and mechanisms for technical assistance to governments at the state and municipal levels.

FIDES worked with funds derived from up to 30 percent of the national value-added tax as well as other funds assigned to it. It was required by law to distribute 70 percent of the total to the states and 30 percent to the municipalities. The amount provided to each state or municipality was based on a formula linking population, territory, and poverty levels.[29] The objective of the funds was to promote regional development and decentralization by providing new investment capital for functions transferred from the national government or by funding administrative modernization projects, personnel expenses that accompanied transferred functions, project design and development, technical assistance to state and local government, and operating expenses.

More generally, the country's block grant program, the *situado constitucional,* mandated that no less than 15 percent of current central government income, as estimated in the annual budget, had to be distributed to the states and municipalities. Through the reforms of 1989, its resources were increased from 15 to 16 percent of current government income with the provision that they continue to increase annually until they reached 20 percent by 1994. Thirty percent of the grant was distributed equally among the states and the remaining 70 percent on the basis of population. This was the principal source of income for the states and localities (see Table 4.2). Half of the *situado* was earmarked for investment projects. These funds provided the basic working capital that the state and local governments needed for their new responsibilities, such as health and education, and a variety of development related expenditures.

In addition, a complex process was worked out to transfer responsibilities to the states and localities and put in place the mechanisms for administrative decentralization. These factors complemented the potential for greater democratic control and responsiveness of the political system. The transfer of funds and functions to the states and municipalities was also important in terms of what different levels of government were contributing to social-sector spending. In 1989, the central government covered 84 percent of government spending in the social sectors, state government accounted for 12.5 percent, and municipalities covered 3.5 percent. In 1994, of the total spent in

**TABLE 4.2**
SOURCES OF STATE-LEVEL INCOME IN VENEZUELA, 1993–1995

| Source | 1993 | 1994 | 1995 |
|---|---|---|---|
| Intergovernmental transfers | | | |
| Situado Constitucional (block grant) | 88.81% | 79.23% | 82.07% |
| Transfer of functions | 0.00 | 1.68 | 7.56 |
| Special funds | 1.34 | 3.89 | 3.76 |
| Credit | 3.18 | 6.34 | 2.69 |
| Subtotal | 93.33 | 91.14 | 96.09 |
| Own resources | | | |
| Income | 0.83 | 1.33 | 0.44 |
| Sales | 0.97 | 0.12 | 0.06 |
| Interest | 1.68 | 1.20 | 0.75 |
| Reserves | 1.00 | 1.17 | 0.90 |
| Other | 2.07 | 1.69 | 1.77 |
| Subtotal | 6.55 | 5.51 | 3.92 |
| Other income | 0.12 | 3.36 | 0.00 |
| **TOTAL** | **100.00** | **100.00** | **100.00** |

*Source:* R. Barrios (1997:133).

the sector, the central government contributed 71 percent, the state governments 24.6 percent, and the municipal governments 4.4 percent.[30]

Meanwhile, the first generation of directly elected governors and mayors was reshaping institutions of state and local government. Armed with new sources of funding, a number of state and municipal executives expanded services to their localities and supported innovations in service provision and citizen participation.[31] In the state of Carabobo, for example, the twice-elected governor and presidential aspirant for the elections of 1998, Henrique Salas Römer, privatized Puerto Cabello, reducing its work force from more than five thousand to less than one hundred and greatly improving the efficiency of the port. He invested heavily in health services and infrastructure development and became a nationally recognized figure in terms of the improvements his administrations introduced. The mayor of a wealthy part of Caracas, Irene Sáez, introduced innovations in public security, traffic control, and public amenities that helped gain her national attention as an effective manager.[32]

The period was rich in such experiences. The hospital in Mérida, in the state of Bariñas, became a model for how local governments could take over central functions for health and deliver much-improved services. Several hospitals in the state of Aragua were turned over to local communities and non-governmental organizations, resulting in improvements in service and efficiency. The city of Valencia, in Carabobo state, greatly improved municipal finances and expanded the tax base significantly. A participatory budget process was successfully introduced in San Félix in the state of Bolívar. The municipal police force in the city of Sucre in Miranda state was developed around a vision of community service, demonstrating to Venezuelans that police forces did not have to be corrupt, inefficient, and ineffective, as citizens had come to expect. The state of Monaguas, through its Century 21 program, set a model for attracting development investment through effective public policy and marketing. In Chacao, a wealthy municipality of Caracas, an innovative and effective independent authority was set up to manage traffic and urban transportation. States and municipalities not only gained national and international recognition for these innovations, they also began exporting their experiments to neighboring states and localities.[33]

The extent of innovation is impressive considering the difficulties the states and municipalities faced in taking over functions previously carried out by the national government.[34] Under the complex formula for transferring responsibilities, the governor was charged with initiating the process by requesting approval from the state legislature; if that approval were forthcoming, the governor had to petition the national executive through the Ministry of Internal Relations. The ministry then convened a mixed state and national commission to develop and negotiate an agreement with the central ministry currently carrying out the function (for example, health), established a transfer program, and submitted the program to the senate for approval. If approved, the mixed commission was charged with developing a formal agreement for the transfer of functions, which in turn had to be signed by the president and the governor. Hence this process depended on the interest of the governor and the agreement of the state legislature in taking on new functions as well as on the willingness of the president, the senate, the Ministry of Internal Relations, and the particular ministry currently carrying out the functions to transfer the activities to the state level.

Added to the difficulty of transferring functions was the provision that the *pasivos laborales* (funds required whenever a public sector employee was dismissed or retired, based on years of service and the most recent salary) had to be assumed by the states for the functions transferred to them, and the virtual absence of taxing power of the states. Even governors who were eager to pursue the transfer of responsibilities learned to be careful about the conditions under which workers were transferred. According to one official involved in such transfers:

> The decentralization law says that when we take over functions, we
> have to absorb all the people who work in the service being decentralized. Well, when we took over the health service, there were
> 10,000 people in the state [employed by the national government]
> working on it. There was tremendous corruption and lots of people
> being paid who never showed up to work. We were constrained by
> the legal obligation to respect their employment contracts . . . [and]
> we had to pay the social benefits owed to all of those who were dismissed, and it cost a lot. . . . We did it because the services offered
> here were so terrible. There were monthly strikes, the hospitals were
> paralyzed, there was no equipment, no medicines, there were power
> outages in the middle of operations, there was no food, no water. . . .
> [But] we stopped before taking on education . . . taking on 18,000
> people in addition to the 4,000 teachers employed by the state. The
> governor wouldn't be able to handle this and doesn't want to take it
> on. Thirteen states have taken over sanitation services and haven't
> been able to get rid of one worker. This is where you see the reproduction of the central bureaucracy at the state level.[35]

Eventually, such difficulties discouraged governors and municipalities from taking on responsibilities for services they were uncertain they could finance into the future. A survey of states in 1996 indicated that the most important problem that kept the decentralization process from going forward was the *pasivos laborales*, followed by high costs and resistance from the central government.[36] Together, a complicated process, almost complete dependence on the national government for funding, and legal obligations in the event of restructuring organizations once they were transferred to the states set some very high barriers to administrative decentralization in Venezuela.[37]

In 1994, the new president, Rafael Caldera, proved himself committed to slowing down the process of decentralization in an effort to return power to political leaders in Caracas. According to some, he represented the conservative backlash against the gains made through political decentralization. His campaign platform supported opposition to the Pérez economic reforms, decentralization, and privatization.[38] The Ministry of Internal Relations was taken over by a COPEI politician known to be hostile to the process, and the Ministry of

Decentralization was reduced to an office within that ministry. Caldera formed an alliance with the traditional wing of AD in congress to alter the policies put in place by his two AD predecessors. In addition, the president and his minister were much less interested in receiving and supporting claims to transfer responsibilities for the provision of services by the states and municipalities. Whereas twenty-seven agreements to transfer functions had been signed between 1989 and the end of 1993, only three additional agreements were signed between early 1994 and the end of 1995.[39] This suggests that, as one observer noted, "decentralization is actually dependent on presidentialism."[40] Just as important, the process remained highly dependent on central financing. Table 4.2 indicates the extent to which state finances flowed from central largesse. Although various types of transfers were mandated by law, the speed and efficiency through which they were transferred remained subject to political influence.

The election of Hugo Chávez in 1998 called the future of decentralization into question again. As promised during his campaign, a constituent assembly was convoked to rewrite the constitution. Advocates of decentralization worried that the assembly, heavily backed with Chávez supporters, would undo the decentralization measures. Anti-reformers sought powers to dismiss all governors and mayors, replacing them with "regional councils." In the end this change was abandoned, although the powers of states and municipalities were defined more narrowly.

The transfer of some functions continued to be attractive to state-level leaders. Now elected rather than appointed, they could promote their popularity through the provision of services that were more efficient than when provided by the central government, and they could begin to build state-level political machines, thus displacing the power of central party elites, by taking control of public jobs and contracts. There was also an incentive to create new municipalities to increase the number of public positions available and significantly increase the amount of centrally provided resources for an area. In fact, state-level personnel expanded from 231,011 in 1991 to 248,455 in 1996, and the number of municipalities increased from 269 in 1989 to 330 in 1995.[41] By the mid-1990s, it was increasingly obvious that political decentralization had unleashed new sources of conflict in the country, as well as new party dynamics, campaign strategies, and political careers.

## Parties, Campaigns, and Careers: New Forms of Competition

Traditional ways of doing politics in Venezuela suffered from the reforms of 1989. Presidential politics were altered because the president could no longer build his personal political machine through the appointment of governors. Governors from the president's party did not even have to be supportive of their national leader because popular election meant that they could run on their own programs and promises and construct their own electoral coalitions and alliances. Moreover, the ability to vote for councillors and legislators by name meant that the central party leadership could no longer demand that those listed on party slates owed loyalty (both for their inclusion on the slate and for their ranking within it) only to them. The links between the national, state, and local parties was also weakened because local party officials could no longer guarantee to deliver votes to the party's national candidates given their loss of patronage possibilities. At the same time, however, limitations on the resources available to governors and mayors made them dependent on the orientations of presidents in power. Presidents who favored political decentralization were more willing to provide national-level resources and disburse funds for state and local government activities than were those who opposed the new institutions. Thus, institutional inventions in Venezuela created new sources of political power at the same time they revealed new constraints on the use of that power—a result of increased political and administrative decentralization and continued fiscal centralization.

*Political Parties: Responding to Reform*

AD and COPEI traditionally dominated the political arena in Venezuela through their control of elected and party positions, as well as their capacity to distribute other forms of patronage. As we saw in chapter 3, democracy in Venezuela meant "partyarchy" or *partidocracia;* partyarchy contributed directly to the gradual delegitimation of the political system in the 1980s and 1990s, reflected in abstention rates that reached nearly 40 percent in the presidential elections of 1993 and remained over 50 percent for state and local elections (see Fig. 4.1).[42] Among the most obvious and critical consequences of the 1989 reforms was the weakened ability of parties to control political processes from Caracas, where party leaders had traditionally pulled the strings of national political life. Direct election of governors and mayors created a situation in which these officials could build bases of political support that were relatively autonomous from party headquarters. Regional and local reputations and actions became the factors that generated votes, not obedience to central party dictates. Moreover, as incumbents could seek reelection and could also run for election for other local or regional positions, career futures depended far less on the center. Consequently, to the extent that gov-

**FIGURE 4.1**

ABSTENTION RATES IN NATIONAL AND REGIONAL/LOCAL ELECTIONS IN VENEZUELA

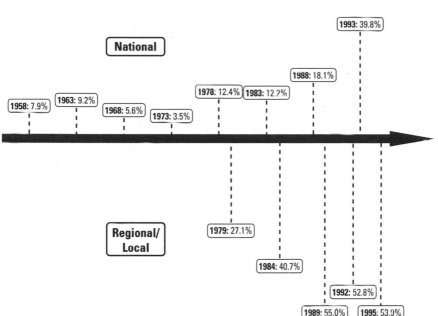

*Source:* http://www.elecciones.eud.com/absten.ntm

ernors and mayors were able to build local bases of support, the relationship with the party leadership in Caracas became more one of bargaining and negotiation than one of submission.

Governors and mayors could no longer be counted on automatically to support the national ticket in political campaigns, deliver votes to the party's candidates at national levels, distribute patronage in accordance with the direction of the party leaders, communicate unquestioning support for national policy preferences of party headquarters, or play by the traditional rules of conflict resolution within the parties. At times, party labels were taken on by candidates only as a matter of convenience. This occurred to such an extent with MAS that it became "the national umbrella organization for several strong regional leaders. . . . No longer is there just one party line, one program, or one clearly defined national image. Much of MAS's success at the national level is due to the popularity of local leaders who are either relatively or completely unknown in the national arena."[43] Moreover, to the extent that state and local officials built regional and local support and became advocates for regional and local interests, Caracas headquarters would begin to give greater attention to state and local concerns as matters of national policy. In short, the direct election of state and local leadership was a direct attack on the Leninist features of the traditional political parties.[44]

Equally important, the 1989 reforms further weakened the capacity of the parties to mobilize organizations of civil society, and it became more difficult for them to control the activities of functional organizations such as community betterment associations, unions, professional organizations, mothers' clubs, and other groups that had traditionally been organized by the parties or closely identified with them through party-based elections of their leaders. In any event, this capacity was in decline prior to political decentralization, due in part to the emergence of organizations intent on resisting government and party control (and therefore mismanagement and corruption) and committed to promoting improvement in local conditions, the environment, the distribution of wealth in the country, or the delivery of public services.[45] Similarly, new types of trade union organizations were formed in the 1980s, with agendas that included claims for autonomy from the traditional parties; members of the party-controlled unions also began to assert demands for greater internal democracy.[46] This process was also stimulated by the decreased capacity of the political system to provide sources of patronage, subsidies, and other benefits in the context of austerity measures.

The loss of the parties' hold on national politics and associational life is mirrored in the increasing abstention rates of the 1980s and 1990s and the decline in the number of people identifying themselves with particular parties in public-opinion polls (see Fig. 4.1 and Table 4.3). The 1989 changes provided added impetus to these trends. To the extent that government performance no longer depended entirely on the center, new foci for lobbying and demand making by a variety of citizen groups emerged around new sites of decision making and administrative control. Moreover, innovative leaders at state and local levels developed new options for service delivery by enlisting nongovernmental organizations and citizen groups whose attention was focused on interactions with government at these levels rather than with Caracas. In addition, the number of political parties vying for votes in local elections burgeoned from 26 parties registered with the national electoral council in 1984 to 155 in 1989 and 491 in 1992. In the presidential and gubernatorial elections of 1993, 274 parties were registered.[47] Several of these parties emerged as splinters of the national parties.[48]

The leaders of AD and COPEI were the most obvious losers from political decentralization. They had long enjoyed highly centralized power over the

**TABLE 4.3**

IDENTIFICATION WITH MAJOR POLITICAL PARTIES IN VENEZUELA

| Date of Opinion Poll | AD | COPEI | Independent | Other Parties | None | No Answer/ Don't Know |
|---|---|---|---|---|---|---|
| 1989 May | 27% | 14% | 38% | 6% | 13% | 1% |
| 1990 January | 22 | 14 | 46 | 5 | 12 | 1 |
| 1992 May | 16 | 15 | 40 | 5 | 23 | 1 |
| 1993 January | 13 | 16 | 41 | 12 | 16 | 1 |
| 1995 March | 14 | 11 | 36 | 13 | 24 | 2 |
| 1996 January | 16 | 10 | 40 | 14 | 19 | 1 |
| 1996 July | 21 | 8 | 33 | 10 | 27 | 1 |

*Source:* Consultores 21. The poll asked, "Do you consider yourself an Adeco, a Copeyano, [names of other parties] or an independent?" (Names of smaller parties varied by poll.)
*Note:* N=2,000.

activities of the parties, the distribution of spoils and government benefits, and the selection of candidates for office from the presidency of the republic to councillors of the smallest and most remote municipalities. The reactions of these leaders to the new context for competition and electoral advantage was slow to emerge, however. In part, the slow response can be credited to the lack of experience with the need to share power; the party leaders were simply unprepared for the reforms and perhaps did not fully appreciate the extent to which they introduced new dynamics into traditional party politics. Moreover, during the period after the reforms were introduced, the Caracas-centered leadership of the parties was riveted by the fast pace of the economic reforms introduced by the Pérez government, the two coup attempts, and the events surrounding the demise of the Pérez presidency. They also had to grapple with the electoral results of 1993, in which AD and COPEI votes combined failed to reach the 50 percent mark for the first time since 1958.[49] And both parties contained reformist wings that were more supportive of decentralization, as well as the traditional leadership in deep opposition to them. These factors allowed the first generation of state governors and mayors to innovate and claim power resources more effectively than was true for subsequent generations.

Central party leaders, however, eventually began to act in accordance with their opposition to the reforms, and both AD and COPEI leadership were aided by the Caldera administration. A principal weapon for slowing the process was the role that congressional and presidential approval played in promoting the pace of decentralization. Thus, the process of acquiring consent to transfer functions and to allow FIDES investments in the states became more difficult and contentious after an initial spurt of activity between 1989 and the end of 1993. Moreover, the two main parties continued to have extensive political machines throughout the country, down to the remotest villages, that linked national leaders with local political bosses and that provided extensive intelligence to the national-level parties. Although no longer controlling the amount of patronage that had been available in the past, national leaders continued to use what access they had to patronage to support these machines. This was particularly true for AD in rural areas, where it had traditionally had its most loyal base of support, and COPEI in the Andean region, where it had emerged in the 1930s and 1940s. Newer or smaller parties lacked these extensive networks of party cells, information, and traditional loyalties. Moreover, state and local politicians seeking to build their own bases of support had either to destroy the traditional machines or capture them for their own purposes. This process took time, and meanwhile, national party leaders continued to be able to mobilize some of their traditional base through their party organizations. AD and COPEI joined forces in a successful effort to separate regional and local elections from presidential elections in 1998. Their purpose in doing so was to use their still-impressive machines to make a good showing in the earlier regional and local contests and thus influence the national election.[50]

The reaction of the party organizations to political decentralization was not simply to resist change, however. More significant in the longer term were efforts to recapture the initiative by adapting to the new rules of the game. In part, this often involved using patronage resources to contest control over newly created units of government. National politicians, for example, saw the creation of new municipalities as a potential site for new clientele relationships. As indicated by one party activist, "Everyone wants his own municipality now, because this means that you get to appoint a driver, an assistant, a secretary, who knows what. . . . The political parties have captured these positions and there is a lot of pressure to make more and more municipalities, even when there is only a small number of people living in an area and even when there is no source of income for the people."[51]

Ironically, the decentralization opposed by the traditional party leaders may have been a factor in protecting AD and COPEI from even greater electoral rejection in 1998. The campaign and election were significantly affected by the candidacy of Hugo Chávez, one of the leaders of the coup attempts earlier in the decade. His populist and anti-establishment campaign resulted in a strong mandate and an equally harsh defeat of AD and COPEI presidential candidates at the polls. At the same time, however, the traditional parties held on to significant support in the gubernatorial elections, an outcome attributed to the local popularity of the candidates, not to their party label.[52]

### Candidates, Campaigns, and Issues

In approaching the campaigns of 1992, 1995, and 1998, the parties became more attuned to candidates and issues that could insert the national parties more effectively in elections at state and local levels. They sought to find candidates to nominate for positions who were traditional centralists, but they also began to court locally popular politicians and to offer them party backing for their candidacies. In the process, they were willing to make bargains about access to patronage and campaign support. The increasing prevalence of public opinion polls and a resurgence in local media activities helped them locate promising candidates for state and local office and to explore with them opportunities for future career mobility that could attach to those who were willing to follow the lead of Caracas. One observer explained the behavior of Luís Alfaro Ucero—the AD general secretary popularly known as *El Caudillo* of the party—in these terms:

> He's the old maximum leader who ruled with an iron hand, but he's not so wedded to the old ways as people think. . . . He watches the public opinion polls very carefully about who's popular and who has the possibility of being a good candidate. When he is convinced that he sees a winner, he then works to incorporate that person into AD. Of course, he's not watching everyone, he's watching that group of people that is already acceptable to him. He certainly has been an opponent of decentralization, but he has realized that he now has to look at it as a way of strengthening the party. He realizes that the party needs a new strategy to adapt to the new era.[53]

Electoral campaigns, then, were where changes and adaptations resulting from the 1989 reforms tended to become most visible. First, even as national leaders attempted to reassert their previous positions of dominance, state and local politicians learned the importance of focusing on state and local issues for their campaigns, regardless of their party identity. The condition of locally provided services such as police protection, road maintenance, trash collection, and health services became hot items for campaign rhetoric and prom

**TABLE 4.4**

ELECTION RESULTS FOR GOVERNORS AND MAYORS, 1989–1998

(Percentage of Total Governors and Mayors by Party)

| Party | 1989 | | 1992 | | 1995 | | 1998[a] |
| | Governors | Mayors | Governors | Mayors | Governors | Mayors | Governors |
|---|---|---|---|---|---|---|---|
| AD | 55.0% | 55.9% | 31.8% | 42.9% | 54.5% | 59.1% | 34.8% |
| COPEI | 35.0 | 37.8 | 50.0 | 45.7 | 13.6 | 27.0 | 21.7 |
| MAS | 5.0 | 3.3 | 16.6 | 6.7 | 18.2 | 5.2 | 13.0 |
| LCR | 5.0 | 0.7 | 4.5 | 1.8 | 4.5 | 2.4 | 0.0 |

*Sources:* Consejo Supremo Electoral (CSE), 1989–95; Consejo Nacional Electoral (CNE), 1996–98.

[a] Elections for mayors postponed.

ises.[54] Some new parties emerged as vehicles for neighborhood concerns.[55] In contrast, before the reforms, campaigns for municipal councils and state legislature often featured rhetoric and promises about inflation rates and trade policy (which, of course, councillors and state legislators had no input into). Similarly, governors and mayors became advocates for state and local issues and often reached a national political audience through media coverage of their campaigns.

The results of contests for governorships and mayors fluctuated considerably by election year, as suggested by Table 4.4. National-level political events no doubt influenced these results, most clearly in 1992 and 1993, when the AD president had lost the support of his party leadership. In 1992, the proportion of Adeco governors dropped from 55 to 32 percent, while COPEI rose from 35 to 50 percent, and those who represented other parties moved from 10 to 22 percent of the total. But these results were probably not simple reflections of perceptions about the national parties or national politics. Public-opinion polls after this election indicate that 60 percent of those who voted for governor did so on the basis of the candidate, not his or her party; 59 percent of those voting for mayor made a similar claim.[56]

The decoupling of national and regional/local politics was also apparent when two governors were reelected by large majorities in 1993, at the same time they were public partisans of the highly unpopular Pérez economic reforms; in those elections, the Adeco mayor of Caracas criticized the reforms but lost his bid for reelection.[57] In addition, local and state elections were sites for novel electoral alliances that were significantly different from national level alliances. In the 1993 elections, center-right COPEI formed alli-

ances in three states with the leftist MAS and made four similar alliances in
1995. AD and COPEI, traditional competitors in all elections since 1958,
formed an alliance in one state in 1995. In the 1995 elections, eleven mayors
were elected from parties other than AD or COPEI in the country's twenty-
seven most populous cities.[58] In 1998, most candidates for governor were
supported by coalitions of several parties. Among these were six AD-COPEI-
Convergencia alliances, five COPEI-MAS alliances, and several URD alliances
with AD or COPEI. In fact, the range of coalition partners varied widely
across states, and few of them made sense from the perspective of national
politics.

*Political Careers in Flux*

Political careers also changed as a result of the reforms. It quickly became
apparent to politically ambitious individuals that state governorships and
mayoralties of large cities could be the launching pad for national political
careers. Traditionally, presidential candidates had emerged from party organizations and had reflected the internal power structure and conflicts within
the parties. Usually, the person claiming the leadership of the party became
the standard bearer in presidential elections. Thus, most presidents, prior to
their election, had been high-level party officials or legislators. In the 1993
campaign, however, three of the four top contenders for the presidency came
from state capitals or the mayor's office. Oswaldo Alvarez Paz had been the
twice-elected and widely acclaimed governor of the petroleum-producing
state of Zulia, Andrés Velásquez had been the governor of the important state
of Bolívar, and Claudio Fermín had been mayor of Caracas.[59] In fact, each of
these candidates owed his political prominence to his electoral history rather
than to his connection to the party machines in Caracas. Fermín and Alvarez
Paz were able to win nominations to head their party's tickets because they
believed the centralized control of party leaders had diminished to such an
extent that an "outsider" could succeed. According to Michael Coppedge,

> Claudio Fermín, the mayor of Caracas, gambled that in this re-
> formed institutional environment the nomination would be won not
> by a national faction that forged deals with regional brokers but by
> someone who could bypass the brokers and attract support directly
> from activists with a good record of governing at the state and local
> level. This strategy worked well for Fermín in AD, just as it did for

COPEI's nominee, Oswaldo Alvarez Paz, the governor of Zulia, who soundly defeated his party's general secretary, Eduardo Fernández.[60]

Equally important, those who had embarked on national political careers under the pre-reform rules were finding it expedient to return to states and municipalities to run for office as a way of acquiring legitimacy and executive experience that would promote their careers nationally. Several national deputies and senators ran for governor or mayor in 1993, and in 1995, even more national politicians sought state and local office.[61] In the pre-campaign for the presidential elections of 1998, the twice-elected governor of Carabobo, Henrique Salas Römer, the mayor of the municipality of Chacao (a part of Caracas), Irene Sáez, a previous governor of the state of Aragua, Carlos Tablante, as well as Andrés Velásquez and Oswaldo Alvarez Paz were all considered serious contenders for the presidency. It was these individuals the party leadership was watching and sometimes courting, and it was these individuals who received media coverage and attention from public opinion polls about their plans and perspectives for the future. Sáez was chosen as candidate by COPEI, and Salas Römer ultimately became the only contender who could seriously challenge Hugo Chávez for the presidency. AD selected its long-time central party leader, Luis Alfaro Ucero, who was roundly rejected by voters.

In this process of change, the credentials for elective office were increasingly acquired in an electoral and campaign arena in which citizens had a capacity to see and judge the candidates rather than in intraparty factional politics. One analyst has argued that state and local elections "renewed the political class" in Venezuela.[62] The overarching issue of the legitimacy of the political system, however, continued to shadow the electoral process. In 1998, great popular support evolved around the presidential bid of Hugo Chávez, one of the most prominent coupmakers of 1992. He was elected by a large margin, leading many to believe that the traditional parties had at last lost their grip on the Venezuelan political system.

These changes in the dynamics of political careers altered national-level discussions about citizen concerns, especially at state and local levels, according to some observers. Thus, the leader of an important legislative commission commented on the deputies who had left congress to run for governor or mayor in 1993 and 1995, "Some won, and when they were no longer governor or mayor, they returned to congress with this experience in their minds. Those who lost state elections came back to congress with a much better sense of what the states and municipalities were all about and what citizens were concerned about."[63] To the extent that such occurrences increased, the nature of the lessons that politicians learned through their careers would be significantly altered from lessons that focused attention on the perspectives of party leaders to those that spanned a much broader field of perspectives. The changed nature of political careers, more than any other consequence of the reforms, indicates the extent to which the reforms of 1989 had increased the degree of pluralism in the political system.

The consequences of the 1989 reforms are significant not only in terms of the political dynamics they unleashed but also in terms of subsequent institutional changes that deepened the extent of democratic accountability in Venezuela. The 1989 voting law established the "named" vote for municipal councillors; voters could now vote for individual candidates on one or more party lists. The law also established a mixed system—55 percent selected on the basis of named votes and 45 percent selected on the basis of proportional representation—for members of congress and state legislatures. In 1992, the proportion of named to proportionally selected local legislators was altered, increasing named councilors to 66 percent of the total and reducing those who were selected by proportional representation to 34 percent. Then, in 1993, the law was amended again to expand the named vote to 100 percent of the municipal council. This law was changed again under the Caldera administration to reestablish the formula that was introduced in 1992: 66 percent named and 34 percent proportional representation. In addition, each state would thereafter be entitled to a minimum of three representatives to congress rather than the previous two. The Supreme Electoral Council, previously composed of party-designated members, would now be composed of six independent members elected by the congress and the rest designated by the five political parties with the largest number of votes in the previous elections. Mayors and governors were elected by simple majority vote throughout this period.

## Conclusions: Rational Politicians, Conflict, and Uncertainty

The new rules of the game introduced in Venezuela did noticeably alter the dynamics of the political process in the country. The crisis of legitimacy that was brought home to the managers of partyarchy through the *caracazo* of 1989 was the most important stimulus to the introduction of the new democratic institutions. The new institutions did not resolve that crisis of legitimacy, but they did help put in place the beginnings of more pluralistic and accountable politics by diminishing the power of the party leaders in Caracas and expanding the possibility for developing new sources of power linked to state- and local-level political competition. The direct election of governors and mayors in Venezuela also did not necessarily produce good—or even improved—government, but it did increase the extent to which citizens could identify the people and the parties responsible for political decision making and the management of public affairs. Indeed, Carlos Blanco, one of the fathers of the political reforms, argued that the concept of leadership was undergoing change as a result of the direct election of governors and mayors. Leadership was no longer measured in terms of rhetoric but in terms of accomplishments, he stated: "A group of people has emerged into political prominence who can say, 'Look what I have *done.*'"[64]

The hypotheses I present in chapter 2 diverge in terms of their predictions about the consequences of political decentralization. Approaches based in economics anticipate the establishment of a new equilibrium. In contrast, the comparative institutionalist approach predicts continued conflict over the rules of the game. Certainly, there is evidence that politicians adapted to the new rules of the game by concerning themselves centrally with efforts to establish electoral advantage over their competitors. At the same time, however, the years after the introduction of the reforms were replete with efforts to stymie or promote their development, to undo or increase their impact, and to adjust to them as parties and politicians contested their reach and meaning. This suggests that the creation of new institutions unleashed new conflicts and resurrected old ones in the political system as center and periphery continued to negotiate over the extent of their power, as governors and mayors began to compete for media and public-opinion attention and power over local resources and decisions, and as party leaders attempted to reconcentrate power in the center.

Two hypotheses drawn from new institutionalism in economics anticipate that institutional change will have an impact on transaction costs or principal-agent problems. The Venezuela case presents a complex picture in response to these hypotheses. The direct election of governors and mayors complicated the electoral process in the sense that it became more pluralistic and thus more subject to change across localities and across time. Elections featured a broader array of electoral coalitions and more diverse ways of becoming a candidate. As a result, citizens needed more information to vote intelligently after the reform than before it. From the perspective of central party leaders and presidents, doing politics also became more complicated, time consuming, and uncertain because it involved more courting and bargaining and the need for more information on the perspectives and personalities of potential candidates and allies. Lines of accountability and loyalty blurred in the new environment. From another perspective, however, the reforms did create the possibility of greater accountability of public officials to voters. In terms of the behavior of officeholders and the identity of those to hold responsible for government performance, citizens had more ready access to pertinent information. The case of Popular Participation in Bolivia provided a similar arena for altered ways of doing politics.

# Political Engineering in Bolivia

## The Law for Popular Participation

The Law for Popular Participation, enacted by the Bolivian legislature as Law 1551 and signed by the executive on April 20, 1994, promised that citizens of the country would henceforth enjoy a more effective form of representative democracy.[1] The law established the municipality as the basic unit for local government throughout the country and authorized the direct election of mayors and municipal councils. It explicitly recognized the legal equality of men and women. It also acknowledged, for the first time in the country's history, the legal standing of indigenous and community organizations and sponsored their incorporation into the new local institutions.[2] As a formal statement of democratic principles and rights to representation, the Popular Participation law was a significant improvement over conditions that had excluded two fifths of the country's population from access to local government.

In addition to a statement of principles, the law had bite. It mandated that 20 percent of national tax revenues be transferred to local governments through a formula based on each municipality's population. Local governments were given responsibility for investment, administration, maintenance, and upkeep of the infrastructure for health, education, local water supply and sanitation, sports, rural roads, culture, and small irrigation works.[3] They were directed to spend no more than 10 percent of the transfers on operating expenses and to invest 90 percent on projects and programs that would spur the development of the local area.[4]

A complementary Law of Administrative Decentralization, passed in July 1995, deconcentrated national-level management of social services (health, education, and social assistance) and devolved administrative responsibilities for transportation, tourism, environment, rural electrification, and investment fund management to the departmental (regional government) level.[5] This same law established elected councils at the departmental level to advise and monitor the activities of presidentially appointed prefects and mandated cabinets for the prefects, made up of nationally appointed ministers of departmental-level bureaucracies. It also dissolved the Departmental Development Corporations (DDCs), the institutions that had had a virtual monopoly on non-central resource allocation in the past. The projects managed by the DDCs were to be gradually transferred to the prefects of the departments and managed until their funding was depleted. In conjunction with local priority-setting and investment decision making, deconcentration and devolution meant that government and its social and development-related programs would henceforth come within the orbit of regional and local control.

As a plan for political decentralization, Popular Participation was designed "to correct historical inequalities between urban and rural areas" by establishing 311 new territorial divisions, the municipalities.[6] Carefully drawn boundaries mixed rural and urban communities to counterbalance the tendency for urban areas—and urban elites—to capture decision-making power and public resources. In the aftermath of this redistricting, 85.5 percent of the municipalities had a rural majority, even though nationally, 58 percent of the population lived in urban areas.[7] In addition, in reference to what were called "territorial base organizations" (OTBs), the law recognized historically evolved but legally invisible self-governing bodies of peasant communities, indigenous peoples, and neighborhood councils (*juntas vecinales*), enabling them to claim jurisdiction over specific territory and to claim representation within the new municipalities.[8] With membership on municipal vigilance (oversight) committees, they were then authorized to play a role in planning and carrying out local investments and monitoring decision making and administration by local government.

The mechanics of elections and accountability were straightforward. Councillors would be elected by proportional representation in the new municipalities, and the lead name on the list of the party obtaining an absolute majority in the popular election would become the mayor. In cases in which no party list received an absolute majority, the council would elect the mayor from among those who came in first and second in the voting. In each municipality, the formally recognized grass-roots organization (the OTB) for each municipal subunit (canton) would elect a representative to a vigilance committee, which was given responsibility for approving all budgetary expenditures and monitoring local government accounts.[9] This was "an effort to marry the imperfect representative democracy of the Bolivian constitution with the 'other' traditions of self-government, those of the indigenous peoples and rural communities," the modern form that party politics had introduced and the traditional form through which local affairs had often been managed in the frequent absence of effective state authority.[10]

For Bolivia, its politicians, and its citizens, Popular Participation was a large step into the political unknown. Traditionally, most public affairs in the country, including the provision of services such as education, health, and basic sanitation, were determined in La Paz. The resolution of even minor administrative matters generally required lengthy journeys to ministry headquarters, time-consuming paperwork, and the mobilization of clientelistic ties. Extensive centralization of decision making and control over day-to-day affairs was complemented by political centralization, as parties focused their attention on capturing control of national political office, from which flowed control over a very large amount of patronage and spoils. As part of the architecture of centralization and patronage, departments and provinces were administrative units of the national government; the president appointed the departmental prefect who, in turn, appointed subprefects for the provinces. Before 1994, municipal governments existed only in the country's nine departmental capitals and the capitals of its 112 provinces. Most of the country's territory and most of its rural people—some 42 percent of the population— had no formal local government.

Even in the limited number of municipalities that existed, citizens had little input; between 1942 and 1985 there were no local elections for municipal councils, and mayors were selected by the central government.[11] Ninety-two percent of the revenue shared with the existing municipalities—equal to 10 percent of national tax revenue, distributed according to a formula based on tax contributions—was concentrated in the country's nine provincial capitals. When local elections were reinstituted in the limited number of municipalities that existed in 1985, eligible voter turnout was a sparse 43 percent, suggesting both a weak legacy of citizen involvement in local affairs and a limited range of activities carried out by local government.

In contrast, Popular Participation put significant resources in the hands of municipal officials as well as control over planning and investment for broad categories of public goods. It also enhanced citizen capacity to hold public officials accountable for their actions. Local elections based on party campaigns were complemented by the locally selected vigilance committees, whose job it was to look over the shoulders of the mayors and the councillors and monitor their use of resources. These committees were also given responsibility for proposing investment projects and participating in their elaboration.[12] In some cases, they could halt the transfer of funds from the central government and the municipal councils could, in some cases, censure and dismiss the mayor.[13] The law thus introduced formal mechanisms for limiting the capacity of individuals, parties, and clienteles to dominate resource-allocation decision making. At the same time, because of increased resources made available to the municipalities through revenue sharing, mayorships and councillorships became more valuable public offices, potentially interesting to the politically ambitious at local levels as well as to national party organizations attracted by the potential to capture new levers of power and patronage.

Bolivia's experiment with democratization was introduced in a country with a weak state and an incomplete sense of nationhood, national political parties held together primarily by the distribution of patronage from the center, politically mobilized interests that were centralized and often stronger and more cohesive than the parties, and a history of economic and political instability. For a century and a half, Bolivians worried about national disintegration and the violence and insecurity that such a situation could unleash. Empirical bases for this concern are not difficult to find: forty-one presidents held office in the century between 1880 and 1980; 118 political parties were created between 1958 and 1989, and seven military governments and two civilian governments came to power between 1978 and 1982, although none of them was able to concert effective authority.[14] In a national poll in 1995, 28.6 percent of respondents identified themselves more strongly with their regions than with the country.[15] In 1996, a department threatened to declare itself independent or to join Argentina or Chile rather than to submit to a loss of representation in congress.[16]

These conditions raise questions about why decision makers in 1994 were not more concerned that political and fiscal decentralization could destroy what little coherence the country had or why they were not more interested in maintaining the levers of patronage and organization they enjoyed. Under existing conditions, rational politicians and institutional designers might well recommend that government centralize and strengthen its hold over national territory and institutionalize political stability before trusting in the capacity of newly created local governments to improve over the performance of the central government. As the following survey of Bolivia's traditional political institutions indicates, there were important reasons, related to political stability and control, to insist on central power and important incentives to prefer central to local power. In fact, these same conditions eventually contributed to a crisis of governance serious enough for political leaders to consider radical new solutions to long-existing problems. Popular Participation, an idea generated by a small team of advisers, was taken up by a national political entrepreneur as a solution to ineffective state management and troublesome demands for regional autonomy. The process of reform, however, was far from participatory, and the change it implied was far from popular. There is no question, however, that it was audacious, given the history of Bolivia's political institutions.

## The Sins of the Fathers

Bolivia's republican past was fraught with even more problems of national integration than that of Venezuela. The battle for independence from Spain, which formed part of the wider Andean struggle led by Simón Bolívar, left behind in 1825 a country divided by geography and ethnicity.[17] For most of the period prior to the 1870s, it is difficult to speak of Bolivia as a country in any sense of the word. It was, until then, little more than a setting for locally centered enclaves dominated by landed elites, rural baronies ruled by warlords, mining camps that maintained their own social and economic order, and indigenous peoples who continued pre-Columbian traditions of self-government. Throughout much of the nineteenth century, state authority did not reach much beyond the cities of La Paz, Cochabamba, Potosí, Santa Cruz, Sucre, and Oruro, and any form of state presence in remote highland areas or tropical lowlands was generally happenstance—a result of mining activities, the presence of trade routes, or the natural course of rivers.

Even this limited presence of the state was undermined by a succession of coups, countercoups, and regional strongmen and by maladministration, ineptitude, and corruption at the center. The geographical penetration of the national state and its capacity to insist on national integrity and sovereignty was so weak that Bolivia lost half its territory to the neighboring states of Chile, Peru, Argentina, Brazil, and Paraguay between 1825 and 1935. These losses, especially as a result of the 1879–84 War of the Pacific with Chile and the 1932–35 Chaco War with Paraguay, resonated in national political discussion as "territorial dismemberment."[18] At the same time, large regions of the country, particularly those in the east, were unconnected to national government and developed strong antipathies toward the central state.[19]

Bolivia's historical weakness as a state and a nation does not mean that there were not numerous efforts to overcome these conditions. In fact, its more recent history can be written in large part as an ongoing effort to build both a credible state and a national identity. In the second half of the nineteenth century, an economic boom based on silver introduced the first efforts in this direction. Between that time and the turn of the century, governments began to create an infrastructure of roads and railways to link the country more effectively to external markets, even while internal links remained largely undeveloped. During the 1880s, as tin mining began to rival silver in economic importance, the country's first political parties emerged, coalescing around interests in land and mining-based industry and defining themselves primarily in terms of commitment to tradition or modernity. These interests, which incorporated rival visions of governance—federal and regional vs. unitary and national—divided elites centered in Sucre and Potosí from those in La Paz.[20] Their politics, however, only served to underscore how limited the debate was at that time; national elections involved only about 2 percent of the population.[21]

Despite small numbers, the divisions between those oriented toward regional power and those who wanted a centralized state were so deep that civil war broke out in 1898. Echoing the dynamics of the political parties, this war was about elite rivalries, and peasants were enlisted to do battle over issues that had little meaning for them.[22] Liberals, demanding federalism, confronted Conservatives; the Liberals were victorious and celebrated their ascension to power by abandoning federalism. In the war's wake, a national and industrial "project" was supported by a thirty-year boom in tin production and exports that in turn fueled the growth of La Paz and linked Bolivia firmly to the international economy. Tin mining became the dominant political force in the period between 1898 and the 1920s; government was successfully captured and manipulated by the industrial interests of the "Big Three" mining baronies of the Aramayo, Hochschild, and Patiño families. In pursuit of these economic interests, the state took on a national goal of development and became, simultaneously, a source of spoils and patronage.[23] As a consequence, and even while the mining and urban economies continued to boom, elite politics gradually degenerated into intense conflict over possession of the presidency and the distribution of the spoils of office. Indeed, although the country had been declared a unitary state and the hold of mining interests over both the state and the economy had been solidified, the dynamics of day-to-day politics undermined the capacity of the state to be either strong or effective. Regionalism also remained strong enough to further inhibit the development of national identity.

Although Bolivia's economic development, based on the expansion of tin mining, lasted until the depression of the 1930s, it had begun to slow down and stagnate by the mid-1920s. Simultaneously, the degeneration of politics into elite and personalistic infighting over control of the presidency accelerated, pitting "ins" and "outs" against each other within and among parties. This dynamic, in the context of a declining economy, helped spawn additional nationalist initiatives among urban and intellectual groups that had not been incorporated into elite politics. Nationalist sentiments figured in the military coup of 1930, in which dissident and nationalist junior officers lent their support to reformist elements among the higher officers. When this leadership proved too accommodating to the mining elites, junior officers staged their own coup in order to push their nationalist agenda. Shortly thereafter, however, the Chaco War further emphasized the failure of the country's leaders to create either a nation or a state. This conflict, in which Bolivia had considerable logistic, matériel, and numerical advantages, was a farce of national incapacity from beginning to end. It ended in humiliation and further loss of territory, more than sixty-five thousand Bolivian deaths and desertions, and even greater economic and political disarray.[24] Once again, the state had proved itself weak and incompetent, feeding increased political instability and greater weakness, as well as heightening nationalist sentiment among urban intellectuals, the military, and increasingly, the working classes.

In the wake of the war, a military government, infused with both nationalism and socialist ideology, introduced greater state involvement in the economy, nationalized oil holdings, and called for corporatist representation of social groups.[25] The constitution of 1938 recognized the obligation of the state to provide for the social welfare of its citizens, and investments increased in the social sectors. Nevertheless, these commitments were poorly fitted for the reality of a country in which most Bolivians were not citizens. According to the same constitution, citizens "are required to . . . be at least 21 years old, know how to read and write, and be enrolled in the Civic Register."[26] By this definition, most Bolivians were excluded from political relevance. In 1940, about 2.8 percent of the population voted in the presidential elections.[27]

The next major effort to create a strong and national state came as a culmination of the increasing mobilization of political parties and unions in a context of increasing disillusion with the capacity of existing political rules to bring about such an end. The Revolution of 1952 began on April 9 as a three-day confrontation in La Paz. Facing each other were the military and its allies in the oligarchy on one side and the Movimiento Nacionalista Revolucionario (MNR), mine workers, and the national police on the other. The issue that triggered the confrontation was a dispute over control of the presidency.[28] The conflict spread quickly to a much larger set of issues, however, feeding on the weakness of the state itself. Union organizations took over mining camps and peasant villages, while armed peasant organizations drove landowners from their haciendas as they took over land and set up self-governing local institutions to distribute and protect the land. The mine owners and landed elites found little protection in a national army that quickly disintegrated; many recruits joined the insurgents or abandoned their arms to locally organized groups of insurgents. Central authority collapsed.[29]

The revolution did not last long, its violent phase over between April and June of 1952, but its impact was profound: major agrarian reform (more than 200,000 rural families benefited when some 30 percent of the country's agricultural land was redistributed); an economy increasingly dominated by the state (by 1963, the state accounted for a third of GDP); a dominant political party (the MNR); a strong and radical labor movement (capped by the peak organization, the Central Obrera Boliviana, or COB); a reformed and modernized military; and a state that was more centralized and that penetrated further into national territory than had ever been the case in the past. For the first time in the country's history, indigenous groups were incorporated into national political and economic life. Moreover, the vote was extended to all adults, and a sense of national identity became a reality for a much larger portion of the population.[30]

The creation of a strong national state was central to the goals of the MNR and the Revolution of 1952. The revolution was successful in this objective in terms of establishing a set of institutions that were widely recognized as legitimately Bolivian and also in the sense of providing the government with control over sufficient economic resources, primarily through nationalization of the mining sector, for pursuing national goals. MNR governments, however, were not successful in creating a strong state in the sense of the capacity to set unambiguous rules of the game or to administer public services effectively.[31] Indeed, in the twelve years of MNR government that followed the revolution, as the state grew in size and responsibilities, party rivalry and political challenges to government increased. Parties competed intensely to dominate an apparatus that could provide jobs, contracts, subsidies, and connections for loyal party members and potential supporters. At the same time, the strength of the unions was a constant threat to the ability of the government to establish and carry out public policies. The military, like the unions, remained an uneasy ally with the MNR-dominated governments in the post-revolutionary period. Regionalism also continued to threaten national coherence.[32] While nominally in control, it was not at all clear that the government could marshal enough force to insist on its right to govern. In 1964, the revolutionary government was overthrown, the victim of increasing intransigence on the part of labor and the military, thereby eroding control not only over the disparate forces that made up its support base but its own mismanaged economic policies and spoils-based administration as well.[33]

Like the MNR before them, successive military governments committed themselves to the creation of a strong and centralized state to counteract the centrifugal forces of regionalism and localism. Through nationalizations and other measures, they increased the size and economic presence of the state. Aided by high prices for petroleum and commercial agricultural products, and the beginnings of the coca boom in the 1970s, military governments borrowed money and invested heavily in infrastructure and industrialization. At the same time, strongly organized labor unions continued to challenge the military, which also needed to manage dissension over national development policy and power within its own ranks.

Political conflict increased in the mid-1970s. Regional economic elites, especially in the rapidly growing city and department of Santa Cruz, added their voices to national political debates.[34] These groups, organized as civic committees, set themselves in opposition to the political and economic mandarins of La Paz and demanded greater regional autonomy and fiscal decentralization. During this period, the military established Departmental Development Corporations in each of the country's nine departments, funded by revenue transfers from the central government and taxes on local natural resources. These development corporations became important as centers of regional economic power and initiative. They were dominated by the civic committees and focused on investments in urban infrastructure such as electricity, potable water, sewers, and roads. The corporations began to play a role in the increasing political mobilization as regional elites used them to achieve local development goals and make demands on the central government for resources and autonomy.

Under the military, the state grew in size and also became as dependent as civilian governments on the distribution of patronage and the dynamics of clientelism.[35] The goal of overcoming a century and a half of weakness continued to elude the generals and lieutenants as well as civilian politicians. The turning point of this difficult period was reached during the administration of General Luis García Meza, when brutality, corruption, and the close connection between the leadership and the country's drug trade fully discredited the military.

The entrepreneurial elites of Santa Cruz, those of the eastern region more generally, and the peak organization representing business, the Confederación de Empresarios Privados de Bolivia (CEPB), played an important role in bringing this period of military rule to an end, as did the COB. Mobilizing against plans by the government to build a sugar mill near La Paz, the civic committee of Santa Cruz, representing the department's business leaders, protested strongly, leading the government to attempt to reorganize the civic committees in all the departments. This, in turn, led to a twenty-four-hour strike, called by the Santa Cruz committee and widely supported in the department.[36] Continuing protests in Santa Cruz and La Paz and an unusual convergence of workers and economic elites in opposition to the military governments eventually brought them to an end.[37] Again, those who dominated the state had failed to provide effective government or legitimate institutions.

### Union Militancy and Party Patronage

The sins of the past that seemed to condemn the Bolivian state to perpetual weakness also influenced the emergence of the country's class-based organizations and political parties and the relationships that developed among these political actors. Although political parties made their official debut in the 1880s, worker's organizations were the first to attempt to mobilize non-elites for political purposes. Labor unions first appeared through an artisan-labor movement in the latter half of the 1910s, and in the early 1920s, railway workers created the first labor federation in the country. This early union movement was strongly influenced by socialism and later by communism. In 1927, a national confederation was formed in order to represent worker interests, but the refusal of political and economic elites to accept such representation in any form encouraged organized labor to use confrontational tactics— general strikes, protest marches, and demonstrations—in order to make their demands known. When Bolivia's economy collapsed in the depression and when unemployment increased even further in the wake of the Chaco War, labor protested more frequently and more insistently. Strikes, marches, and demonstrations punctuated life in the cities on a daily basis.[38] Over time, exclusion from power and the use of direct protest that was in turn met with repression meant that the labor organizations emerging out of the 1920s and 1930s were strident, class conscious, and alienated.

The 1940s were a period of even greater mobilization as labor became "the most coherent radical force in the country."[39] In 1944, the Federación Sindical de Trabajadores Mineros de Bolivia (FSTMB) was formed, and, through the leadership of Juan Lechín Oquendo, became the principal force for the political and economic enfranchisement of workers. Centered among workers who lived in concentrated and remote locations, ties of loyalty and commitment were strong. This union faced continuous and violent repression; its history, along with that of the other major unions—railway and factory worker organizations—is replete with confrontations between striking or protesting unions and forces representing the government. The "Massacre of Potosí" in 1947, the "Massacres of Catavi" in 1942, 1947, and again in 1949, and the "Immolation of Villa Victoria," which commemorate such confrontations, became an enduring part of union martyrology. Equally telling, leaders of the union movement were routinely rounded up and imprisoned or exiled. The result of this history was a union movement that was ideological, militant, strong, practiced in carrying out strikes and protests, and able to survive clandestinely. It also had leadership from its own ranks: miners and other workers who did not rely on the leadership of urban intellectuals in the same fashion that the political parties did. Rural organizations emerged later than those of industrial workers, but by the 1940s, a number of rural syndicates had been formed. In the aftermath of the Revolution of 1952, these organizations initiated a far-reaching agrarian reform, largely in the absence of government. As indicated, the COB was formed just after the revolution and became the most important voice of organized labor in the country. Within a short time, membership in the COB was obligatory for all labor unions. Well into the 1990s, labor unions continued to elicit more confidence from Bolivian citizens than any other political or economic institution in the country, with the exception of the mass media.[40] The unions were central and ubiquitous actors in Bolivian politics, and few proposals for change could effectively survive their opposition.

In contrast to the emergence of a mass-based and militant labor movement, the emergence of nationalist and reformist political parties came later in Bolivian history and was much less successful in terms of creating strong and coherent organizations.[41] Political mobilization centered primarily in La Paz, where reformist professionals and merchants, revolutionary socialists, and radical students joined nascent workers' organizations in protesting the backward condition of their country, the dismal state of its economic development, and the limited extent of political participation. The political parties that emerged in the 1930s and 1940s began as elite organizations. Over time, they became mass parties with multiclass support but still with elite leadership. Their ideologies, generally leftist, were decidedly nationalist and statist. The MNR, the party that spearheaded the Revolution of 1952 and, since then, becoming the most prominent political party, was formally organized in 1941. Established by young urban intellectuals, it proclaimed both nationalist and socialist objectives for "affirming and defending the Bolivian nation." Initially, as a party of urban elites, it demonstrated some reluctance to mobilize a mass base beyond the periodic need to rally votes to its cause. Nevertheless, as rival parties emerged and began mobilizing support from among those who had been largely excluded from politics in the past, the MNR turned to wider publics to gain support for its cause and to mobilize displays of power. The structure of the MNR reflected the atmosphere of repression in which it emerged—it was based on a series of cells, designed to persist despite repression, and incorporated paramilitary commandos whose job it was to resist and harass government.

As a force proclaiming nationalism and socialism, the MNR actively sought alliances with labor and encouraged its mobilization. As part of this strategy, it provided an umbrella for the FSTMB's creation. Nevertheless, from the beginning, the labor organizations resisted the control of the MNR, seeking instead the capacity to negotiate independently on issues as they emerged. MNR and labor militants formed the core of the resistance that resulted in the revolution, but they never acknowledged a united leadership. In fact, the mining unions were far in advance of the MNR in taking control of the mines and forcing their nationalization, and the rural unions were far in advance of the MNR in taking over land and forcing the agrarian reform by fiat. The COB, acknowledging affiliation but not union with the MNR, was able to demand control of several ministries in the first revolutionary government and dictated the terms for the relationship of labor to the nationalized industries. Asserting the principle of co-government, the COB insisted on naming labor ministers and others for the cabinet and the right to representation in the leadership ranks of the party.[42] Similarly, it demanded worker control in the mines. In rural areas, regional and local *caciques* (bosses) were forces to be reckoned with. By the late 1950s, national political figures were required to court their support and, at times, needed invitations to "intrude" into the areas the *caciques* controlled.[43]

As the MNR struggled to "lead" the revolution and then to keep at its head, ceding control of key policy areas was one way of maintaining support. Just as important, MNR governments became skilled at responding to specific needs of specific groups and at distributing jobs and resources to their supporters in an effort to establish and maintain internal order. Over time, this response became more embedded in the dynamics of everyday politics, and eventually support for the MNR reflected response to the particularistic needs of organized groups rather than identification with a program or even a leadership group.[44] This dynamic held the seeds of the systematic weakening of the party over time as its power became increasingly dependent on spoils and parceling out policy areas to its supporters. Other parties also mobilized and contested elections around the desire to control patronage and spoils, affirming that, as one observer noted, "power in countries like Bolivia is the power to appoint people and provide jobs."[45]

Whereas in Venezuela the strongly organized political parties set out to create and incorporate all other organizations that were politically relevant, in Bolivia the parties never matched the loyalty and militancy of the labor unions. Thus, the relationship between parties and workers' organizations was much more based on negotiation and pact-making than on co-optation and control. Mobilizing the vote involved bargains, horse-trading, and promises about public policy and spoils. The currency for strengthening the party was domination of the national executive, and there was clear incentive to increase the extent to which the government set policies that rewarded important supporters and managed as much patronage as possible. The dynamics put a premium on a large and active state as well as a centralized one. They did not require that the state deal effectively with public problems, however.

### Political Pacts, Economic Reform, and Centralized Decision Making

In 1982, democracy was reinstated in the country, but it was a crisis-ridden and fragile system. Between 1982 and 1985, Bolivia seemed to be repeating the dynamic of the past as general strikes, mass protests, marches, hunger strikes, and denunciations brought government to a standstill. Hernan Siles Zuazo, of the Unidad Democrática y Popular (UDP) Party, attempted to govern with a shifting coalition made up of center-left parties, but conflict within the coalition impeded any effort to address problems of either political or economic instability. Moreover, the COB systematically opposed any efforts to respond to the mounting economic crisis.

Among the numerous problems faced by this administration, the massive foreign debt accumulated by the military regimes of the 1970s created the most immediate sense of crisis. Not only did the debt become due, part of a larger international crisis that reverberated through Latin America in the aftermath of Mexico's 1982 announcement that it could not service its massive foreign debt, but the price of Bolivia's main export, tin, plummeted in October 1985. At the same time, the price of natural gas, another important export, dropped significantly. The external debt placed an extreme burden on the government and on a country that was poor and underproductive by any measure. Inflation reached extraordinarily high levels in 1984 and 1985. Table 5.1 indicates the extent of the economic crisis in the first half of the 1980s, when growth fell precipitously and inflation skyrocketed. During this difficult period, only the underground economy, spurred by booming drug production, made it possible for large numbers of Bolivians to sustain themselves from one day to the next.[46]

The government of Hernan Siles Zuazo might have been able to deal more effectively with the country's economic policies had not political conflict and partisan rivalries demanded most of its attention. The streets of La Paz and other large cities were rarely free of protesting labor unions. General strikes proliferated, and the main political parties took advantage of the situation to attack each other. Congress was in gridlock; ministers and cabinets lasted only weeks or even days in office. In fact, the situation of the economy became so grave, the political stalemate so deep, and the level of political conflict so great that the government agreed to call elections a year early.[47]

These years of deep crisis and the failure of government to manage the situation were, however, years in which various political interests began to discuss the structural problems of the country's economy and political instability. Modern entrepreneurs from Santa Cruz, for example, began meeting with modernizing groups within the major political parties and some of the more technocratically inclined administrators at high levels in government.[48] Among the concerns they shared was the relationship between the history of populism and state intervention in the country and the gradual discovery of how economic liberalism and effective representative government provided a distinct way of thinking about the relationship between state, market, and civil society. They carried these concerns into the elections of 1985.

The victors in this election were the old revolutionary leader, Victor Paz Estenssoro, and the party that had led the Revolution of 1952 and that had instituted the statist and populist development strategy the country had followed in the succeeding thirty years.[49] The new government immediately convened an economic team, including Gonzalo Sánchez de Lozada, an entrepreneur-turned-politician from Cochabamba.[50] This team called in Har-

## TABLE 5.1
### ECONOMIC INDICATORS IN BOLIVIA, 1980–1995

| Indicator | 1980 | 1981 | 1982 | 1983 | 1984 | 1985 | 1986 | 1987 | 1988 | 1989 | 1990 | 1991 | 1992 | 1993 | 1994 | 1995 |
|---|---|---|---|---|---|---|---|---|---|---|---|---|---|---|---|---|
| GNP per capita[a] | 550 | 610 | 550 | 490 | 460 | 450 | 490 | 620 | 730 | 730 | 710 | 720 | 740 | 770 | 770 | 800 |
| GNP per capita growth rate (%) | 6.6 | 10.9 | −9.8 | −10.9 | −6.1 | −2.2 | 8.9 | 26.5 | 17.7 | 0.0 | −2.7 | 1.4 | 2.8 | 4.1 | 0.0 | 3.9 |
| GNP growth rate (%) | 1.6 | 1.0 | −6.8 | −3.8 | 13.7 | −13.2 | −1.7 | 4.7 | 4.1 | 3.4 | 5.7 | 5.1 | 4.0 | 4.0 | 4.6 | 3.9 |
| Annual inflation | — | 32.0 | 123.1 | 276.7 | 1,308 | 11,480 | 277.0 | 14.5 | 16.0 | 15.3 | 17.1 | 21.0 | 12.4 | 8.8 | 7.4 | 10.7 |
| Govt. deficit (−) or surplus as % of GNP | 30.6 | 29.9 | 24.2 | 14.9 | 10.1 | 12.3 | 8.3 | 11.8 | 14.5 | 16.3 | 20.0 | 24.9 | 31.2 | 32.2 | 33.2 | — |
| Total external debt (TEB)[b] | 2,702 | 3,219 | 3,329 | 4,069 | 4,317 | 4,805 | 5,575 | 5,836 | 4,901 | 4,132 | 4,275 | 4,061 | 4,235 | 4,307 | 4,871 | 5,266 |
| Total public debt as % of TEB[c] | 80.8 | 84.6 | 85.2 | 80.0 | 78.1 | 73.1 | 73.0 | 79.2 | 84.5 | 82.9 | 86.2 | 86.9 | 86.6 | 85.8 | 84.5 | 84.5 |

Source: World Bank (1997).
[a]Current U.S.$.
[b]Millions of Current U.S.$.
[c]Includes public guaranteed debt.

vard's Jeffrey Sachs, who advised shock therapy and later recommended that the president put Sánchez de Lozada, minister of planning, in charge of the economic team and the country's economic policy.[51] In an intensive period of less than three weeks, this team hammered out the Nueva Política Económica (NPE), a shock program aimed at halting the spiraling inflation and putting in place the basic principles of a market economy.[52] On August 29, 1985, the president announced Decree 21060, which put the program into effect and signaled that both the government and the MNR had turned their backs on the nationalist and statist past.

From a macroeconomic perspective, the NPE was a stunning success. The core of the program was aimed at controlling hyperinflation. This strategy brought a rapid and welcome degree of stability to an economy that had generated the second-highest inflation rate in modern history.[53] Within two months, monthly inflation had been reduced to about 2 percent, and by 1987, it had declined to an annual level of less than 15 percent. Growth recovered in that year also, and per capita GDP showed strong gains (see Table 5.1). The NPE included devaluation, a wage and salary freeze, liberalization of the domestic economy, an end to price controls, and massive downsizing of the large state enterprise sector. It also sought to open the economy to international trade and capital.

Paz Estenssoro and Sánchez de Lozada also had a deeper goal in mind in terms of reestablishing the authority of the state and responding to extensive corruption in government. They sought to reverse the historical legacy of a state whose existence was threatened by its own weakness. According to Sánchez de Lozada, "Rather than a strictly economic program, the NPE is a political plan that aims at reestablishing principles that are fundamental to the functioning of the Republic and without which we run a grave risk of following a path of national state disintegration."[54] In contrast to the approach of political leaders of the past, however, the solution to strengthening the state lay in making it smaller and giving it fewer responsibilities.

The rapid success of the program in curtailing inflation gained Bolivia considerable international attention. The costs of the therapy were extremely high, however, as tens of thousands of people lost their jobs and as government was unable to provide traditional forms of social welfare services to urban and lower-middle-class constituencies. As a response to the hardship in the wake of the economic reforms, the government created one of the earliest and most successful models of a social adjustment fund, which, through a process of funding local-level development and employment-generating schemes, brought work and other benefits to an estimated 1.2 million people.[55]

Politically, the NPE was as significant as it was in the economic realm. What made it possible was a formal pact, the Pacto por la Democracia, between two principal political parties, the MNR and the Acción Democrática Nacionalista (ADN), in which the parties pledged to support the reforms and a state of siege that enabled the government to control (and repress) opposition.[56] The pact, signed on October 16, 1985, created a model of striking a bargain on the contents of the economic program in exchange for representation in government ministries and in the cabinet.[57] When the government of Jaime Paz Zamora took over in 1989, it engineered a pact known as the Acuerdo Patriótico, which committed the pacting parties, the Movimiento de Izquierda Revolucionaria (MIR) and the ADN, to continue the main lines of the NPE in exchange for a carefully engineered division of government offices.[58] While less successful than the Pacto por la Democracia in terms of maintaining a firm governing coalition, the Acuerdo Patriótico was equally important in resolving a basic political problem in Bolivia, that of concerting enough power to govern.[59] The traditional politics of patronage were thus put to use in the service of economic reform.

Both the NPE and its successor program in the Paz Zamora government were carried out through centralized executive decision making. This was most clear in the government of Victor Paz Estenssoro, when a small group of technocrats designed and implemented the major policies for stabilization and the initial efforts to replace the state-centered development strategy of the past with a more market-oriented strategy. Indeed, those designing the program believed that solutions to the economic problems were technical and should not be subject to political negotiations.[60] The Pacto por la Democracia and the Acuerdo Patriótico ensured that congressional input into economic policy would be limited to approving the plans of the executive and that there would be little debate.[61]

Technocratic decision making was also accompanied by harsh political measures carried out against politically mobilized groups, particularly labor. To stop a marathon of general strikes and street protests, Paz Estenssoro declared a state of siege in September 1985 and ordered the arrest and internal exile of large numbers of union leaders, including the grand figure of Bolivian labor, Juan Lechín Oquendo. As many as twenty-three thousand miners in the state-owned mining companies were dismissed, and thousands more lost their jobs because of the crisis. The government responded with the Social Emergency Fund but not with any conciliation on the main lines of its economic policy.[62] The Jaime Paz Zamora government also adopted the state of siege and sent labor leaders to prison and to internal exile. It is not too much to claim that the NPE and its successor were designed and implemented in authoritarian style.

Clearly, the political agreement on the NPE needs to be understood from the perspective of the hyperinflation—a situation so painful that a large number of politically relevant groups, as well as the population more generally, agreed that "something must be done" and were willing to give government some latitude and significant support to do it, even at the cost of new hardship. And the NPE bought political tolerance because it produced noticeable positive results in short order in controlling inflation, despite the repression of labor protest. The importance of Victor Paz Estenssoro and General Hugo Banzer Suárez as leaders of their parties also enabled them to have considerable control over their MNR and ADN followers in congress.[63] Indubitably, the underground economy increased the sustainability of households, many of which also benefited from the highly innovative and rapidly instrumented Social Emergency Fund. Nevertheless, against the backdrop of the extreme political instability of the period leading up to the Paz Estenssoro government and against the backdrop of extended incapacity to deal with the mounting economic crisis, the NPE was an important moment in Bolivian history. But the political lessons that could be drawn from the NPE and its continuation under the next government were stark: centralization of power, technocratic decision making, repression of opposition, and distribution of patronage could respond to intransigent problems of political stability in the country, at least in the short term. Each of these factors, however, could also be linked to the persistence of political instability over the longer term.

From the perspective of Popular Participation, the reform program of 1985 is also important because it brought national attention to Gonzalo Sánchez de Lozada, the single most important person in propelling NPE forward, and because of the political conditions it laid for the elections of 1989. Those elections, in which Sánchez de Lozada ran and lost a presidential bid as the candidate of the MNR, thrust the candidate into a period of personal reflection about Bolivia's past and future and his own role as a reformer. These reflections led to a fundamental questioning of the lessons about centralization and stability that could be drawn from the NPE experience.

## Success, Defeat, and Rethinking History

The NPE made Gonzalo Sánchez de Lozada a national political figure.[64] As the architect of the economic reform program, he gained national and international attention as a reformer who represented a new entrepreneurial and technocratic elite in the country and in the MNR.[65] He had strong backing among the modernizing entrepreneurs of the country, new technocratic elites in the public and private sectors, and both technocrats and leftist intellectuals who had been part of the emergency adjustment fund experience. Equally important, he became the standard bearer of the reformist flag within the MNR, the figure who championed a new vision of Bolivia's development that was in tune with the neoliberal ideology sweeping policy circles throughout Latin America at the time.

Within the MNR, the vision guiding the NPE reformers was very distant from the traditions of the revolution and its beneficiaries. It was market-oriented and international where the MNR tradition was statist and national-ist, liberal where the MNR had been protectionist, and capitalist rather than socialist.[66] For the reformist wing of the MNR, Sánchez de Lozada was an ideal person to lead the party in the elections of 1989. Energetic, attractive, and personable, he promised to bring considerable popular support to the party. While his candidacy was not automatic and he faced opposition within the MNR from those who supported its traditional, statist, populist, and clientelist bases, Sánchez de Lozada had strong support from Paz Estenssoro and the reformists within the party.[67] Few were surprised when he was con-firmed as the MNR candidate on September 5, 1988.

The election campaign went well for the MNR. Sánchez de Lozada cam-paigned on a platform of continuing the economic reforms and moving the Bolivian economy into a more competitive position internationally. Socially, the party promised renewed efforts to create employment and to deal with massive problems of poverty. Public opinion polls, which gave Sánchez de Lozada the lead, were proved accurate on election day. The MNR carried the popular vote with 23.07 percent of the total, against 22.70 percent for ADN candidate Hugo Banzer and 19.64 percent for the MIR's Jaime Paz Zamora. It appeared that the success of the NPE, the MNR, and Sánchez de Lozada was vindicated in the popular election.

This prognosis did not take into consideration the details of the country's electoral process, however.[68] Under the rule in effect at the time, when no candidate wins an absolute majority of the popular vote, Bolivian presidents were elected by congress from the top three winners of the popular vote.[69] This electoral process worked to the advantage of those candidates and par-ties that actively sought out congressional and party coalitions and that were ready to make deals to share the presidency and the benefits of control over the executive branch, including the distribution of ministerial posts and ex-tensive patronage over public-sector jobs. The MNR campaign, however, had been characterized by negative personal attacks on the other candidates, which now made it difficult for the party to gain support from the ADN or the MIR.[70] In addition, a series of new political parties was vying for power, some of them representing populist movements, such as the Unión Cívica de Solidaridad (UCS) and Conciencia de Patria (CONDEPA), and some of them representing ethnic and regional movements, such as the Movimiento Revolucionario Tupac Katari de Liberación (MRTKL, or Katarista Party), and this added to the complexity of the negotiations. Moreover, perhaps because the logic of the congressional process was not fully understood or because Sánchez de Lozada was overly confident after the results of the popular vote, he was reluctant to negotiate aggressively to form a coalition. The other candidates were not so shy. After intensive bargaining, the ADN and the MIR joined forces to elect Jaime Paz Zamora president and to share in executive power and patronage. The MNR was thrown into the opposition.

The consequence of this political process was significant for Sánchez de Lozada on a personal level. Having emerged as a winner from the NPE and the popular election, he now became the outsider and the loser. According to many, this moment of disillusion and loss had a profound impact. The almost-president entered a period of deep depression. According to one associate from this period, "He learned a great deal from the events of 1989. He was the winner of the popular elections but he was not the winner in the subsequent congressional vote. He went into this process very much on his own, thinking he had won and that that was enough. When he lost, he really learned the importance of seeking political accords, agreements. He spent time after his loss thinking about how and why he lost."[71] Another adviser suggested a deeper kind of disillusion: "The 1989 defeat in congress had a real impact on him in the sense that he realized that a formal democracy was not what he thought it was."[72] At one level, the defeat carried an important lesson about the importance of coalition building and alliances in politics, about the need to give and receive, to negotiate and bargain. For a nontraditional politician who had not emerged from years of toil within the MNR as its traditional leaders had done and whose political career had engaged him in policy roles that brought both success and prominence, this was a valuable lesson for the future. At another level, the failure to win the election caused Sánchez de Lozada to question his and his party's assessments of the reality of Bolivia and their ideas about how to solve its problems.

After the election, Sánchez de Lozada turned to the Fundación Milenio, a think tank created by him and several close associates to carry out studies and make recommendations about political reform, the reform of the state, and sustainable development. The ex-candidate wanted help in considering the economic, social, and political situation of the country and in developing a vision of "what ought to be" in considering a second presidential bid in 1993. With Sánchez de Lozada as president, the foundation assembled an international board of advisers, including Juan Linz of Yale University, Arturo Valenzuela of Georgetown University, Carlos Nino of Argentina, and Bolívar Lamounier of Brazil, to provide insight into how the structure of government could be changed to provide for deeper democracy and greater control over the country's development. This group met five times between 1991 and 1993 for five-day retreats with Sánchez de Lozada, his advisers, and at times with leaders of various political parties. In addition, the national group met frequently with specialists called in to discuss particular issues.[73] By all accounts, the young technocrats and modernizing politicians brought together in the foundation fundamentally challenged the central beliefs of Bolivia's postrevolutionary politics: a centralized state, a statist development strategy, a paternalist approach to the country's indigenous population and rural hinterlands, and nationalist protection of industry.[74]

A number of those who joined the work of the foundation were young elites who had been actively engaged in the social adjustment fund carried out during the implementation of the NPE. Through that work, and the extensive travel and local-level experience that it required, they became familiar for the first time with the level of poverty and backwardness that structured the lives of most of the Bolivian population. They witnessed the exploitation, paternalism, and prejudice that, even in postrevolutionary times, characterized the interaction between the Spanish-speaking population and the indigenous groups who made up more than half the population.[75] Others, educated abroad, were influenced by the enthusiasm for market- and outward-oriented development strategies that were strongly supported by international financial institutions and the economics profession more generally. According to one central participant in the foundation's discussions,

> There were two or three areas in which we were particularly interested. We believed that the government should completely cease being a producer of goods and services and that this activity should be carried out by the private sector. We also wanted to open up the country to the rest of the world and make Bolivia part of the modern trend toward globalization. The third thing we wanted to do was to redesign the state, to increase its efficiency and organize it along efficiency grounds rather than functional ones. We wanted to get

away from the rigid centralized system that had been in place. The state in Bolivia suffers from a paradox. On the one hand, it is very paternalistic in terms of taking on problems, but on the other hand it is very limited in its capacity to respond to real problems.[76]

Clearly, Sánchez de Lozada's own experience helped them question the strongly embedded economic and political traditions of the country. Raised and educated in the United States (he studied philosophy at the University of Chicago), he was less bound to view the country through the lenses of its postrevolutionary political culture.[77] An entrepreneur from Cochabamba, he was less tied to the clientelistic political traditions of La Paz. Of a technocratic bent himself, he was interested in the results of empirical analysis and social science research.[78] Moreover, he had strong opinions that helped shape the issues considered within the Fundación Milenio. He was appalled by conditions of poverty and backwardness in the country, particularly among the indigenous population that was still primarily rural; he was deeply critical of the level of corruption in government; and he was impatient with nationalist sentiments that he believed constrained the capacity of Bolivia to become part of a new global economy.

An important product of the foundation's work and Sánchez de Lozada's leadership was the Plan de Todos, an electoral platform that outlined the central problems of the country. The studies undertaken by the foundation staff convinced them that the highest priorities for the future of the country were those that would respond to unemployment, low salaries, lack of access to decent education and health services, corruption, and the failure of the country's development to reach the countryside. The Plan de Todos outlined three strategic pillars to deal with these problems. First, it promised a solution to unemployment, low salaries, and corruption through the privatization of a large number of state-owned enterprises—a process dubbed "capitalization" to counter nationalist concerns about selling what was regarded as the national patrimony. Second, the capitalization of these enterprises would generate funds for a social development foundation that would respond to the needs to improve education, health, and social services, particularly in the poorest areas of the country. At the same time, distributing shares of the enterprises to the population would redistribute wealth in the country. Third, the plan called for popular participation of communities in their own development planning as a way of localizing the benefits of development investments.

With this plan in hand, Sánchez de Lozada went on to win his party's nomination as presidential candidate, hire a public relations firm from the United States to advise on campaign strategy, and canvass the country for votes.[79] The MNR campaigned through an electoral coalition formed with the MRTKL, which sponsored the vice-presidential candidate. The campaign was slick and often bitterly personal, the tactics borrowed from recent U.S. elections, and in the end, the MNR and the MRTKL were successful. Sánchez de Lozada garnered 35.56 percent of the popular votes, avidly sought governing alliances with the UCS and the Movimiento Bolivia Libre (MBL), and proceeded to win the congressional vote.[80] He took office on August 6, 1993, along with his running mate, Vice-President Victor Hugo Cárdenas of the indigenist MRTKL, with a majority coalition in both houses of congress behind him.[81]

## Democratization by Central Plan

The Plan de Todos gave high priority to a decentralization plan called Popular Participation, which was promoted as the basis of a new participatory democracy in the country. In reality, however, the proposal was vague, calling for organized communities to "define their priorities, demand their needs, and supervise the implementation of their decisions through the People's Committees that will be organized" for various local services. The definition of the real content of Popular Participation was left until after the election.

In the wake of his victory, Sánchez de Lozada moved quickly to set up commissions to draft the legislation for the reforms outlined in the Plan de Todos. For Popular Participation, he set up a committee after the election and prior to taking office that was to begin to sketch out the plan more fully. The committee consisted of a number of close advisers who later became ministers in his government as well as leaders of two of the parties in alliance with the MNR. In addition, he called on a young academic from the Santa Cruz region, Carlos Hugo Molina. Molina had participated in the Fundación Milenio and had encouraged the team to consider municipalization as a form of political decentralization. He had been a critic of the MNR and the political system more generally but also an advocate of municipalization for some years.[82] A representative of a small political party, the MBL, which represented democratizing leftist intellectuals, and the leader of the MRTKL participated in discussions, bringing with them considerable knowledge of the indigenous forms of organization and local self-government, as well as knowledge of a tradition of peasant and ethnic claims for local autonomy.[83] This committee drafted the first version of the Popular Participation Law and then turned over its activities to a technical team headed by Carlos Hugo Molina.

In September 1993, under the direction of Carlos Hugo Molina, the team began meeting daily to delve into the details of how Popular Participation would work. The president was often in attendance, dedicating three hundred hours of his time to this working group over the next several months.[84] According to Molina, the group had great scope for thinking creatively about political decentralization: "The president laid down two initial conditions: we were to develop a radical process of political and economic decentralization, and it was to be irreversible."[85] Ultimately, the team that designed popular participation generated thirty-two drafts of the new law over the course of six months of almost daily meetings.

The composition of the design team, particularly the presence of Carlos Hugo Molina, was important in moving the group toward serious consideration of municipalization. Molina had made a name for himself as one of the few advocates of municipalization in the country.[86] As an academic, he had studied municipal government and how it might work, but there were few who took this option seriously. According to some, "His was a voice in the wilderness—no one was listening," even though a number of intellectuals were engaged at that time in a lively discussion of indigenous and rural forms of local-level governance, and some organizations had actively pressured for government recognition of traditional community problem solving, conflict resolution, and social-control systems.[87] Now heading the design team considering Popular Participation, Molina was in an influential role to turn discussion toward this alternative. The president, initially favoring direct decentralization to the level of small communities, was eventually persuaded by the municipal alternative.[88]

Sánchez de Lozada became a strong advocate of the plan that emerged.[89] In his view, the kind of radical municipalization envisioned in the Popular Participation initiative promised to solve at least three problems of the political system. The first was nationalist legitimacy. The president believed strongly that the historic problems of a weak Bolivia— having a presence and an identity throughout the national territory—continued to exist. There were still regions in the country where the notion of "Bolivia" was not fully adopted as a statement of identity. The president worried about the borders of the country but also about the impact of religious movements in some of the hinterlands that threatened the sovereignty of the Bolivian state.[90] Thus, the historic concern of nationalism, which in the past had been approached through the lenses of centralization, was given a new twist: municipalization with significant support from the central government offered a way of penetrating the national territory more fully and realizing the existence of a national state that provided a lifeline for local development. According to a participant in these discussions, "In the early 1990s, it was essential to lessen the demands and pressure on the central state. It was also imperative to get the presence of the state known and understood throughout the country. This was not so much a concern for security in the traditional sense, but because of a concern for political security."[91] For the president and members of the design team, creating a municipal level of government with significant resources at its service and local decision-making autonomy would achieve the historic mission of making a Bolivian nation-state a reality.[92]

Second, the president was keenly concerned about the level of corruption that characterized government in Bolivia. As we have seen, the evolution of the political system from the nineteenth century on had generated a clientelistic and prebendal system in which jobs, contracts, favors, and bribes constituted the normal business of government. Even if the legacy of public corruption could not be overcome, Sánchez de Lozada argued that "it is better to have widespread local corruption than corruption centered in the capital cities of the country," and that "it makes a difference if the thief who is robbing you is in your local community or in a distant capital.[93] Municipalization, in this view, did not necessarily offer an immediate remedy for corruption, but it did bring corrupt acts closer to the people, who were in a better position to monitor them and hold corrupt public officials accountable. Failing this check, he argued that at least local corruption distributed jobs and circulated money in a local economy rather than only in the major cities. In an effort to restructure the state, stripping the central government of most of its control over public-goods provision and development investment, Sánchez de Lozada was convinced that Popular Participation would eventually result in more responsive and less corrupt government. In his words, "There is no way of putting an end to corruption or controlling it in a centralized government. You know, it is one thing not to steal yourself, it is another thing to keep others from stealing. Decentralization of power was important in order to have social control, local control, at the grassroots level, where people can keep an eye on things."[94]

Third, the president saw in municipalization a way to counteract centrifugal tendencies that came from the departmental capitals. For almost two decades, politicians and economic elite groups in several of the nine departmental capitals had been pressing for decentralization.[95] Pressure was particularly strong from prosperous regions such as Santa Cruz and Beni that had grown rapidly since the 1960s and that now sought freedom from La Paz and greater control over fiscal resources. But to those committed to Popular Participation, decentralization to regional levels threatened not only a serious divide between the prosperous eastern part of the country and the much more backward western region, but it also placed tremendous power in the hands of regional economic elites. Sánchez de Lozada and other leaders of the MNR were convinced that decentralization to departmental governments was a recipe for the dissolution of the country. As expressed by one member of the design team, "the departmental capitals are the centers of nuclei of power, and we saw their desire to have direct elections of departmental government as a way of concentrating power at the departmental level. . . . The elites are concentrated in the major cities. The opposition to national politics is found there."[96] Another participant concurred, "If we had gone in the direction of federalism, which is what the regional oligarchical elites wanted, the country would have been destroyed."[97] For the creators of Popular Participation, decentralization to the departmental level worked against one of their principal goals—governability—by encouraging regional separatism.

They believed that regional control would also exacerbate the urban bias of development in the country.[98] According to Sánchez de Lozada, "I thought it was important to break down federalism in this country; it was important that the country not be separated into different regions. Those cities only saw the rural areas as a hinterland, they were never going to do anything for the rural areas. We were protecting ourselves from the pressure groups in those urban areas. We were very conscious of the fact that if you cede power, you get stronger, you get power," in the sense of increased governability.[99] According to one of the design team members, "The Popular Participation Law and the Law of Decentralization are basically about governance, finding a way to decentralize power without destroying the capacity to govern."[100] For the president and the working group, municipalization offered a way of dividing the country to such an extent that the potential for national dissolution was much reduced and the potential power of regional elites diluted.

From the perspective of the president, centralized power faced several threats: a weak central state, incomplete nationalism, extensive corruption with a resulting loss of legitimacy for government, and pressure from economic elites for regional solutions to economic growth and development. Municipalization promised to bring local government closer to the national government. It also promised to strengthen (and save) the state by reducing its functions, to remove from the hands of central officials many of the policy-related benefits they traded for personal and partisan advantage, and to side-step demands for regional autonomy that could threaten a much deeper division of the country into have and have-not regions. Reformers at the national level were thus proposing a never-before-attempted alliance with local governments and communities against centralist elites in national government and federalist economic elites in the departments.

The design team met, deliberated, planned, and drafted detailed legislation in isolation from public discussion or debate. The leadership of the MNR was not involved in the working group and drafts of the law were kept strictly confidential. The unions were also kept outside the discussion. Even ministers were denied access to them.[101] In the process of considering various options for making Popular Participation work, the group did consult at a general level with some party and union leaders, with civic committees in various regions, and with some representatives of organized interests in the country. These meetings proceeded, however, largely without more general public discussion, and after the main ingredients of the plan had been determined. On February 21, 1994, the president sent the law to congress, along with a letter introducing it as "the most important redistribution of political and economic power in the republic since the Revolution of 1952."[102] After that, the design team coordinated an intense process of discussing the initiative with organized groups throughout the country.[103] In technocratic fashion, they produced a matrix of the features of the program and the reactions of each of the groups they polled. These data allowed them to consider adjustments in the legislation that would gain support or at least tolerance from various groups.[104] It also provided information that would help them devise a communications strategy for winning support for their plan.

After the law was sent to congress, considerable discussion appeared in the press. Many commentators voiced skepticism about the intentions of the new law. Others argued against it on the grounds that the "logical" step to take in decentralization would be to the departmental level.[105] Although left outside the design process, the workers and the economic elites reacted strongly. The unions and the civic committees were strongly opposed to the new law. Because they were organized along functional lines, the unions believed they would lose their claim to represent large numbers of people; Popular Participation structured interest representation along geographic lines in the territorial base organizations (OTBs). The powerful national peasant union, the Confederación Sindical Unica de Trabajadores de Bolivia (CSUTCB), which provided the only governance structure for many rural communities in the highland areas of western Bolivia, was particularly concerned about the OTBs. Popular Participation, it believed, would place representatives of territorially defined organizations on the vigilance committees instead of union representatives. Moreover, the rural unions had long benefited from unofficial local autonomy that was the product of a weak state and were concerned that if they were not part of the implementation of Popular Participation, the organizations that did end up representing the communities would be hand-picked by government or would be dominated by the political parties.[106] In response, in May 1995, the government signed an agreement with the CSUTCB confirming an interpretation of the new law that allowed them to seek legal status to represent peasant communities. The rapid implementation of the plan also began to make some headway in reversing the negative perspectives of the peasant unions. In many cases, they were able to claim successfully to represent the local communities.

The COB, with strong support from the teacher's union, was quick to include Popular Participation as one of the "three damned laws" of the Sánchez de Lozada presidency, along with an education reform and the plan for capitalization of state-owned enterprises. The workers' unions were convinced that their preeminent position in representing group interests in the country was threatened by the new law.[107] Proponents of the reform believed the COB had set about a deliberate campaign of disinformation and active resistance to the plan, inspiring skepticism about the real intent of the government. Efforts to communicate and negotiate about the democratizing intentions of the planners were also far from credible because the government was, at the same time, continuing its efforts to repress the unions and their leadership. In fact, opposition to Popular Participation was part of a more general reaction against anything that the MNR government proposed. Since 1985, the party, when in power, had pursued a pattern of hostility and active repression of labor and was now reaping the political consequences of this history.

Regional economic elites were clear losers in Popular Participation. From the outset, led by the civic committee of Santa Cruz, they were opposed to a plan that would bypass the departments in favor of more local government. An early draft of the municipalization plan, leaked to the Santa Cruz group in November 1993, created an outcry against a "secret process" through which the government was undoing movement toward departmental decentralization. They also scorned the capacity for local government in a country as poor and backward as Bolivia. In many of the new municipalities, illiteracy rates were high, few spoke the national language, and the idea of producing plans and budgets on a regular basis could only raise eyebrows. At the end of the year, in a meeting with the vice-president, the civic committee was promised that nothing would be done in terms of departmental decentralization until there was broad agreement on the initiative. In the end, however, Popular Participation included major changes that they opposed: municipalization, elected mayors, and grants based on population.[108] In April 1995, the civic committees again demanded regional decentralization. These demands not only went unheeded but claims for regional power also suffered an additional blow through the July 1995 Law for Administrative Decentralization, which dissolved the Departmental Development Corporations. At the same time, however, this law deconcentrated spending in several policy areas to the departmental level and brought extensive new resources to it.

Although there was strong opposition to the legislation, debate in congress was minimal, lasting less than a day. The law was passed on April 20, 1994. In its wake, an implementation unit and then the National Secretariat for Popular Participation were established. Carlos Hugo Molina was given responsibility for implementing the plan rapidly. Among his initial tasks, however, was managing the widespread skepticism and lack of understanding of the new law. In an atmosphere of general distrust of government and pervasive hostility to politicians, it was hard for average citizens to be enthused about the new law, even if they understood it. Opposition political parties appeared largely indifferent to the new law. The result of a process of closed-door decision making and lack of full debate about the initiative was a piece of legislation with an uncertain future.[109]

## Conclusions: Motivations and Solutions

Popular Participation was not an obvious solution to the problem of a weak state and incomplete political institutions in Bolivia. Those who planned and promoted it, of course, were convinced that it was a modern solution to an old problem, one that turned the traditional solution—centralizing power to increase strength and legitimacy—on its head. But the new logic required some faith in the positive outcomes of testing the unknown. Municipalization would strengthen the state only if that state could be effective in creating the municipalities, reaching them with a clear understanding of their new responsibilities, training their officials in how to carry out those responsibilities, and providing regular and reliable distribution of development resources. Similarly, municipalization would result in decreased corruption at the center only if resources were disbursed in a timely and equitable way and if the transactions between the municipalities and the central government remained free of partisan favoritism.

Moreover, despite the president's belief that local corruption would be better and more amenable to correction than central corruption, such a bromide remained more in the realm of faith than observed reality. And although municipalization robbed the regional capitals of control over development resources, there was nothing in the legislation to prevent the capture of poor and rural municipalities by the larger and richer departmental and provincial capitals, or the fortuitous advance of richer areas ahead of poorer municipalities. The new approach had one powerful argument in its favor, however, in that the traditional approach to Bolivia's political problems of a weak state and incomplete political institutions—centralization—had a long history of failure. Municipalization was a radical alternative to a poor substitute.

This case provides a second lens for assessing hypotheses about the motivations of politicians and the factors that influence the kinds of institutional reforms they champion. The architects of Popular Participation believed that by decentralizing power, they could strengthen the power and legitimacy of the Bolivian state. Concerns for the immediate electoral advantage of the politicians involved could not be easily linked to their actions. Sánchez de Lozada could not be reelected, and Popular Participation was, in any event, of ambiguous advantage to him or his party in the short or even medium term. In a rapidly urbanizing country, the rural support base of the MNR was becoming less important. This support was eroding in any case through the expansion of populist and indigenist parties. The party was not a participant in the critical design phase of the new law, and a concern of its creators was to ensure that societal groups had more control in the municipalities than the parties.[110] In this case, it is not reasonable to argue that the president had short-term electoral gains in sight. Nor was the solution a rational maneuvering within institutional constraints. Instead, it was an definitive effort to break away from those constraints and set new institutions in place.

If hypotheses derived from rational choice analysis do not provide a good explanation of the Bolivian case, the social conflict hypotheses from comparative institutionalism also propose dynamics that are not in tune with what occurred. The municipalization idea did not emerge out of the conflict of groups nor was its adoption primarily a result of negotiation and bargaining between group interests. Groups became involved in the discussion of the reform and conflict emerged over the proposal, but these occurred after the president had committed himself to reform. The option most pressed upon the designers by groups in society was that of decentralization to departmental levels. It was this alternative that was most clearly rejected.

The history of municipalization cannot be told without reference to the concerns of Sánchez de Lozada about the integrity of the Bolivian state. His interest in championing a new solution to the chronic weakness of the state was related to his conviction that it faced a crisis of legitimacy. Ineffectiveness, corruption, and regional separatism threatened the potential to govern and to deal with the deep problems of the country's economic and social development. Giving up power to local government, according to the president, was the only way to ensure that the Bolivian state had a future.

Equally interesting, the work of a team of analysts in the Fundación Milenio and then of a design team called together to put flesh on the bones of an idea in the early months of a presidential administration are important for understanding what solution got proposed for a problem of concern to the president. Other options existed—decentralization to the regional level the most obvious and most often supported alternative among them—but the study and deliberations of the team were central in developing the logic of a new approach. Their deliberations were clearly not responsive to mobilized pressure from interest groups in the society; if anything, they were a reaction against them, if the role of the unions, civic committees, and the pressure for departmentalization is considered. The shape of the reform was fundamentally set by the interests of the design team and its leadership. Like the Venezuelan case, then, this was also an elite project. The design team consulted various interests, but only with the idea of adjusting their detailed solution so that it would become more palatable, not as a way of assessing the viability of other options. The choice of institutions cannot easily be explained as a negotiated or imposed solution to political conflict. More directly, the deliberations of the team suggest much more of an institutional design process, in which discussions dealt centrally with issues of accountability, monitoring, and incentives. Chapter 6 assesses the extent to which Popular Participation was able to fulfil the expectations of its creators.

# A New Conundrum

## National-Local Politics in Bolivia

**P**opular Participation was designed, approved, and introduced in a matter of eight months in 1993 and 1994. In Bolivia, political decentralization was the outcome of a centralized design process involving a small number of officials who worked in close collaboration with the president. It was introduced and voted on in the congress with minimal discussion. It was publicly opposed by powerful groups, but to little effect. It was then put into operation in rapid order. In the early days of the program, it was much more widely discussed in public, but most of the commentary about the new scheme was skeptical.

And indeed, there was much to be skeptical about. Most of the 311 new municipalities did not exist. Any simple assessment of the country's geography suggested that many of those to be created would come into being in remote areas in which there was virtually no experience with budgeting, planning, or managing and monitoring projects. The amount of money to be transferred to the municipalities was considerable, and there was a real question about the absorptive capacity of many local communities. While some municipalities-to be had extensive experience with traditional forms of local problem solving and conflict resolution, they had very little or no experience with the selection of local officials in Western-style elections or the use of significant amounts of capital for investment projects.[1]

The capacity of the national government—to draw new municipal boundaries; to educate local populations about the new institutions; to hold local elections; to train newly elected public officials in their responsibilities; to help grass-roots organizations such as local village councils select representatives to form the vigilance committees and train the new committees; to transfer funds, expertise, and responsibilities for the provision of public services; and to monitor the use of funds—could only be questioned. Despite all that needed to be done, Bolivia continued to have a weak state that carried out even routine activities with great inefficiency. Moreover, these activities were to be challenged by labor unions that feared losing power to the newly recognized community-level organizations and regional economic elites who felt betrayed by the new program.

In addition, the new law was to be carried out in an atmosphere of generalized ignorance about its contents and intent as well as deep suspicion of government and the ruling party. A national poll in mid-1995 indicated that 19.5 percent of respondents believed that corruption was the greatest political problem in the country; 15.2 percent believed it was poor management of government; 17.6 percent thought it was "politicking"; 7.5 percent identified "they never fulfill their promises" as the main problem; and 5.5 percent blamed the deceitfulness of politicians—a total of 65.3 percent of the respondents. Economic instability, narcotrafficking, unemployment, and education all fell below these responses. Almost 73 percent of the respondents said that corruption was worse than it had been in 1985.[2]

While the requirements of implementing the new law were astonishingly difficult, an extraordinary fact about the Bolivian experience is that the municipalization law was put fully into effect in short order. Within twelve months, nearly two hundred new municipalities had been created.[3] The urban bias of decentralized investments was altered rapidly. In 1993, 92.1 percent of funds allocated to non-central levels of government was concentrated in nine departmental capitals (85.1 percent was concentrated in the three largest cities); by 1995, only 39.0 percent was destined for these cities.[4] Elections for municipal councils and mayors were held in December 1995; of 1,625 councillors elected, 437 represented indigenous or peasant communities.[5] In 73 municipalities, these indigenous or peasant councillors held a majority. Indicating a rapid process of local capacity building, 296 municipalities developed operating plans and budgets in 1995. By mid-1997, 13,827 territorial base organizations representing indigenous communities, peasant villages, and urban neighborhoods had gained the legal recognition necessary to speak for their communities within the new municipalities.[6]

The first transfer of funds to the newly installed local governments was made in July 1994. Table 6.1, which indicates the distribution of public in-

**TABLE 6.1**

DISTRIBUTION OF PUBLIC INVESTMENT IN BOLIVIA, 1993–1997

(Percentage of Total)

| Level of Government | 1993 | 1994 | 1995 | 1996 | 1997 |
|---|---|---|---|---|---|
| Central government | 72.5% | 65.5% | 53.4% | 29.3% | 20.9% |
| Regional cofinance | 7.2 | 13.1 | 8.8 | 13.5 | 14.4 |
| Departmental administration | 17.9 | 12.0 | 13.4 | 34.9 | 43.4 |
| Local administration | 2.4 | 9.4 | 24.4 | 22.4 | 21.3 |

*Source:* Ministerio de Desarrollo Humano (1997:140).

vestment to various levels of government, shows that 24.4 percent was transferred to the municipalities in 1995, the first full year of the implementation of Popular Participation. This figure compares with a transfer of only 2.4 percent of national investment in 1993. Municipal investment doubled as a percentage of GNP.[7] The percentage of resources allocated through the departments also increased extensively in 1996, just after the administrative decentralization law transferred a number of investment responsibilities to the departments. In addition, co-financing of development investments increased through a series of funds managed at the national level. Together, these reallocations left less than 21 percent of all public investment in the hands of the national government. Popular Participation accounted for about 43.9 percent of municipal investment in 1995 (see Table 6.2).[8]

Much of the rapidity of the implementation of the law was due to the high priority the program had for the Sánchez de Lozada administration, the personal prompting of the president, and the "true believer" commitment of the leadership and staff of the new Secretariat for Popular Participation. It was also due to a belief among the law's designers and implementers that delay and lengthy preparation would work against the viability of the law. They were convinced that it was better to rush it into reality and let local governments flounder and learn by doing than to lose momentum through careful planning, training, and step-by-step implementation.[9] They believed that the "build capacity and then decentralize" approach adopted by many other countries masked the reluctance of political and administrative elites to carry through with such initiatives or was a naïve strategy that ignored the extent to which time allowed opponents of reform to regroup and stall the implementation of change.

The promoters of Popular Participation had some important allies in ad-

**TABLE 6.2**

SOURCES OF FINANCE OF MUNICIPAL INVESTMENT IN BOLIVIA, 1994–1996

| | 1994 | | 1995 | | 1996 | |
| Source of Funds | U.S. Dollars | % | U.S. Dollars | % | U.S. Dollars | % |
|---|---|---|---|---|---|---|
| Popular Participation | 21,275,519 | 64.66 | 107,333,773 | 43.88 | 115,891,644 | 43.37 |
| Own resources[a] | 8,443,453 | 25.66 | 42,592,263 | 17.41 | 3,422,423 | 1.28 |
| External credit | 1,897,347 | 5.77 | 18,287,193 | 7.48 | 29,301,395 | 10.97 |
| Other resources[b] | 1,125,210 | 3.42 | 46,260,787 | 18.91 | 45,100,391 | 16.88 |
| Community funding | 101,232 | 0.31 | 2,968,008 | 1.21 | 7,053,125 | 2.64 |
| Donations[c] | 66,238 | 0.20 | 26,292,491 | 10.75 | 34,315,430 | 12.84 |
| Transfers from Treasury | 0 | 0.00 | 874,036 | 0.36 | 2,111,914 | 0.79 |
| **TOTAL** | **32,904,999** | **100.00** | **244,608,551** | **100.00** | **267,196,321** | **100.00** |

*Source:* Ministerio de Desarrollo Humano (1997:75,77).

[a] Income from taxes on housing and vehicles, airplanes and ships; income from sale of goods and services, and municipal patents; donations from the community and money from the previous administration.

[b] Includes prefectures, investment and development funds, capital transfers from not-for-profit institutions, short and long-term subsidies, subventions, and credit.

[c] Donations from local and foreign institutions.

dition to presidential support. The rapid pace of its introduction was matched by the mobilization of donor funding for training and monitoring activities. Between 1994 and 1996, the program received almost $50 million in external credit and more than $60 million in grants from organizations like the World Bank, the European Community, the Inter-American Development Bank, and the United Nations Development Program (UNDP). Bilateral assistance came from development agencies in Denmark, Spain, Switzerland, the Netherlands, and the United States (see Table 6.2). Moreover, the program received financial support and technical assistance to collect data on the use of funds by the municipalities on a sustained basis. Major studies were undertaken by UNDP, the World Bank, the Swedish International Development Agency, and the U.S. Agency for International Development. Although the international agencies were not central participants in developing Popular Participation, they were eager to be involved in its implementation.

Moreover, because the Secretariat for Popular Participation was staffed by young, well-trained technocrats, it had in place, from the beginning, a sophisticated monitoring and evaluation program. The municipalization experience was widely viewed as innovative because it included political decentralization as a central element to accompany the much more frequently recommended administrative and fiscal decentralization. Its novelty attracted extraordinary interest among researchers, both Bolivian and foreign, who flocked to the offices of Popular Participation, the finance ministry (where funding was managed), the Social Policy Analysis Unit (UDAPSO), and the municipalities to explore the process and impact of the new law. They were joined by researchers and advocates of ethnic revivalist movements, who were eager to monitor the impact of autonomy and resources on indigenous communities. It was, above all, a well-watched and supported experiment in democratization.

In fact, the first several years of Popular Participation resulted in important political changes toward more responsive and democratic government in the country. First, although local experience with development investment differed widely, the program encouraged more responsiveness to local needs and interests in many municipalities. Second, just as political parties in Venezuela were slow to understand the implications of the new institutions for their own future, so some Bolivian parties found it difficult to move quickly to take advantage of the new arena of local politics. Nevertheless, as the parties began to recognize the opportunities and risks of Popular Participation, they focused greater attention on local politics and local elections and sought to assert control over new forms of political interactions. In doing so, however, they often had to trade their traditions of party militancy and central control for popularity at the local polls. Third, local electoral campaigns began to reflect the salience of local issues for voters, and these in turn had some limited influence on national elections. Fourth, the career paths of aspiring politicians began to reflect greater diversity, as new posts created new opportunities for pursuing political careers. This chapter explores changes in the relationship between national and local politics in Bolivia.

## Fiscal Decentralization: The Uses and Abuses of Power

Under the municipalization scheme, local governments were to receive grants from the central government that amounted to 20 percent of national income. Translated into municipal coffers in 1995, this meant about $21.30 per capita, a figure that was programmed to rise to $28.60 per capita in 1997.[10] In 1995, almost $200 million was transferred to the local governments to cover expenses associated with health, education, public sanitation, roads, irrigation, and other development-related activities. There were few constraints on the use of the funds, other than the proviso that no more than 10 percent could be used on current expenses and that 90 percent had to be directed to development investment (changed to 15 percent and 85 percent, respectively, in

**TABLE 6.3**
MUNICIPAL INVESTMENT BY SECTOR IN BOLIVIA, 1994–1996
(Percentage of Total)

| Sector | 1994 | 1995 | 1996 |
|---|---|---|---|
| Urbanization | 50.0% | 48.6% | 32.7% |
| Education | 14.5 | 16.8 | 21.3 |
| Basic sanitation | 10.7 | 16.9 | 16.6 |
| Transport | 8.0 | 5.2 | 10.2 |
| Multisector | 6.2 | 3.2 | 1.9 |
| Energy | 5.5 | 2.9 | 2.6 |
| Health | 2.8 | 3.3 | 6.7 |
| Hydro resources | 1.1 | 1.3 | 3.7 |
| Agriculture | 0.8 | 1.7 | 4.1 |
| Tourism and industry | 0.2 | 0.2 | 0.2 |
| Communication | 0.2 | 0.1 | 0.1 |
| **TOTAL** | **100.0** | **100.0** | **100.0** |

*Source:* Ministerio de Desarrollo Humano (1997:87–89).

1996). The funds were allocated through a formula based on a municipality's population and were transferred to local governments twice a year.[11] The secretariat and the Ministry of Finance monitored the use of funds, but the real responsibility for their use and abuse was left to the mayors, the councils, and the vigilance committees. As indicated in Table 6.3, local government priorities for the first year and a half of the program (six months in 1994 and all of 1995) showed a decided preference for "urbanization" (urban works and housing). In 1995, this category absorbed 48.6 percent of the funds; basic sanitation came next with 16.9 percent, followed by education with 16.8 percent.

The designers of Popular Participation, who had a strong preference for investment in the social sectors and basic needs, were disappointed with the results of eighteen months of investment. "Urbanization" included such politically visible investments as beautifying public parks, installing street lighting, building basketball courts, and constructing municipal offices and community centers. For most communities, these were investments in real needs, of course, but they were also needs whose importance often paled beside investment in public health in a country in which the rural infant mortality rate varied between 117 and 132 per 1,000 births (depending on location), or investment in education when the rural illiteracy rate was 37 percent.[12] For many in the central administration of the program, as well as its proponents in the Ministry of Finance and UDAPSO, investments in urban works raised concerns that municipalities would not make the best investment decisions and that elected local officials would choose what was popular and tangible (a public park, for example) rather than what was more important but less immediately visible (lower infant mortality, for example). Some program designers believed that high levels of investments in urban works gave credence to critics of Popular Participation who argued that the funds would be squandered by corrupt local officials on projects of little development significance.[13]

Indeed, such was the disappointment of central administrators in the priorities of local decision makers that a new regulation was put in place in December 1995 that 30 percent of investments had to be directed to "human development" if municipalities wanted to be eligible for matching grants from other programs. As indicated in Table 6.3, this change appeared to have had considerable impact on the distribution of investment funds in 1996, even while it may have stripped local communities of an opportunity to learn from experience and to begin to hold local officials accountable for their decisions about local priorities. On the one hand, the new regulations were evidence that, for its designers, Popular Participation was an experimental framework that would need to be adapted to experience as it was implemented. On the other hand, it also suggests a traditional recourse to centralized decision making and control when initial expectations were not met by the reality of local government behavior.

Despite the general trends indicated in Table 6.3, evidence on expenditures for 1995 also indicates that municipalities differed considerably in terms of their priorities. The twelve capital cities of the departments allocated 68 percent of their investments to urban works, 6 percent to education, 2 percent to health, and 15 percent to basic sanitation. In contrast, in the rest of the country, 299 municipalities invested 23 percent in urban works, 30 percent in education, 6 percent in health, and 20 percent in basic sanitation.[14] Similarly, per capita investment in education and health was much higher in non-capital city municipalities than in the capital cities. Non-capital city municipalities invested $9.32 per capita in education and $1.70 per capita in health, compared with $3.14 and $0.73 per capita, respectively, in departmental capitals.[15]

The vigilance committees, the feature of the Popular Participation Law that was expected to ensure the democratic accountability of public officials between elections, were another source of difference among the municipalities. As indicated, these committees, formed by representatives of grass-roots organizations, were charged with proposing local development projects, participating in annual development planning, and monitoring spending by the mayor and council. And as anticipated, the vigilance committees in many municipalities had little experience in the determination of investment priorities among communities and no knowledge of planning or budgetary processes, although many of them had long been actively engaged in community-level governance. A survey carried out in 138 rural municipalities in 1996 indicated that slightly more than half the vigilance committees were actively engaged in budget discussions; 32 percent had supervised projects; and 39 percent had been involved in enforcing allocation guidelines.[16] While these data show that half of the committees were not yet functioning as intended, they also suggest that considerable progress had been made in involving the grass-roots representatives in decision making and monitoring activities, despite their widespread lack of experience.

Early evidence also suggests that some vigilance committees were playing an important role in the allocation of resources. One 1996 study indicated that smaller and more rural municipalities were quite responsive to the constituencies represented in the vigilance committees, which acted as lobbyists for local needs.[17] In larger and more urban municipalities, however, more interests were engaged in lobbying for resources, and traditional political elites had considerable influence over local decision making in these environments. Vigilance committees were only one among a variety of actors involved.[18] These urban committees, formed primarily of representatives of *juntas vecinales* (neighborhood councils) were thought to be particularly weak, divided, and riddled with clientelism and thus in a poor position to counter the power of the elected officials and organized interests that lobbied for benefits outside the formal structures of the vigilance committees.[19] Another study indicated that the presence of strong vigilance committees in rural areas was correlated with higher levels of investment in social services and in productivity-enhancing investments.[20] In yet another study, strong vigilance committees were associated with more equitable distribution of resources between urban and rural components of municipalities.[21]

From a design perspective, a deeper problem became apparent as the program advanced. The vigilance committees were expected to perform their functions without remuneration, while mayors and city councillors received pay for their official duties. Thus, the committees—and individual committee members—if they were to operate at all, had to be motivated by community spiritedness, political partisanship, or some similar energizer. For some observers, this made the vigilance committees more vulnerable to corruption in allocating and monitoring investments or to co-optation by elected politicians. Combined with lack of experience, this imbalance in the incentives for committing to the new structure of local decision making was a defect that constrained the democratizing effect of the change. At the same time, proposals for providing vigilance committees with a small budget from municipal resources were questioned because of the potential misuse of funds to co-opt members of the oversight groups. For many who assessed the first years of municipalization in Bolivia, the vigilance committees were the weak link in making the new process work well and in deepening the extent of democratic accountability in the political system.[22]

Despite such problems, local groups were beginning to hold local officials accountable for their actions. The Popular Participation law authorized vigilance committees to bring charges of irregularities against elected officials. Based on such a petition, the national executive, through the Ministry of Finance, could investigate and require municipalities to take remedial action; in cases in which they did not comply, the matter would be referred to the senate, which would have the discretion to freeze the transfer of funds to the municipality until the problem was resolved. A survey in 1996 indicated that one in five of the vigilance committees had initiated such petitions.[23]

In addition, in cases in which the mayor did not receive an absolute majority in municipal elections, the vigilance committees could bring charges against this official during his or her first year in office. Some anecdotal evidence suggests that vigilance committees at times acted to control the abuses of power and decision making of these public officials. In some communities, however, researchers reported that changing mayors after a year reflected a traditional *cargo* system found in many Amerindian communities. Under such a system, respected community members are elected to assume responsibility for the public and spiritual life of a community; the honor of the office is rotated annually because of the financial burden such service imposes on the individual (and family) assuming this responsibility. In some rural municipalities, then, becoming mayor may have become the equivalent of an annual *cargo*, with community tradition mandating that a year in power is sufficient for any local leader.[24] In still other cases, charges against incumbents appear to have been the result of partisan divisions between the mayor and council on the one hand and the vigilance committees on the other.

Municipal councils were also part of this dynamic, taking action to remove mayors from office. In 1997, 29 percent of mayors were removed, and in 1998, 25 percent suffered this fate.[25] In the large cities, relationships between mayors and city councillors were particularly contentious. The mayor of La Paz, Ronald Maclean, was ousted from office after a year, to be replaced by a council member who was later indicted for corruption and replaced by yet another councillor. In the meantime, the courts ruled that Maclean's removal had been unjustified. The denunciation of local officials appeared to conform to a variety of local circumstance, as communities sought to manage new ways of participating in local decision making and as parties and individual politicians sought to acquire advantage in the local arena. More generally, however, the experiment with Popular Participation indicated that it was possible for local communities to begin to hold public officials to account. Grassroots organizations, which in many cases had long histories of community-level problem solving and conflict resolution, acquired new leverage as they were incorporated into an institution that provided formal mechanisms for participating in both local and supralocal decisions.[26]

## Political Parties Test New Rules

In December 1995, 1.8 million Bolivians went to the polls to elect mayors and municipal councillors, as well as departmental councillors. These elections were the first to include single adults between the ages of 18 and 21 and the first local elections for many citizens.[27] According to the law, those running for municipal offices had to do so as candidates of registered parties, each of which presented lists to the electorate. Thirteen political parties participated. Interest in these elections was considerable; the abstention rate, which in 1993 (prior to Popular Participation) was 46.7 percent, dropped to 36.4 percent, despite the enfranchisement of so many new voters.[28] Equally important, organizations that had opposed Popular Participation, such as the confederation of rural unions, CSUTCB, backed their own candidates running under party labels and campaigned actively in many local areas for positions in local government.

This election put the parties in a position to benefit from a large number of new positions created by the need to select incumbents for some twenty-nine hundred municipal and departmental posts. In addition, the parties had new opportunities to become important players in local politics by influencing the selection of representatives of grass-roots organizations that would form the vigilance committees in each municipality. And given that there were some twenty-seven hundred non-elective municipal positions to be staffed, the parties might be able to provide a significant number of jobs to their supporters. Most important, they could benefit from controlling positions involved in making decisions about millions of dollars that had to be allocated under the Popular Participation Law. Although the parties had been marginal to the formulation of the municipalization program, they recognized its importance for their access to positions and resources. At this point, the Popular Participation Law had been in operation for a year and a half, and millions of dollars of new investments had flowed into the municipalities. This point was not lost on those competing in the elections.

Bolivia's principal political parties never reached the degree of consolidation and centralization achieved by parties in Venezuela. Nevertheless, many of them had internal organizations that allowed them to compete regularly and competitively in national elections. As noted in the previous chapter, many of the traditional parties had begun life as outgrowths of elite politics, generally formed by young intellectuals searching for ways to define a vision of Bolivia as a nation. Over the years, periods in office and in opposition had transformed them into clientelistic machines, kept operative from election to election through the distribution of patronage and the promise of patronage to come. As we saw in chapter 5, by the 1980s, national policy preferences were traded for positions in government through formal pacts among the parties.

The major parties were highly centralized. Their national officials were militants in the sense of having spent their professional lives within the ranks of the party. They were key actors in developing party platforms, selecting candidates, and negotiating support with interest groups such as those representing workers, peasants, ethnic communities, and economic and regional elites. Traditionally, the parties had responded to central direction and to national issues as well as to priorities identified by their party leaders. They were oriented toward national elections because national positions controlled access to jobs and resources that could be of benefit to the parties. Many parties lacked local party organizations and the internal capacity to create local organizations. In many areas, they simply depended on their historical ties to functional corporatist organizations—like the links between the MNR and the unions, for example— to mobilize the vote. They were, above all, clientelistic parties with centralized leadership and national orientations.[20]

Popular Participation presented a considerable challenge to these nationally oriented parties and their leadership. Given the extent to which municipalization decentralized resource allocation and empowered local governments and community organizations, local elections became, almost overnight, critically important for capturing political power and patronage. The new structures for local representation, however, were defined in geographic terms, not corporatist or functional ones. Moreover, a larger number of electoral arenas and the possibility of defining local- rather than national-issue agendas offered opportunities for increased intraparty competition. Reformist wings had emerged in almost all the old established parties in the 1980s, generally dividing allegiances between the traditional nationalists, who favored a state-oriented development strategy and vertical relations within the parties, and the reformists, who favored more market-oriented development strategies and greater internal party democracy. The tension between the traditionalists and the reformers within these parties was far from resolved when Popular Participation was introduced.[30]

The 1995 elections indicated that parties differed in their ability to adapt to new rules of the game. The more institutionalized parties were slow to appreciate the importance of finding locally attractive candidates to fill their lists. The MNR, an older party with a more entrenched bureaucracy, left candidate selection up to its departmental chiefs, who drew on their clienteles at the municipal level.[31] These officials sought candidates among the local party faithful and relied on the party's links to functional organizations rather than searching for individuals who had emerged as local or "natural" leaders in the municipalities. The MNR leadership considered this to be a winning strategy, expecting that their traditional support in many rural areas would carry them through to a very strong showing in the elections. Its traditional opposition also anticipated an MNR victory in these elections.[32] In contrast, smaller and newer parties took the initiative in searching out candidates who were well known at local levels and who promised to be good vote-getters. The MBL led other parties in adapting its electoral strategy to local interests in the 1995 elections.[33]

Thus, as the traditional parties gradually became more aware of the importance of the 311 new electoral arenas, in many cases they found that others had gotten there first. The space created for new positions of power was already at least partly filled with candidates from various ethnic movements, from smaller and more agile political parties, or from local-level organizations that "adopted" existing parties. Table 6.4, which compares the results of the presidential elections of 1993 with the results of the municipal election of 1995, indicates a disconnect between national and local party support.[34] The older parties—MNR, MIR, and ADN—showed lackluster results; newer parties—MBL, CONDEPA, and UCS—improved on their earlier performance. The MNR declined from almost 36 percent of the vote to about 21 percent, while the MBL garnered approximately 13.3 percent of the vote compared to about 5.4 percent in the presidential elections. Several smaller parties, particularly the ones that had emerged in the 1980s as initiatives representing

**TABLE 6.4**
ELECTION RESULTS BY PARTY IN BOLIVIA, 1993 AND 1995
(Percentage of Total Votes)

| Party | National Elections 1993 | Local Elections 1995 |
|---|---|---|
| MNR-MRTKL | 35.56% | 21.32%[a] |
| ADN | 21.05 | 11.43 |
| CONDEPA | 14.29 | 15.47 |
| UCS | 13.77 | 17.45 |
| MBL | 5.36 | 13.28 |
| MIR | 10.52 | 9.30 |
| Ethnic minority parties | 0.00 | 6.01 |
| Other partios (5) | 0.00 | 5.74 |

*Source:* Ministerio de la Presidencia (1997).
[a] MNR contested this election without an alliance with MRTKL.

"movement politics" (e.g., parties seeking to strengthen the political voice of the country's ethnic communities), also made a showing in these elections. These parties were quick to recognize that capturing local office could mean much in terms of opportunities to put development resources in the hands of those who had been excluded from political and economic power for four hundred years. Often, their candidates were the "natural" leaders who were already prominent at the village level for their participation in decision-making and conflict resolution. The older parties suffered from a paradox suggested by a Bolivian researcher who commented, "We have modernized our political system, but the parties have not modernized themselves."[35]

The parties that were more locally responsive and least encumbered by party bureaucracies, and thus more willing to back locally attractive candidates, proved more able to mobilize votes at local levels. Nevertheless, while the MNR emerged from the elections a loser in terms of its prior performance, it emerged as the largest vote-winner in 120 municipalities and was able to claim 484 of the 1,624 council seats (29.8 percent), more than twice the numbers obtained by its closest rivals—the UCS, the ADN, and the MBL.[36] Moreover, in only 13.8 percent of the municipalities did any party win an absolute majority, leaving 86.2 percent of the mayors to be selected by the newly elected councils. In the end, considerable pact-making in this post-election phase of politics left the MNR in control of 38.91 percent of the mayors' offices. The MBL acquired 14.47 percent; the UCS, 12.54 percent; and ADN, 12.22 percent (see Table 6.5).

**TABLE 6.5**
COUNCILLORSHIPS AND MAYORSHIPS BY PARTY IN BOLIVIA, 1995

| Party | Percent of Councillors Elected | Percent of Mayors Elected and Negotiated |
|---|---|---|
| MNR | 29.80% | 38.91% |
| UCS | 14.59 | 12.54 |
| ADN-PDC | 14.47 | 12.22 |
| MBL | 13.49 | 14.47 |
| CONDEPA | 8.93 | 8.36 |
| MIR | 8.81 | 5.79 |
| IU | 3.69 | 3.54 |
| MRTKL | 2.03 | 1.61 |
| Other parties (5) | 4.19 | 4.17 |

*Source:* Calla Ortega and Calla Ortega (1996:19, 25–26).

## Local Elections, Local Issues

What is interesting in assessing these municipal-level agreements is the extent to which they diverged from the pacts made at national levels. In the presidential elections of 1993, the presidency was decided by the congress on the basis of two governing pacts formed by the MNR, UCS, MBL, and the MRTKL.[37] ADN and MIR led the opposition in national politics. These alliances were not widely reproduced in local elections. At local levels, in the aftermath of the 1995 elections, intense negotiations over who would assume mayorships resulted in UCS-ADN alliances in some municipalities, MIR-MNR or MIR-MBL alliances in others, and an occasional ADN-UCS or UCS-MIR alliance. One department featured a UCS alliance with CONDEPA in one municipality, UCS with MRTKL in another, and UCS, MNR, and ADN in another. In the Chapare, an unusual MNR–ADN–MIR–UCS–CONDEPA alliance was formed to limit the mayorships that would be controlled by the regional Izquierda Unida (IU) Party. In the capital city of La Paz, an ADN–MNR–MBL–UCS alliance decided the mayoral election.[38] In fact, the postelection winning alliances featured just about every possible combination of political parties, including those between major national parties and small regional ones and between major national rivals. Moreover, in working out some of the local negotiations, elected officials at times declared themselves independent of their parties or went directly against the wishes of their national parties in forming alliances. This was all the easier given that the major costs of the elections were borne by the candidates rather than by the parties.

These results suggest the locally relevant content of local elections, the disarray of the political parties in responding to new opportunities, and their willingness to sacrifice national alliances for locally relevant electoral calculus in individual cases. Local concerns rather than centralized parties clearly emerged the winners in the politics that surrounded the 1995 elections, compared with the difficulties encountered by all the parties in contesting at these levels. In some municipalities, local organizations drew up slates of candidates they favored and negotiated with political parties in terms of their willingness to support these candidates.[39] In some cases, such groups merely "borrowed" the labels of established parties to run their own slates of candidates.[40] Many of those who ran for election disclaimed party membership prior to the campaign, even though they were legally bound to run for election under party labels.[41] And that 437 of the councillors elected were either indigenous or peasants indicated strongly the local nature of the elections.

Again, these factors suggest the extent to which the dominance of national parties was unsettled through the Popular Participation Law and the extent to which, at least in the short term, what was local influenced electoral outcomes. One analyst claimed that the 1995 elections were "the most important in the entire history of Bolivia" because of their democratizing impact, although others were concerned about the capacity of party negotiation to undo the results of popular voting and to heighten uncertainty.[42] The national leader of the MNR lamented the extent to which it was being transformed from "a party of militants into an electoral party" through the impact of local elections.[43] An extensive analysis of the impact of Popular Participation at the local level indicated that the MNR's legacy of centralization was at fault for its loss. In this regard, that MNR had introduced Popular Participation was an issue of little importance:

> No longer are all the best cards in the hands of the politicians, and no longer does the MNR have a monopoly of reformist credentials. Politicians now have to win votes, and they win votes at the local level primarily by showing that they are serious about local issues. . . . The MNR has failed to recognize these changes in the rules of the game. An immediate effect has been that it has lost votes to newer organizations that understand the situation better, like the MBL. This, rather than necessarily the electorate's view of the Gov-

ernment's *policies,* is what explains the most dramatic feature of the December 1995 election results: the very poor showing of the party that (in theory) made it all possible, the MNR.[44]

In response to the electoral loss, the MNR and other parties created committees, task forces, and focus groups to help them assess their future strategies for local elections.[45]

More generally, while a good deal of campaign competition was an age-old rivalry between the "ins" and the "outs," the issues around which this competition played out were local: the probity of one candidate vs. another, the claim to power of one group vs. another, the need for better roads vs. the need for repairs to the schoolhouse, or the claims of rural vs. urban interests. National themes, such as privatization, education reform, neoliberal economic policies, Popular Participation itself, were much less in evidence. As suggested by the national leader of the MNR after the electoral dust of 1995 had settled, this party had learned important lessons about future campaigns: "Tactics have to do with local issues, finding solutions to garbage collection, potable water, light, electricity, the police in the local area, keeping the health system working. This is going to be how the MNR moves into the [next] elections, by taking up these issues."[46] A possible exception to this trend was the campaign in the coca-growing region of the Chapare, where coca-growing peasants had become mobilized in opposition to the government's anti-drug policies. The Asemblea por la Soberanía de los Pueblos (Assembly for People's Sovereignty, or ASP), adopting the label of a small party, Izquierda Unida (IU), fielded candidates and ran a campaign focused on national drug eradication policy.[47] The party and the *cocaleros* (coca growers), won control of eleven municipalities and their leader ran successfully for the national congress in 1997. Nevertheless, this example also suggests that the issues to emerge in local elections would be those that local constituents considered the most important.[48]

## New Routes to Power

The political consequences of popular participation also signal the development of new career trajectories for aspiring politicians in Bolivia. Of course, municipalization increased the number of political offices available to potential politicians. Prior to 1994, non-national elections in Bolivia featured contestation over some 262 positions, including posts in capital city councils and councils at the departmental and provincial level. After the Popular Participation law was put into effect, the number of local and regional offices to be filled every three years increased by a factor of eleven, to more than 2,900 positions. In this regard, the initiative radically increased the opportunities for democratic representation in Bolivia.

Moreover, municipalization offered many opportunities to launch political careers independent of the traditional political parties and their national leadership. In many cases, as we have seen, the parties sought out the attractive local candidates. In contrast to most prior practice, candidates did not, in anticipation of a nod from national headquarters, apprentice themselves as worker bees for the parties. This put them in a relatively strong position in terms of negotiating with the parties for locally desired benefits. Once in office, these more independent public officials had opportunities for using investment and patronage resources traditionally captured by the national parties to build their own political bases. A variety of alternatives were possible from this point. For instance, locally elected leaders could make use of the resources they commanded to build local machines and personally loyal followers—a new arena for traditional clientelist politics in the country.[49] Another possibility was for local communities to become increasingly agile in putting effective electoral pressure on mayors and councillors to be responsive to their needs. As indicated above, this occurred in a number of municipalities that had a prior history of strong grass-roots organizations and that had promoted strong vigilance committees. Still another possibility was that the traditional parties, faced with the challenge of controlling local officials, would gradually co-opt the local leaders and turn them into national party operatives at the local level. In this case, the politics of clientelism would probably be established. The post-electoral alliances that determined the occupants of many of the mayoral posts in 1995 suggested that this would not be an easy task to accomplish because the national parties were, at least in these early days of Popular Participation, caught off guard by local elections.

In the short term, local elections increased opportunities for locally prominent politicians to build support and to launch themselves onto a national political canvas. A vice presidential candidate in 1997 had been mayor of Santa Cruz. Two prominent potential presidential candidates for elections in 2002 gained national exposure as mayors of large cities. The 1995 municipal elections were the vehicle through which the coca growers' peasant union achieved enough national prominence to launch their leader into congress. In many areas, those aspiring to assume positions as mayor first served as municipal councillors. The traditional parties, if they reached out to find politically attractive candidates to run under the party banners, could anticipate some renewal of their leadership cadres from those whose political experiences and careers differed considerably from those of the traditional party leaders. More immediately, however, the emergence of new and more local bases for political careers began to change perceptions of aspiring politicians about the best routes to political power. According to one observer, predicting the emergence of a "new political class" from the decentralization experience, "Local politics is where the action is these days."[50] Or, as a leading politician indicated, "Political careers are changing. New generations are coming up through the municipalities, particularly through the larger cities. Congress is now becoming like a political museum in terms of being a very unpropitious place for launching or furthering a political career."[51]

## Conclusions: New Arenas for Conflict and Competition

As in the case of Venezuela, then, the consequence of political decentralization in Bolivia was to unsettle traditional forms of party management, electoral mobilization, and candidate choice and to increase considerably the routes by which aspiring politicians could capture political office. This pluralization of candidacies and the need of national political parties to be more attentive to local-level dynamics and issues clearly increased the potential for democratic responsiveness and accountability in Bolivia. It did not necessarily increase the coherence of political participation or political debate, however. Many parties emerged more democratic but weaker from municipalization. Electoral campaigns became more focused on local issues but possibly also more susceptible to personalism at local levels. The paths to political prominence became more varied but also more subject to failure and reversal.

As predicted by rational choice perspectives, the political parties clearly revised their strategic calculations about winning elections in the face of institutional change. They sought out candidates they expected to be attractive to local constituencies, often with little regard to the candidates' histories of party militancy or service. In the post-election negotiations over mayorships, they forged alliances that were difficult to understand from the perspective of national politics. At times, local operatives made these alliances in direct opposition to the preferences of party leaders. Moreover, allies in one municipality could easily be the competition in the neighboring municipality. These actions suggest the extent to which the parties were able to learn the new rules of the game introduced by Popular Participation.

At the same time, however, the parties did not always respond quickly to change. They seemed uncertain about the implications of institutional change for winning elections, and the initial response of several parties was to rely on traditional practice in the selection of candidates. When they did begin to evince revised electoral calculations, they often did so more in response to the success of their more agile competitors than to their own analysis of the way the rules had changed. Indeed, adaptation to new rules took some parties longer than others, as the more traditional and organizationally "heavy" parties were slower to respond to the new opportunities provided by Popular Participation than were newer and smaller parties.[52] Similarly, increased risk in predicting political outcomes encouraged a period of experimentation and local flexibility that also increased the instability of political outcomes. This was particularly true of the political jockeying for alliances that followed the elections. "Rational" electoral calculations reassert themselves in the aftermath of institutional change, the Bolivian case suggests, but not immediately and not without considerable stumbling about to learn what is "rational" in the new context.

Aspiring politicians also adapted to the new rules of the game, apparently adopting electoral strategies based on locally important issues that were likely to win them votes in electoral contests and in post-election negotiations. Groups supporting various potential leaders often negotiated skillfully with parties about how their slates would be filled. Similarly, once in office, politicians appeared to be responsive to the most well-organized and audible groups, whether this was a strong vigilance committee representing grassroots organizations or more established elites and interests that had long benefited from resource allocation decisions. Again, however, the case indicates that municipalities differed in terms of the ability of their leaders to take advantage of new opportunities and the capacity of vigilance committees to become effective organizations pressing for local development needs.

Were transaction costs lowered in the aftermath of change in Bolivia? The tasks facing the traditional political parties and their leaders, like those of their Venezuelan counterparts, became more difficult, ambiguous, and time-consuming in the wake of institutional change. In contrast to their previous ability to dominate candidate choice, issue selection, and campaign strategy from national headquarters, the parties had to become much more engaged in collecting local-level information, selecting locally attractive candidates whose political personae they did not necessarily know or trust, and negotiating locally relevant alliances with other political parties. Moreover, even in victory, they could not be certain that their local candidates would use the resources of public office to increase the political base or popularity of the party. Many candidates simply put on a convenient party label for the purpose of election, with no deeper commitment to the leadership or the ideology of the party. For the traditional parties, this was interpreted as abandoning their identity as membership parties to become more loosely defined as electoral parties.

For local politicians, doing politics also became more complicated as new actors emerged at local levels to make demands on them. Routes to political office became more complex, replacing selection based on party service with the need to attract multiple constituencies, the possibility of moving through new levels of office, and the increased risk of competition. The parties could no longer provide them with relatively reliable information on how to acquire and maintain power or how to move upward in the political world. In office, their control over political resources might be monitored more closely by grass-roots organizations and the vigilance committees. At the same time, of course, they also gained greater space for maneuver with the political parties and the potential to mobilize personal followings that could then be used to acquire party sponsorship. Greater complexity and uncertainty, then, was accompanied by greater capacity to maneuver through the political thickets. It would be hard to conclude, however, that the costs of doing politics were lowered in any systematic way.

From the perspective of principal-agent problems, local elections and the ability to participate in the selection of the vigilance committees probably increased the capacity of citizens to hold public officials accountable and gather information on their performance in office. Clearly, for the 42 percent of the population that had had no access to local government and that was the most distant from national government, local elections and decision making about development investments were a major step toward access and empowerment. In this regard, perhaps the most notable achievement of Popular Participation was to open up new spaces for the practice of politics and enhanced opportunities to make a difference at local levels through such involvement. While many local communities had strong traditions of local-level problem solving and governance, they generally had few resources and no national support for bringing about significant change in their development trajectories. With Popular Participation, they gained both resources and legitimacy to attempt this difficult task.

While Popular Participation introduced a new strategic context for rational political behavior, it also unleashed dynamics consistent with the comparative institutionalist hypothesis about the consequences of change. Overall, the introduction of a new institution created a variety of ripple effects for parties, politicians, and citizens. Most of these changes indicate the creation of new sources of conflict and the emergence of new political actors, new claims for resources, and new sites for contestation. Elections and the interaction of the councils, mayors, and vigilance committees proved to be new spaces for contestation. The efforts of central administrators to control the local use of resources, the parties to reassert control over candidates and campaigns, and the grass-roots organizations to influence investments all suggest the extent to which new institutions can generate new forms of conflict or serve as arenas for old conflicts.

Conflict about the rules also emerged in terms of whether the new rules would be carried out. This conflict was led by those who perceived that Popular Participation caused them to lose power—the civic committees and the party hierarchies. In this regard, the presidential elections of 1997 were not propitious for Popular Participation. The MNR fielded a lackluster candidate and reaped considerable ire for the rapid pace and uncertain results of many of the reforms introduced by the Sánchez de Lozada administration. The MBL performed so poorly in the elections that it virtually disappeared. The ADN put forth General Hugo Banzer who, from the beginning, was predicted to win, in part because the leaders of two populist parties, the UCS and CONDEPA, had died and the parties were not able to find nationally known figures to replace them. Banzer won. Although his party was committed to the continuance of the neoliberal economic policies in place since 1985, it did not have a very specific plan of government.[33] This was probably not a major problem, however, given that the congressional coalition to elect the president was an unwieldy one that made it difficult to take action on any policy front.

Popular Participation, like other initiatives, suffered from this situation. The law continued in effect and investment resources continued to flow to the municipalities, but the activism and support of the Sánchez de Lozada years was lost. A policy of "do nothing" slowed the momentum of change and inhibited the development of local-level capacity. The loss of the top-down direction that characterized the Sánchez de Lozada administration hindered further progress of bottom-up politics. In addition, the Banzer administration reintroduced the initiative to decentralize to the departmental levels.[34] Nevertheless, the rules of the game continued in effect: resources distributed to the municipalities for investment, municipal elections, local-level decision making, and monitoring of public officials. In terms of the most important political dynamics, therefore, the sustainability of the new rules of the game seemed secure. Moreover, in the aftermath of the election, both the MNR and the MIR introduced primary elections within the parties, suggesting a further weakening of the centralized system of control. Barring a change in regime, political decentralization was becoming an embedded part of everyday politics in Bolivia.

# Pacting Institutional Change in Argentina

On August 22, 1994, the Argentine congress approved a constitutional reform that, among other things, mandated the direct election of the *intendente* (mayor) of Buenos Aires, the capital and largest city of the country.[1] The city was given responsibility for overseeing certain essential services, establishing its own codes and legislation, and administering local judicial matters. The election of the mayor, to be carried out as soon as possible after the approval of the reform, was to be a prelude to drafting a city constitution. When this document was completed, a city legislature would be elected and given the job of developing the institutional structure for the new city government and passing the laws and regulations it would carry out.

On June 30, 1996, citizens of Buenos Aires voted for mayor for the first time. On October 1, 1996, delegates signed a constitution for the newly named Autonomous City of Buenos Aires. And then on October 26, 1997, citizens voted for a sixty-member city council, which began to meet in December to establish the institutional framework for governing the city.[2] Through these actions, a significant change in the national constitution was put in practice.

At the time of the constitutional reform granting it autonomy, Buenos Aires was critical to Argentine politics. For a century and a half, the city had figured in national politics as a center of power—and as a threat to other parts of the country because of that power. Its leadership was selected by the president of the country; the mayor was constitutionally designated as the "chief of the capital." Political control over the city provided an extraordinary number of public positions and public contracts to distribute. Political parties maintained their headquarters there. Citizens of the city elected senators and deputies to the national congress, and the national media covered their campaigns as issues of national importance. Granting autonomy to this hub meant giving up considerable influence over the course of national development and an extensive amount of patronage and political capital.

A reform granting autonomy to the city was certainly significant in its own right, but it was also part of a larger package of reforms of great importance to the institutional structure of the Argentine political system. The 1994 constitutional reforms included replacing an electoral college with direct election of the president and vice-president, limiting presidents to four-year terms of office while allowing for their immediate reelection, electing senators directly and adding a third senator from each province, changing the terms served by senators from nine years to six, creating the post of prime minister, giving congress greater power to appoint and remove supreme court justices, circumscribing the use of presidential decrees, creating an auditor general's office and a public ombudsman, and providing for citizen-initiated referenda and initiatives.[3] Together, these changes fundamentally recast many of the most important institutions of governance in the country. They also significantly redistributed political power.[4]

The constitutional reform was agreed to by the major political parties and adopted within a set of rules agreed to by major political actors. In the context of Argentine history, this was a remarkable achievement; all prior constitutions had been imposed on the losers of electoral competitions or regime changes. For instance, a failed constitution of 1826 was an effort to impose the rule of Buenos Aires on the rest of the country's provinces. The most legitimate of the country's several constitutions, that of 1853, was the product of a military victory of one faction over another. In the 1930s, military governments used a constitution that allowed them to restrict participation and to ban the largest political party, the Unión Cívica Radical (Radical Party), from electoral competition. The 1949 constitution endorsed Peronism and laid the basis for persecuting Radical Party leaders, who did not vote for the constitutional change in congress. In 1957, a new constitution was imposed upon the vanquished Peronist Party and excluded it from participating in elections. The 1972 constitution was imposed by the military. A coup in 1976 reimposed the 1853 constitution but without permitting elections or democratic rights. The pattern set by this history was significant: the winners wrote the rules of the game and were generally committed to excluding the losers from competition over power. In 1994, however, the two main political parties, the Radicals and the Peronists, agreed to a significant reform of the reintroduced constitution of 1853 and made changes that expanded participation and broadened the base for political debate.[5] In doing so, they agreed to a set of principles that could significantly constrain their own power when in office.

Interestingly, however, Argentines were not particularly impressed with the significance of these most recent constitutional changes. While the part of the constitutional reform that dealt with the autonomy of Buenos Aires and the direct election of its chief executive was an issue that had long been desired by citizens of the capital city, it was not an issue around which interest or community groups had mobilized. Nor was it an issue that political parties had championed. Politicians had not made constitutional reform into a campaign issue. When asked where the reforms came from, citizens regularly dismissed them as the product of a cynical deal entered into by two party bosses, President Carlos Menem of the Partido Justicialista (Peronist Party), and Raúl Alfonsín of the Unión Cívica Radical.[6] Each, according to the dominant interpretation, wanted something badly enough to bargain away a large number of changes wanted by the other. Popular commentary was almost unanimous that Menem emerged the winner from this game, having gained his most coveted goal of becoming eligible to run for reelection.[7] Most agreed that this outcome denied Alfonsín his major objective— limiting the powers of the presidency—although the agreement did provide him an opportunity to demonstrate that he remained the maximum leader of his party.

Most Argentines, in describing what to them amounted to a cheap political deal, dismissed the longer-term potential of the reforms to alter the nature of politics in the country. They pointed to the fact that many of the constitutional changes, in order to go into effect, required enabling legislation. In the absence of presidential or legislative initiative, many of the institutional inventions adopted by the constitutional convention would remain on paper only. Generally, then, popular perspectives on constitutional reform emphasized the role of politicians, and Carlos Menem in particular, in pursuing the immediate goal of maximizing politicians' power. For most, Menem's actions provided a textbook case of a rational, power-oriented politician doing whatever was necessary to maintain his position. Alfonsín was widely thought to have gotten the best deal he could under disadvantageous circumstances.

Indeed, the political agreement on which the constitutional reforms were based provided considerable support for this interpretation. On November

14, 1993, Carlos Menem, then the president of Argentina, and Raúl Alfonsín, the president who had been elected when democracy was reestablished in the country in 1983, signed a joint statement known as the Pacto de Olivos, after the presidential weekend retreat where it was signed. The Pacto listed issues on which there was agreement between the parties for reforming the constitution. The signing ceremony itself was a quiet affair, with few people and no press present.[8] When news of the pact leaked to the media, most Argentines were taken by surprise. They had not been aware of the negotiations and had had no part in any public discussion about constitutional reform. They reacted negatively to the party bossism implicit in it and the way it was negotiated.[9] Despite widespread criticism of the process, within a short time, President Menem asked congress to approve a constitutional convention to write the terms of the pact into the basic law of the land. The new constitution was approved eight months after the pact was signed. Carlos Menem was free to run for reelection, which he promptly did, winning by a handsome majority in elections in May 1995.

But there was more of a story to the constitutional reform than a tale of bossism, ambition, and paper reforms. This case certainly demonstrates much more short-term electoral maneuvering than was evident in the cases of Venezuela and Bolivia. In addition, however, there was a history to the pact that included some nine years of discussion, consensus building, and study among a group of influential public intellectuals and politicians. This history suggests that the Argentine reform, like those in Venezuela and Bolivia, was an elite project designed out of concern for the functioning of democratic institutions in the country. Second, while it was true that many of the changes had to be legislated, thus becoming subject to the preferences of politicians who might not want them to go into effect, this was not true of all of the reforms. In particular, the autonomy of Buenos Aires and the direct election of the mayor were put into effect, as was the election of additional senators and the revised electoral calendar. Third, even if the pacting politicians were motivated by short-term political gains, it is not at all clear that they made a good bargain when they agreed to the creation of new political institutions. In the case of Buenos Aires, they gave up significant sources of patronage at the same time that they established a platform for a rival to presidential power who could command extensive media attention and build a local constituency through the use of resources that used to be presidential. They provided a stronger voice for the most dynamic sector of political life in the country, the urban middle class, and opened up significant opportunities for new kinds of political parties to enter national politics. Whatever the designs of the negotiators, some new institutions began to take on a life of their own.

In a context in which political leaders were clearly and publicly identified as personally ambitious, and in which political parties were extremely sensitive to the need to accumulate and invest political capital, why would deep changes in the structure of power be agreed to? Given the particular problems confronted by political leaders and institutional designers, why was this particular constitutional reform seen as a solution? Much more than the cases of Venezuela and Bolivia, the analysis of the agreement to alter the constitution in critical ways emphasizes the electoral calculations of the parties and their leaders and indicates that the immediate context determined the strategies they selected to get what they wanted. But the immediate goals of politicians are more able to explain the timing of reform than its content. The end result of the dynamics among parties and their leaders went far beyond such calculations because they created institutions that would shape future interactions within the political arena. Neither Menem nor Alfonsín could have predicted at the time how these institutions would affect him or his party in the future. Moreover, the issue of the autonomy of Buenos Aires and the direct election of its mayor would likely not have been on the reformist agenda without a long history of the relationship of the city to the rest of the country, of the structure of party competition, or of the nature of presidentialism in the country. The chapter shows that the content of the reforms agreed to was significantly shaped over time by a formally constituted design team and its informal successor that were both deeply aware of these institutional legacies. I conclude with a tally of wins and losses for political actors in light of the longer term implications of the reform.

## The Roots of Political Conflict: Who Represents the Nation?

Historically, Argentina was a country as poor and as marked by *caudillismo* and localism as Venezuela and Bolivia, at least until the 1860s. It is thus somewhat surprising that by the early twentieth century, Buenos Aires had become a symbol of centralism and empire to the rest of the country, that by the 1940s, two powerful political parties had emerged and become consolidated around their insistence that each represented the true national destiny and will, and that by the 1970s, a presidential system could have taken on characteristics of "hyperpresidentialism." As the Argentine political system developed, control over Buenos Aires, party rivalry, and presidential power all encouraged a situation in which the capital city was firmly entrenched as a focal point of national politics. It would take the combination of a task force of political and intellectual elites and considerable conniving among politicians to contribute to a process that ultimately resulted in the creation of a distinct kind of political role for the capital city.

### Buenos Aires and Empire: Conflicts with the Interior

Argentina began its history as an independent republic by disintegrating. Within a few years of its formal declaration of independence from Spain in 1816, provincial *caudillos* controlled large expanses of the interior of the country; the central government, located in Buenos Aires, was only a minor player in national politics.[10] Indeed, much of the energy of the new country was expended on a series of wars with Spain and the neighboring countries of Brazil, Uruguay, Chile, and Peru. In these wars, Argentina was largely successful, a record in sharp contrast to internal conflicts over the unification of the country. For the first seventy years of the country's history, centralists fought for the creation of a liberal republican government while federalists resisted both central authority and liberalism.[11] From this early history, the province and the city of Buenos Aires symbolized imperialistic tendencies of the center to dominate the regions in the minds of suspicious provincials, who remembered the city as the colonial headquarters under Spanish rule.[12]

During the first decades of independence, the federalist preference for strong provinces and a weak center was predominant as provincial governments formed a series of agreements and alliances with each other and let the province of Buenos Aires carry out foreign policy on their behalf. In fact, the country was largely defined by a series of semi-autonomous units that emerged around regional, primarily subsistence, economic activities. Among the initiatives to pull a country together out of the regionalism of the early republic, national constitutions were written in 1819 and 1826, but these had little impact on the coherence of the country as a political unit. Buenos Aires refused to join the country formed under the 1819 federalist constitution, and the unitary constitution of 1826 ended in provincial rebellion against it. In 1831, the coastal provinces bound themselves into a loose confederation, but they were not able to convince the interior provinces to join them, nor did they survive long as a unit. More generally, unitarism and federalism served as labels for shifting alliances of those who were in a position to try to assert central power and those who sought to resist it. *Caudillos* provided a semblance of order in the fourteen provinces, collaborating with one another in issues related to foreign affairs and, at the same time, preventing the loss of local autonomy. The idea of "Argentina" as a nation was not regularly reflected in official language until after 1860.[13]

From the earliest days, political struggles turned on the role of Buenos Aires—the province and the city—as a national center of political control. By the early decades of the nineteenth century, almost all trade was carried out through the port of the city and was taxed by the province. In fact, underlying many conflicts of the early national period was the effort to gain access to that source of wealth, a conflict that increased as Buenos Aires prospered and the interior became more impoverished.[14] The earliest of the national *caudillos,* Juan Manuel de Rosas, rose to power in the 1830s as the governor of Buenos Aires Province and, from that position, parlayed the province's economic advantages and its responsibility for foreign affairs into the capacity to dominate the other *caudillos* and provide a semblance of national order, all the while denouncing the unitarists for their liberal political orientations.[15] Rosas was overthrown in 1851 by dissatisfied provincial *caudillos;* among their grievances were the economic advantages provided to the province of Buenos Aires by the Rosas dictatorship. This most important province almost undid the next effort to establish a constitutional government by withholding approval of the 1853 constitution, modeled on the federalist system of the United States. The reason for this opposition was whether Buenos Aires, the city, would be declared the national capital. If it became the capital, customs revenue from the port would be claimed by the national government—and lost to the province.[16] Buenos Aires was not part of the union until 1862, even while the city continued to benefit from the free-trade policies adopted by the national government. Until 1880, the national government met in Buenos Aires "as guests of the provincial government."[17] In that year, a battle between the province and the national government finally forced the province to cede the city of Buenos Aires to the national government.

Long after Rosas' demise, the economic forces unleashed by the development of the port region consistently strengthened the city vis-à-vis the rest of the country. Taxes on trade ensured its wealth; openness to Europe made it a center of education and intellectual life as well as of economic life. In the mid-nineteenth century, British immigration and investment centered in the city, and gradually, the province of Buenos Aires came to dominate trade relations with the rest of the country. In 1852, the city had a population of 85,000 people; by 1875, there were 200,000 people living within its boundaries. The first of the national newspapers, *La Nación,* was founded in the city in 1870. By the late nineteenth century, when technological innovations in shipping and refrigeration radically increased the export potential of the country, the city of more than 650,000 people was in a strong position to exploit the agricultural wealth of the country through its port and trade with Europe. Shortly after the turn of the century, a third of the industrial establishments of the country were located in the capital.[18] By the early years of the twentieth century, the political and economic power of Buenos Aires had asserted itself to such a degree that little autonomy was left to the interior provinces. Eventually, it became difficult to separate the power of the province and the city from the power of the country.

In the decades after 1880, rapid economic growth and extensive foreign investment, primarily from Britain, and a major influx of immigrants, primarily from Italy and Spain, further cemented the centrality of the capital city to national economic and political fortunes.[19] Its commercial expansion was matched by the commitment of its presidentially appointed *intendentes* to make it a cosmopolitan center modeled on the great capitals of Europe. Earlier investments had given the city gas lighting, a sewer system, and running water. Urban planning from the 1880s on gave it impressive civic buildings, public parks, wide thoroughfares, paved streets, schools, cultural centers, and the University of Buenos Aires.[20] Soon, it was dubbed the "Paris of the South" and boasted a population of more than 1.5 million inhabitants by 1914.

Although the trade economy of the coast was initially built on wheat, meat, and wool from the provinces, there was no question that Buenos Aires was the hub, just as all the new railway lines being built converged in the capital city and just as the city grew twice as rapidly as other urban areas in the country. During this period, Argentina became the tenth wealthiest country in the world, and from this period on, the preeminence of the city was never threatened, however much it was resented in the rest of the country. It had become the seat of empire.

At the same time, however, tensions began to emerge between the old oligarchy, the new urban middle class, and the new working class of immigrant origins, and their political conflicts were often played out within the boundaries of the capital city and, more generally, of Buenos Aires Province.[21] While the elites held on to power from the citadel of their Buenos Aires social clubs, symbolized most significantly by the exclusive Jockey Club and the Rural Society, the middle class established political party headquarters in the same city. The Radical Party developed its strongest base of support in the city, where the largest middle class in Latin America was concentrated.

The political weight of Buenos Aires was strengthened further when Juan

**TABLE 7.1**
PRESIDENTIAL ELECTIONS IN BUENOS AIRES PROVINCE AND THE FEDERAL CAPITAL,
1983–1995
(Percentage of Total Votes)

| Party | 1983 | | 1989 | | 1995 | |
|---|---|---|---|---|---|---|
| | BA Province | Federal Capital | BA Province | Federal Capital | BA Province | Federal Capital |
| PJ | 39.90% | 28.10% | 49.90% | 36.70% | 51.8% | 41.7%[a] |
| UCR | 49.75 | 66.00 | 28.90 | 36.30 | 13.9 | 10.7 |
| FREPASO | — | — | — | — | 29.8 | 44.5 |
| Others | 10.35 | 5.9 | 21.20 | 27.00 | 4.5 | 3.1 |

*Sources:* Fraga (1992 and 1995); 1995 data from Centro de Estudios Unión para la Nueva Mayoría.
[a] Includes 16 percent from votes of parties in alliance with the Peronist party.

Domingo Perón (1947–55) mobilized the urban working class—much of it foreign born or first generation, and much of it from the rural hinterland of the country—into political relevance. Like the Radicals, the Peronists established their strongest base in the capital city and its environs. When there were elections, and when the Peronists were allowed to participate in them, they regularly won national elections, while the Radicals generally polled strongly in the city of Buenos Aires. In the post-1983 democratic regime and until 1995, the Radicals continued to demonstrate that they had considerable support in the city, even though their support diminished over time. The Peronists continued to do well in Buenos Aires Province, particularly in congressional elections (see Table 7.1, Figure 7.1, Figure 7.2). During this era, the city became the center for the emergence of more than thirty-five hundred organizations representing civil society, suggesting the degree to which citizens were active participants in a variety of activities, many of them political.[22]

As an economic and social center, Buenos Aires was unrivaled. By the 1990s it contained 2,248 pre-primary, primary, and secondary schools and accounted for 50.8 percent of the output of general hospitals in the country. Two thirds of the largest industrial firms were located in the city.[23] More than one hundred thousand people were contracted by the national government to work in the city administration, which had an annual budget of $3 billion.[24] At the same time, the city had no police force of its own nor did it have a separate court system.

Historically, then, control over Buenos Aires was a theme with deep roots and meaning in the country. Those who sought political power sought to

**FIGURE 7.1**

CONGRESSIONAL ELECTIONS IN BUENOS AIRES PROVINCE, 1983–1997

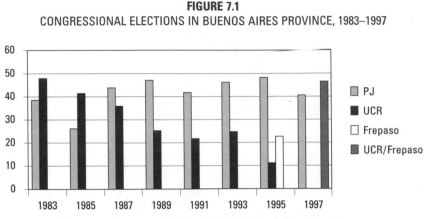

*Sources:* Fraga (1992 and 1995); 1993 and 1995, Centro De Estudios Para La Nueva Mayoría.

**FIGURE 7.2**

CONGRESSIONAL ELECTIONS IN THE FEDERAL CAPITAL, 1983–1997

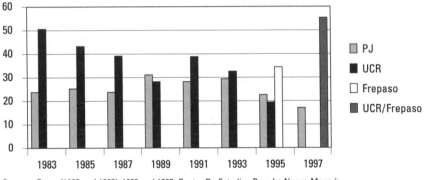

*Sources:* Fraga (1992 and 1995); 1993 and 1995, Centro De Estudios Para La Nueva Mayoría.

control the city and its economic riches and potential. Those who lived within the city were equally interested in maintaining their political dominance over it and the country's hinterland. They welcomed efforts to make it the preeminent urban area in the country. In the provinces, politics was often defined by opposition to the center, and the main political parties were divided by internal rivalries about the relative weight of the city and the interior. Providing autonomy to the city was giving up a valuable political resource and opening up the potential for unanticipated consequences in terms of elections and policies adopted by the city.

## Parties, Leaders, and the Pact

Raúl Alfonsín and Carlos Menem were in positions to seal the Pacto de Olivos because they spoke for the Peronist and Radical Parties. Raúl Alfonsín was a venerable leader of the Radical Party. He began his political career in Buenos Aires province, then moved on to the national legislature in the early 1960s and made an unsuccessful bid to be his party's presidential candidate in 1973. He was an outspoken critic of the military regime in power between 1976 and 1983 and was elected by an absolute majority of voters in the first elections of the modern democratic era. By the 1990s, he continued to be widely respected for his commitment to consolidating the democratic regime and advancing the causes of human rights and democratic governance. His years in office had been marred by the inability to manage economic crisis and by worsening conditions of life, but he was nevertheless honored for the role he played in the reestablishment of democracy in a country that had been ravaged by seven years of brutal military government.[25] Within the Radical Party, he imposed greater centralization of decision making and insisted on a strong leadership position for himself.

Carlos Menem had worked his way to the top of the Peronist Party from an outpost as the twice-elected governor of the poor and remote province of La Rioja.[26] Trained as a lawyer, he became active in the Peronist Party during a military dictatorship in the mid-1950s. In the reintroduced democratic regime between 1973 and 1976, he was elected governor of La Rioja; when that government was overturned in a coup, he was jailed for four years. Reelected governor in 1983, he began a rapid rise to national political prominence. He became a presidential candidate in July 1988 through strongly contested primary elections—the first ever held by the Peronists—and was not the candidate of choice for a considerable number of party elites who backed Antionio Cafiero, the governor of Buenos Aires Province. After the election, the Peronists were internally divided in their support of Menem, given his role in introducing neoliberal market reforms in a country still deeply immersed in a statist development strategy.[27] The party, after all, still revered Juan Perón for his role in expanding the state's role in both economic and social welfare activities in the 1940s and 1950s. But even those who opposed Menem's leadership were awed and even frightened by his political skills. He was able to relate directly to voters throughout the country at a time when the traditional parties were being heavily criticized for their remote and boss-led styles. At the same time, he was widely known to be a savvy political manipulator whose instinct for power rarely failed and who almost always came out ahead in political conflicts.

The parties Alfonsín and Menem represented were also actors in the undramatic events at Olivos. The Unión Cívica, established in 1889 as a "loose combination of malcontents of various kinds," emerged with a constituency among those who were excluded from political participation by the traditional oligarchical elite.[28] It was the first organized opposition party in the country, and in its first decades, many of its adherents were more revolutionary than reformist. Because the party was based in Buenos Aires, its national impact was limited until it developed a network of party organizations in the provinces, a task not completed until twenty years after its founding.

In 1912, a series of electoral reforms named for the president who introduced them, Roque Saenz Peña, opened up participation in the political system by providing for the secret ballot, effective registration of voters, compulsory voting by citizens, and a form of proportional representation that benefited the party with the largest number of votes. These laws provided the Radicals with the context for victory in the presidential elections of 1916, when 30 percent of the adult male population voted.[29] Once secure in the presidential office, the party was able to take advantage of presidential prerogatives and appoint Radicals to key positions in provincial and national government and to intervene widely in provincial affairs. These activities were pursued with the intent of building the support base and power of the party, but they also added to the centralization of power in Buenos Aires and provided the basis for building a party based on clientelism and the distribution of patronage.[30] Thus, the party that was the political expression of the urban middle class, the largest in Latin America at the time, became the dominant political voice in the country in the first decades of the twentieth century. It was a voice of provincial domination by the national government and of clientelism in the interest of maintaining power.

The Radical Party played a historic role in the emergence of democracy in early twentieth-century Argentina and linked its historic mission to this process.[31] It continued to fill the role of democracy's advocate and protector in the 1930s and 1940s, when military governments and persecution of organized political movements and their leaders were punctuated by civilian interregnums tolerated by the military. When Perón came to power in the 1940s, and during military regimes in the 1960s and the 1970s, the Radical

Party continued to identify itself with the politically incorporated middle class and with norms of formal democratic rule. While in opposition, the party's leadership was harassed and repressed by those in power, whether they were Peronists or the military. The party came to see itself as the democratic alternative for Argentina, the party that had been in opposition to both militarism and Peronism and that had a history based on the creation and defense of democratic institutions. Then, in 1983, the election of Alfonsín was a moment of national euphoria, as the party that had traditionally championed democracy and constitutionalism was elected with a majority of 51.7 percent of the vote. Alfonsín's administration, despite mounting economic crisis, reinforced the identity of the party with this tradition.

At the same time, the Radical Party bore the marks of an organization embedded in the realities of Argentine politics. Of all the parties in the country, it had the most well-developed organizational structure and the most strongly developed system of rules and procedures for its internal operations, even while its most revered leaders were strong, personalistic, and even authoritarian. It tended to suffer from internal divisions, particularly when it was in the opposition. Its electoral and organizational strength lay in the more urban areas of the country, particularly Buenos Aires, but it was also a force to be contended with in the smaller towns of the interior. In free elections, of which there were few in the twentieth century, the Radical Party rarely polled less than a quarter of the vote and often managed to achieve 30 to 50 percent of the vote in multiparty contests (see Table 7.2). When in power, it cemented its support through the distribution of patronage and spoils; clientelism structured the inner workings of the party. Its ideological commitment to the process of democratic government was mediated by its traditions of strong and personalistic leadership, its reliance on the distribution of public resources to maintain support, and its clientelistic network of party loyalists. Overarching these characteristics, however, was a sense of historic mission that was taken on as an identity by the party faithful.

The Peronist Party was, if anything, more marked by a sense of historic mission than were the Radicals. When Juan Domingo Perón joined in a conspiracy to overthrow the government in 1943 and then to run for election in 1946, no such party existed. It was the artifact of close followers of Perón who believed that the mobilization of the urban working class, the principal vehicle for Perón's rise to power, needed a structure that would be committed to the leader and that would ensure electoral success.[32] Without a party, the Peronists were dependent on the labor unions and their leaders, who could not be trusted to support Perón first and their own ambitions second. From

**TABLE 7.2**
PRESIDENTIAL ELECTIONS IN ARGENTINA, 1916–1995
(Percentage of Total Votes)

| Year | UCR | PJ |
|------|-----|-----|
| 1916 | 45.6% | — |
| 1922 | 47.8 | — |
| 1928 | 57.4 | — |
| 1931 | a | — |
| 1937 | 40.0 | — |
| 1946 | a | — |
| 1951 | 31.8 | 62.5 |
| 1958 | 44.8[b] | — |
| 1963 | 25.2 | — |
| 1973 | 21.3 | 49.5 |
| 1973 | 24.4 | 61.9 |
| 1983 | 51.7 | 40.2 |
| 1989 | 32.4 | 47.3 |
| 1995 | 16.2 | 47.5 |

*Sources:* Fraga (1989:10–14); 1995 data from http://www.georgetown.edu/pdba/Elecdata/Arg/arg95.html.
[a] Independent UCR factions only.
[b] UCR Intransigente.

its founding in 1946, then, the Peronist Party was designed to be a party for a leader, the movement of the working class united behind a populist leader whose responsibility it was to promote the welfare of organized labor.[33] From that time, the Peronists considered themselves the legitimate standard bearers for the political incorporation of the working classes and the only force capable of responding to their needs. Much of the party's electoral strength, however, was a result of extensive clientelistic ties to remote areas of the country as well as to the urban centers that concentrated the industrial working class.[34] This sense of mission tended to reinforce the role of the leader within the organization and his role in articulating what the ambitions of the supporters were.

After the exile of Perón due to the coup of 1955, the leader continued to manage his party from Spain, publicly above the infighting among labor leaders and party bosses in Argentina, and personally intervening to resolve conflicts among them. When another military government stepped aside for the reestablishment of democratic government in 1973, Perón selected a candidate who won the election and then forced his resignation and a call for new

**TABLE 7.3**
CONGRESSIONAL ELECTIONS IN ARGENTINA, 1983–1997
(Percentage of Total Votes)

| Party | 1983 | 1985 | 1987 | 1989 | 1991 | 1993 | 1995 | 1997 |
|---|---|---|---|---|---|---|---|---|
| PJ | 38.6% | 34.9% | 42.9% | 46.4% | 40.4% | 42.5% | 43.0% | 36.2% |
| UCR | 48.0 | 43.6 | 37.3 | 33.1 | 29.1 | 30.2 | 21.7 | 6.8 |
| FREPASO | — | — | — | — | — | – | 21.1 | 2.4 |
| Alianza UCR-FREPASO | — | — | — | — | — | — | — | 36.4 |
| Others | 13.4 | 21.5 | 19.8 | 20.5 | 30.5 | 27.3 | 14.2 | 18.2 |

*Sources:* Fraga (1992 and 1995); *El Cronista*, October 3, 1997; 1997 data from http://www.elecciones97.com.ar/.

elections, in which he led the Peronist ticket and won. The partisan infighting among party and labor leaders was significant but various factions momentarily united around the triumphant reassertion of the right of the workers to participate in politics.[35] Seven years of hard-fisted military dictatorship that followed the 1976 overthrow of the Peronist government dealt harshly with the party, the unions, and their leaders. The party, although strong as a movement capable of mobilizing extensive support, was in reality a weak organization, with a minimal amount of internal institutionalization, subordinated to leadership-defined goals and strategies, and often overshadowed by the power of labor-union leadership.[36]

Electorally, the Peronists were a majoritarian movement, at times described as hegemonic. When free elections have been permitted, they have polled between 40 to more than 60 percent of the vote in presidential elections and have often won control of the congress (see Tables 7.2 and 7.3).[37] Peronist assumptions of electoral success were so strong that the 1983 election of Alfonsín shocked them into a serious assessment of the party's internal rules and factionalism and its campaign strategies.[38] As was true of the Radicals, they were apt to use their periods in office to distribute positions to their supporters and to use public resources for partisan ends. They provided extensive latitude to their leadership to define programs, policies, and strategies. Internal rivalries, numerous provincial power brokers, and efforts to acquire leadership positions within the movement were characteristic of Peronism. Thus, along with a tendency toward authoritarian leadership, the party was also characterized by periods in which party leaders—and potential leaders—rose and fell swiftly.

It is not too much to claim that these two parties, which together polled

92 percent of voters in the 1983 presidential elections and 80 percent of them in 1989, defined Argentine politics until the 1990s. Both parties emerged as movements to claim political representation for excluded sectors of the population. Both considered themselves the historic embodiment of a strongly held political mission. Both provided their leaders with extraordinary capacity to speak on behalf of this mission—or to turn their backs on it, as in the case of Menem's neoliberal conversion after his election in 1989. And, equally important, each party practiced the politics of exclusion as a way of vanquishing the other. In the 1958 and 1963 elections, the Radicals supported the constitutional proscription on the participation of the Peronists in elections. When in power, the Peronists worked hard to hinder the Radicals from free participation in elections. These, then, were parties that confronted each other electorally and strategically.[39]

By the 1990s, however, Radicals and Peronists were increasingly challenged by the emergence of new parties that mobilized new interests into political relevance. Among the most notable was the Frente Grande, a coalition formed of dissident Peronists and parties of the left for the 1993 elections, and FREPASO (Frente del País Solidario), which emerged for the 1995 elections and absorbed the Frente Grande.[40] These parties were predominantly electoral parties rather than membership parties or movements. Their primary intent was to mobilize voters around particular issues, and their strategy was to use modern means of communication and campaign strategy for this mobilization. In some ways, this made them more agile and adaptive to changing political times than the Radicals or the Peronists, and more able to identify issues of concern to large groups of citizens that were not addressed by the traditional parties. The traditional parties increasingly shared a sense of threat from the emergence of these new political forces. The electoral record of FREPASO (see Tables 7.2 and 7.3) indicates that they had good reason to fear the emergence of this party.

Thus, the signing ceremony on November 14, 1993, was, despite the absence of the press, a historic event that was filled with symbolism. Alfonsín, the party boss and committed democrat, and Menem, the consummate political operator and Peronist-turned-neoliberal, each symbolized the critical changes in Argentina in the 1980s and 1990s. Alfonsín evoked the return to democratic government and the end to the suffering imposed on the country under the generals. Menem was identified with radical change in economic policies—from statist, inward-oriented, and populist to market-oriented, outward-directed, and austere—that had tamed hyperinflation and encouraged economic growth after years of stagnation and crisis. They symbolized the role of personalist leadership in each of the parties, providing Menem the capacity to speak for the Peronist movement, despite its internal divisions, and allowing Alfonsín to reassert publicly his leadership over a movement that was increasingly in a minority position in national politics. They also symbolized the history of inclusion and exclusion that lay at the center of twentieth-century political conflict in the country. The pact indicated mutual acceptance of the legitimacy of the other in the political arena while still excluding the participation of newer political forces. And, as described in subsequent pages, Alfonsín and Menem symbolized the strong interests each had in particular parts of the pact and the role each had played in getting to the agreement.

## Presidentialism

In the 1990s, Argentine politics were widely characterized as hyperpresidentialist, a reference to the strongly presidentialist nature of government structure, as well as to policy making under Carlos Menem, which had further increased the centrality of the president to all issues of politics and policy. Hyperpresidentialism can be traced to the constitution of 1853, whose creators purposely designed a presidency that would have sufficient power to overcome internecine conflict and unite the country under a strong and stable government. One constitutional scholar referred to the intent, based on the model in the 1813 Chilean constitution, to create a "sort of elected king— an office that was democratic in its origin but absolutist in its exercise."[41] Accordingly, this document, which was reintroduced in 1983, allowed presidents to appoint cabinet and other officials without congressional approval, to rule by decree in a broad range of circumstances, and to declare states of seige under certain circumstances, providing them with extraordinary powers and limiting the protections available to citizens under the law.[42] The national government, acting through the executive branch, had the power to dismiss elected officials at the provincial level.[43] The constitution also gave presidents veto power over legislation or specific measures within legislation.

Although not outlined by the constitution, Argentine practice emphasized the development of most legislation and policy in the executive branch and the position of the president as the leader of his party in the legislature. Under military regimes, presidentialism incorporated the legislative process by proscribing the powers of congress and, by domination of appointments and activities, the powers of the judicial branch.[44] When democratic governments replaced military governments, separate powers were reestablished, but the initiative in legislative and judicial matters tended to remain within presidential prerogatives. This tendency was exacerbated by parties that were weak relative to their leadership and by the more generalized tendency for issues to migrate to the office of the person known to have the power to do something about them. As a consequence, formal and informal lobbying by interest groups focused on the executive and the office of the president.

An important basis for maintaining a hyperpresidentialist system was the use of public resources and public positions for partisan purposes. As indicated previously, both the Radical and Peronist Parties actively maintained their base of support through the management of patronage and the distribution of contracts, favors, special deals, and access to those in power. The city government of Buenos Aires, for example, provided the appointive position of mayor and some 120,000 public-sector positions, ranging from street-cleaning jobs to high-level executive ones, as well as an annual budget of $3 billion for managing, provisioning, and servicing the city.[45]

Hyperpresidentialism was also an artifact of particular leaders and particular circumstances. After 1985, President Alfonsín increasingly centered policy making and political management in the president's office and distanced himself from his party and the legislature.[46] Even more notably, the economic-policy transformation put in place by President Menem after 1989—and particularly after 1991, when Domingo Cavallo became inister of the economy—was largely carried out by presidential decree powers. Much of this heightened central control was a result of the economic crisis itself, which, as in large numbers of other countries, opened up considerable space for political leaders to "do something" in response to emergency-like conditions. Nevertheless, in the case of Argentina, the closed decision-making style of the Menemist-Cavallo economic policy reform, and the fact that those within the closed circle of decision makers were more often technocrats and "outsiders" than Peronists, increased the extent to which Menem became the embodiment of hyperpresidentialism. The use of constitutionally permitted "decrees by necessity and urgency" was extraordinary by historical standards; Menem had recourse to more decrees than all other presidents in the history of Argentina combined.[47] His political ambitions for reelection, which were well known to the public, his power-maximizing political machinations, and his flamboyant public personality added to the perception that his use of presidential powers had surpassed and increased the momentum of historical tendencies.[48]

Combined with political parties that defined themselves as exclusive carriers of historical truths, hyperpresidentialism in Argentina tended to increase the difficulty of achieving political consensus. Presidential initiatives were often opposed more because they were identified with the hegemonic projects of political parties and the efforts of authoritarian leaders to impose their will on the opposition than on the basis of their intrinsic content. As a result, Argentina's strong presidents tended to have only weak capacity to achieve agreement on public-policy issues, a condition that increased the tendency to rule by decree and centralize decision-making power in the executive. Obviously, the potential for policy gridlock was greatest when presidents did not have majority support in the legislature.

Interestingly, however, hyperpresidentialism played a key role in the concerns that brought the two most important players to the table to sign the Pacto de Olivos. As leader of the principal opposition to Menem, Alfonsín was deeply concerned about the need to "attenuate the presidency" by setting up a series of controls over executive power.[49] In contrast, Menem was almost exclusively focused on the possibility of reelection. Certainly, the desire of a president to stay in office is understandable in a system that grants extraordinary power to the president. That this motivation should be so strong as to encourage him to agree to a wide range of other changes that would constrain his powers is less easily understood. The political interactions that led up to the Pacto de Olivos and its conversion into a constitutional reform provide part of the answer to this puzzle.

## Finding the Right Moment: Studying, Proposing, and Negotiating Reform

The Pacto de Olivos surprised most Argentines. It should not have. Discussions about constitutional reform could be traced back at least twenty years.[50] During that period, groups and individuals had argued that such action was necessary. And although public opinion universally credited the pact to personal political ambitions, prominent legal and constitutional scholars, other academics, and leading politicians had long discussed the idea. These intellectuals and leaders generally agreed that constitutional reform was a necessity for the country's institutional development. In the mid-1980s, this consensus was strengthened and reiterated when a high-level commission was established by the president and set to work studying the problem. When the commission issued its report, there was considerable agreement about what kinds of institutional changes were most important for the country. Commission members broadly supported these recommendations, regardless of their political affiliations. The fate of those proposals in the 1980s and 1990s, however, was determined not so much by the consensus that underlay them as by immediate political circumstances.

## The Council for the Consolidation of Democracy: Generating Consensus

On December 24, 1985, shortly after mid-term elections confirmed a congressional majority for the Radical Party, President Alfonsín announced the creation of the Council for the Consolidation of Democracy. The president established this council of public and academic luminaries and politically important individuals to provide advice to the executive branch on institutional reforms to strengthen democracy and modernize government in the country.[51] Its members, who were to have the rank of secretaries of state, were instructed to carry out studies and organize meetings to explore institutional changes that could contribute to these ends. The council was to consider reforms that required broad social consensus if they were to be accepted.[52] It would convene subgroups to explore general areas of concern to the future of the country and would be supported by a full-time technical team.

Included among possible subjects for the council was assessing the need for a reform of the constitution of 1853. Revising the constitution was not an unusual event in Argentina, of course, nor was generating new foundational documents.[53] In the second half of the twentieth century, several such initiatives were undertaken. In 1949, a new constitution was introduced. In 1957, a constitutional convention had made a number of changes to the basic law, and a military government introduced a revised constitution in 1972, just before the reestablishment of democratic government. In 1974, President Perón set up a commission to study the possibility of writing a new constitution; this work was abandoned in the wake of his death in the same year.[54] Alfonsín's 1985 initiative put the issue on the public agenda again. The charge to the council members was considerable. They were to "contribute to the development of a transformative project . . . focused on the modernization of cultural, scientific, educational, productive, and governmental structures of Argentine society."[55]

The official explanation for the council underscored the extent to which the Alfonsín administration took seriously its role in institutionalizing the transition to democracy in the country and the importance of constructing durable and legitimate institutions for the future. Constitution writing was a major commitment to this role. Nevertheless, considerable public opinion at the time distrusted the official claims, suspecting instead that the initiative was a result of Alfonsín's aspirations to run for a second term of office, especially in the aftermath of the Radical Party gains in the recent elections.[56] Without a constitutional revision, he was barred from this possibility.

Carlos Nino, a legal scholar of note and a Radical, chaired the commission. Its eighteen members included distinguished political, academic, cultural, and legal figures, among whom were prominent Radical and Peronist leaders, as well as those representing smaller political parties, the social Christians, the socialists, and provincial parties.[57] The inclusiveness of the commission was related to the need to generate the support of two thirds of the congress in order to establish a constitutional convention. Throughout its deliberations, the council emphasized the importance of a broad social consensus on constitutional change that would provide a basis for accepting the legitimacy of such a document. The council, which made recommendations in reports produced in 1986 and 1987, was concerned primarily with institutional reforms that would alter the relationships among the three branches of government and make government itself function more fluidly.[58] Presidentialism was of considerable concern, in part because of the concentration of power and the potential for its abuse that it encouraged, but also because of the tendency in highly centralized systems for bottlenecks to occur as decision making migrated to the top of the political system.

The commission met frequently during 1986 and 1987. It generated many of the suggestions that were later incorporated into the Pacto de Olivos: the creation of the office of prime minister, second-round presidential elections, and changes in the judicial system. These proposals were strongly supported by the Alfonsín administration, whose minister of interior repeatedly referred to the necessity of modernizing the country's institutions to make democracy more effective.[59] Interestingly, the Peronist leadership was similarly supportive of the need for reform, many of them citing Perón's efforts to reform the constitution in 1974 and his insistence that a broad political consensus was needed in order to carry it forward. In 1986, Peronist deputies stated their approval in a congressional statement and reiterated this support in a series of public statements in 1987.[60] They indicated only vague support for the reforms that in any way weakened the presidency, however. Despite the appearance of broad consensus, opponents of reform within the two major parties and outside them criticized altering the 1853 constitution because many of its principles had been honored in the breach. Better, they argued, to enforce the document fully than to alter it.[61] Others disagreed on the timing of the reform.

The ability of Alfonsín and the Radical Party to carry through on their initiatives, however, was severely curtailed by the returns of 1987 elections for governors and half of the provincial and national legislatures. In their wake, the party lost its absolute majority in congress and remained in control of only two governorships; the Peronists captured sixteen governorships and made significant gains in congress and in provincial legislatures. Military uprisings in April 1987, in January 1988, and again in December 1988, along with mounting economic turmoil, were partly to blame for the Radical loss. After the elections, Alfonsín had to cobble together transitory alliances and respond piecemeal to escalating economic and political problems.[62]

The elections reinforced the sense among those most committed to a constitutional reform—those who had been involved in the commission's discussions between 1985 and 1987—that a constitutional reform could only be carried further through some kind of pact between the two major parties. Thus, in 1987, Alfonsín's advisers who were most involved in the on-going reform initiative opened discussions with advisers of the newly elected Peronist governor of Buenos Aires province and Peronist Party president, Antonio Cafiero. At that time, Cafiero, by virtue of his dual posts, was the most likely candidate for president in 1989. In late 1987, Cafiero announced his readiness to negotiate a reform of the constitution. He moved the process further when he met with Alfonsín in January 1988 to consider how they should proceed with this initiative.[63] In early 1988, the Radical Party established a constitutional reform commission to study the possibilities for change; at the top of its list of reforms was the issue of presidential power. This commission recommended that a national referendum should be held on the issue.[64]

At this point, however, the consensus generated by reformers from both parties began to break down because of divergent electoral aspirations. The Radical commission was primarily concerned with developing rules that could constrain the presidentialist nature of the old constitution; after the 1987 elections and in the context of increasing economic and political instability, it was widely expected that the party would lose the presidency in the 1989 elections.[65] In contrast to the Radicals and reflecting its presidential expectations, Peronist recommendations were geared toward protecting the power of the president, including permitting reelection and dissolving the electoral college.[66] A series of party statements and exchanges with the Ministry of the Interior produced declarations of support and initial plans to set up interparty technical groups to further the proposals for reform.[67] Both parties affirmed the need for constitutional reform in their party platforms for the presidential elections of 1989, but by this time, it was clear that their priorities for reform differed considerably.[68]

*Losing Momentum: Candidates, Elections, and Party Leadership*

The agenda of constitutional reform experienced a four-year period of ups and downs between 1989 and 1993, a period in which the electoral strategies of the political parties and their candidates had much to do with this trajectory. These strategies, in turn, were significantly affected by the conditions in the national economy and the political instability attendant upon an escalating burden of economic woes. The Alfonsín administration was increasingly unable to control either the economic or the political situation, and the campaign of 1989 was carried out in a context of increasing economic instability. Inflation climbed steadily between 1981 and 1985 and again from 1986 to 1989, growth declined, and the external debt grew steadily, from nearly $46 billion in 1983 to more than $65 billion in 1989 (see Table 7.4).

These economic problems were matched by extensive political turmoil. Strikes and protests mounted daily as inflation exceeded 3,000 percent in 1989.[69] In the meantime, internal party competition in the Peronist Party toppled Cafiero from his leadership position and awarded the nomination as presidential candidate to Carlos Menem.[70] In the context of rapidly accelerating economic crisis, the Radicals, represented by Eduardo Angeloz, had little hope of doing well in the elections. In the event, Menem won with 47.5 percent of the vote against the 32.4 percent of the Radicals. In the face of mounting protest against the increasingly difficult economic situation, Alfonsín agreed to end his presidency five months before the official timetable and hand over power to his successor to deal with both the economic and the political crises. In July 1989, Carlos Menem assumed power as president of a nation torn by political dissent and protest and rocked by economic decline, high inflation, and mounting unemployment.

This economic crisis and attendant political unrest consumed the focus and energies of the new government.[71] During the initial two years of the administration, President Menem surprised the country and the world as well by his rejection of the Peronist tradition of statism and populism in favor of neoliberal solutions to the economic crisis.[72] Between mid-1989 and early 1991, the government imposed austerity, rapidly privatized large numbers of state-owned industries, liberalized trade, downsized the public administration, instituted tax reform, and devalued the currency. The style set by this presidency also became clear; presidential decree powers were the normal mode for carrying out the sweeping economic-policy reforms. Peronists were generally excluded from economic policy-making circles, in what appeared to make of them mere "guests of the government they had elected."[73]

**TABLE 7.4**
**ECONOMIC INDICATORS IN ARGENTINA, 1980–1995**

| Indicator | 1980 | 1981 | 1982 | 1983 | 1984 | 1985 | 1986 | 1987 | 1988 | 1989 | 1990 | 1991 | 1992 | 1993 | 1994 | 1995 |
|---|---|---|---|---|---|---|---|---|---|---|---|---|---|---|---|---|
| GNP per capita[a] | 2890 | 2790 | 2610 | 2810 | 2830 | 2660 | 3020 | 3600 | 3940 | 2950 | 3270 | 3920 | 6110 | 7260 | 8160 | 8030 |
| GNP per cap. growth rate (%) | — | −3.5 | −6.5 | 7.7 | 0.7 | −6.0 | 13.5 | 19.2 | 9.4 | −25.1 | 10.8 | 19.9 | 55.9 | 18.8 | 12.4 | −1.6 |
| GNP growth rate (%) | — | −7.0% | −6.6 | 3.4 | 3.3 | −7.7 | 9.1 | 2.4 | −1.5 | −1.0 | 4.7 | 10.3 | 9.9 | 6.5 | 7.1 | −5.1 |
| Annual inflation | — | 103.6 | 161.6 | 344.4 | 637.5 | 671.5 | 89.8 | 131.5 | 342.2 | 3084.6 | 2314.5 | 172.1 | 24.3 | 11.3 | 3.9 | 3.0 |
| Total external debt[b] (TED) | 27,157 | 35,658 | 43,634 | 45,920 | 48,857 | 50,946 | 52,450 | 58,458 | 58,741 | 65,257 | 62,233 | 65,403 | 68,345 | 70,576 | 77,434 | 89,747 |
| Public debt as % of TED | 37.5 | 29.6 | 36.4 | 55.4 | 54.6 | 73.3 | 78.1 | 84.2 | 80.9 | 79.4 | 75.4 | 72.7 | 69.7 | 73.7 | 72.1 | 69.3 |

*Source:* World Bank (1997).

[a]Current U.S.$.

[b]Millions of Current U.S.$.

President Menem acquired authorization to increase the number of supreme court justices from five to nine, which allowed him to appoint four new members and ensure that the court would not stand in the way of his economic program.

The constitutional reform project necessarily took a back seat to more pressing economic and political problems through the first years of the 1990s. Although the minister of the interior established the Commission for Institutional Reform early in the new administration, which was directed to make wide-ranging proposals about electoral processes, political party regulation, federalism, state institutions, and the national constitution, little political momentum was behind this initiative.[74] Moreover, aside from the necessity of dealing with the economic crisis and its political consequences, a 1990 effort to reform the constitution of the province of Buenos Aires to allow the governor's reelection also dampened the willingness of the Peronist Party to move forward with the reform project. Although the province was controlled by the party and had long been a party stronghold, a referendum to approve a new constitution failed to win. At the same time, elections for half of the provincial and national legislatures and all provincial governors in 1991 went badly against the Radical Party, weakening its power to move a reformist agenda forward.

In 1992, however, President Menem reopened the question of constitutional reform. The initial year of policy change under Domingo Cavallo had restored stability to the economy and a modest measure of growth (see Table 7.4).[75] The success of this reform program allowed Menem to return to his political agenda. The party's juridical commission published three endorsements of constitutional reform in 1992, and the initiative received overall party support on June 23, 1992, when the Peronists approved the findings of this commission. Nevertheless, internal divisions emerged within leadership cadres of the party about how and when to pursue the reform. Some favored moving ahead with a national debate and referendum; others wanted to wait until after the 1993 mid-term elections.[76] Meanwhile, the Radical Party began to have second thoughts about the wisdom of moving forward with the reform, because Menem's supporters in the Peronist Party were promoting it and were in a powerful position to win their goal of presidential reelection.[77]

Increasingly, the debate between the parties focused not on the extensive range of recommendations put on the table by the Council for the Consolidation of Democracy but solely on the issue of presidential reelection. Leading presidential contenders within both the Peronist and Radical Parties were less than eager to permit Menem a second chance at the presidency. Particularly in the context of a backlash against Menem's use of power in the economic reform program, hyperpresidentialism was increasingly considered a disease that needed a cure by the Radicals and opponents of Menem within the Peronist party. Menem and Cavallo were clearly identified with the neoliberal wing of the party, whereas many Peronist leaders continued to support the idea of a state deeply involved in managing the economy. In addition to harboring a very distinct view of the role of government, many were angered at their exclusion from policy-making positions in the government.[78] Menem and his supporters, however, became even more single-minded in seeking the possibility of reelection.

These positions became marked as elections neared in 1993. The Menemist wing of the Peronist Party decided to use these legislative and provincial elections as a test of the economic policies being carried out by the government. During the campaign, constitutional reform was portrayed as part of the requirements for the sustainability of economic reform, which was producing a positive turnaround in the country's economy at this point. Others now began adding their particular concerns to the constitutional reform package. During this period, Menem's minister of interior, Gustavo Béliz, a young reformer concerned about more efficient management in government and greater political transparency, began efforts to introduce legislation to alter electoral processes, increase internal democracy in the political parties, provide for the election of the mayor of Buenos Aires, and allow citizens of the capital to be consulted through referenda, legislative initiatives, and recall of elected officials.[79] These proposals added emphasis to a number of the initiatives already on the agenda for constitutional change.

As the presidential elections of 1994 neared, the importance of constitutional reform increased for Menem. Within the councils of his advisers and within his party, concerns focused on finding a strategy to get authorization for his reelection bid. The Peronists, who did not have a two-thirds majority, proposed that this meant two thirds of those present at the time of voting rather than two thirds of the total number of members. In response, leaders of the Radical Party set themselves firmly against the interpretation that two thirds of those present could approve the call for a convention.[80] Facing this barrier in the congress, the president's party began to float the idea of a plebiscite to approve the need for a constitutional convention, thus skirting the issue of legislative action. The problem with this route, similar to that of interpreting the two-thirds rule loosely, was the likelihood that the legitimacy of any resulting constitutional reform would be called into question by any who did not agree with the content of the reforms as well as by any who were strict in their interpretation of the constitution. In the end, the party decided to wait for the results of the October 1993 elections to determine its reformist strategy.

Those elections were prejudicial for the Radical Party, underscoring its secondary place to the Peronists in electoral competitions since 1987 (see Table 7.3).[81] The Peronist Party won almost 43 percent of the vote, slightly increasing its representation in congress; the Radicals won 37 percent. This result increased the Peronist effort to push for reelection while the Radicals were split in terms of their position on the reform. Radicals with strong presidential aspirations were firmly opposed to reform because of Menem's likely reelection. Others were more convinced that the full package of constitutional reform measures was critically important to the democratization and modernization of the country and therefore supported action. This ambivalence encouraged party leaders to begin considering negotiation with Menem: the Radical Party would be in a minority position at least until 2001 in the senate, and its capacity to influence legislation in either house or have influence with the supreme court was severely constrained into the future. The president of the senate, Menem's brother, was assiduous in promoting legislation calling for a constitutional convention. As a result of Peronist commitment and Radical ambivalence, this step was approved by the requisite two thirds of the upper house on October 21, 1993. The next step in the formal process was to obtain a two thirds majority vote in the chamber of deputies for the same law.

Recognizing the difficulty of mobilizing enough support in the lower chamber for such a vote, the government proposed to call a plebiscite on the need for constitutional reform with the intention of influencing the vote in the lower house of congress. The Radical Party, unable to forge a common stance on reform, decided to allow its members to decide at the district level whether they would support moving forward with a plebiscite or not. At this point, and in the context of a divided party in which presidential hopefuls were attempting to take over leadership of the party, Alfonsín became more open to dialogue with Menem. He was among the most firmly opposed to the hyperpresidentialism represented by Menem and increasingly spoke of the importance of constraining the presidency through measures to ensure greater judicial independence, a stronger role for the legislature, greater citizen participation, and greater autonomy for the provinces. A plebiscite, he believed, would rob the party of considerable capacity to negotiate for these points.

During this period, Alfonsín's close advisers began a series of meetings with a team of Menem's advisers to explore possible sources of consensus on how to encourage the reform.[82] Radical presidential hopeful Fernando de la Rúa accused Alfonsín of "selling out his party" as it became clear that he was willing to trade the reelection clause for a series of constitutional constraints on the presidency. Despite this opposition, the majority of the party backed Alfonsín by renewing his election as head of the party and implicitly giving the go-ahead to proceed with discussions with the Menemist advisors.[83]

## Menem, Alfonsín, and the Pacto de Olivos

In late 1993, those who met to discuss moving ahead with constitutional reform were well aware of the accord reached between the parties in 1988, just prior to the 1989 election of Menem and the escalating economic crisis. This prior agreement had included modifying the presidency, increasing the independence of the judiciary, strengthening the role of congress and the control of citizens over their elected representatives, and improving the federalist system. Those at the table in 1993 had been involved in these earlier discussions, and in fact, several had been considering the reform since the days of the Council for the Consolidation of Democracy between 1985 and 1987. As negotiators, although representing the parties that traditionally confronted each other at national and provincial levels in Argentine politics, they had become colleagues in terms of their understanding of the reform proposals.

These officials were also advisers who were close to and trusted by the respective leaders of their parties. As such, they had considerable room to set the agenda of reform, as long as each of the leaders was able to achieve his central goals. Issues not related to the core interests of Menem and Alfonsín "gave those negotiating and drafting the constitution considerable liberty in the whole area of institutional design," according to one of the chief architects of the constitution:

> There was much room for negotiation here and there was also a long history of relationships among us personally, Peronists and Radicals, that helped us negotiate and draft with a great deal of trust and sharing of views. We often held similar views and were engaged in a real dialogue about institutional design that went far beyond the basic core interests of the presidents and their advisers. In this process, we

were thinking much beyond the timeframe of the leaders and were given considerable scope for considering how institutions could bring longer term democratization to the country. Behind the *Pacto* and the constitutional convention was almost a decade of discussion [among us].[84]

As they reinitiated discussions, they began to understand their job as defining a "nucleus of basic agreements" that could be subscribed to by both leaders.[85] If they could define these issues and get the leaders and party officials to agree to them, then the constitutional convention could move forward quickly, and the reform would be protected from the kind of gridlock and opposition that often accompanied the interaction of Peronists and Radicals. Their idea was that the nucleus of basic agreements would not be debated at a general level and the convention could focus on defining more precisely the terms in which these issues were stated.

The basic issues around which there was agreement included the principal objectives of Menem and Alfonsín, of course, but also a series of principles about democratic governance that these advisers had discussed over the years and in which many of them believed strongly. A number of the issues that they defined related primarily to how to increase the degree of democracy in the country, how to engineer a better balance among the branches of government, and how judicial independence could be achieved. This group of advisers drew up the terms of the agreement in an intense series of meetings in November. These meetings, in fact, were the principal negotiations for the constitutional reform, rather than the negotiations that took place during the constitutional convention of the following year. In determining the list of changes for the basic agreement, both parties made trade-offs. The Peronists accepted the prime ministership and the direct election of the mayor, as well as allowing for a third senator from each province, selected from the minority party, in return for the reelection of the president. The Radicals accepted reelection because they believed they were getting a broad range of assurances that in the future, the power of the president would be more fully constrained.

On November 14, Menem and Alfonsín signed the Pacto de Olivos, committing both parties to a major constitutional reform that would redesign key institutions of Argentina's democracy. The day after the accord was signed, the government suspended Menem's plan to hold a plebiscite. On December 1, the negotiators presented a more detailed draft of their agreement that was to be presented to the two major parties. The accord, entitled "The Nucleus of Basic Agreements," included a first section with a series of steps that would weaken the presidentialism of the system.[86] The second section dealt with shortening the presidential term and reelection. The sixth addressed the direct election of the mayor of Buenos Aires and the city's autonomy. On December 13, Menem and Alfonsín signed this agreement. Then, the chamber of deputies on December 22, 1993, and the senate on December 29, approved a law calling for a constitutional convention.[87] On April 10, 1994, 213 representatives to the constitutional convention were elected from the two main parties, and 82 from other parties. The debates at the convention were not negligible, but with the nucleus of basic agreement subscribed to by the two principal parties, they concerned the fine print of the reforms. The new constitution, still carried along by the agreement of Olivos, was dutifully ratified by two thirds of the members of congress on August 24, 1994.

## Conclusions: Principles and Personal Stakes

The critical incident in the constitutional reform that led to a series of significant changes in the country's political institutions, then, was the pact of 1993 and the process of discussion and negotiations that led up to it. Analysis of this event and what lay behind it thus provide a third lens for understanding the motivations and choices involved in institutional change. As indicated at the outset of this chapter, Argentines were almost unanimous in explaining the reforms in terms of the personal ambitions of the two main protagonists. From this perspective, the response to the question of why the reforms occurred is simple: Menem wanted reelection, and Alfonsín wanted to assert his position as leader of the party, to control the power of Menem and improve the chances that his party would continue to play an influential role in national politics. One political leader summed up this perspective:

> Menem wanted reelection. We all knew that. And he was determined to get it either by a special law that would alter the constitution or through a plebiscite. The UCR was very weak as a party then; it was really a series of small parties within the party. Alfonsín finally decided that, on the basis of the political rationality of the situation, it would be best to get as much as possible out of Menem in exchange for reelection. So this was the basis on which we all went forward with the pact and the constitutional reform.[88]

There is ample evidence that these perceptions go to the heart of much that occurred. Certainly, Menem made no secret of his interest in reelection nor did Alfonsín or the Radicals hide the fact that they were in a difficult position. The reform had not happened earlier, despite fairly widespread consensus on the recommendations of the Council for the Consolidation of Democracy, because the moment was not right—Menem was not at the center of the Peronist Party nor in office, and the Radicals were not frightened. When the context changed, so did the impetus for reform. One analysis suggests that the two leaders were engaged in a game of "chicken," each interested in negotiating but each eager to gain as much as possible from such negotiations. They continued down the road of personal ambition toward each other until a near-collision led both to the negotiating table.[89] Another analysis indicated that the reform occurred when Menem was in a position to maximize his gains and Alfonsín wanted to minimize his losses.[90] In public opinion, it was widely perceived that Menem as an individual won and that Alfonsín, even while restoring his position as leader of the party, lost in terms of his concern to constrain the presidency. This history certainly conforms to a rational choice perspective on why political leaders would support power sharing.

There are, however, issues of relevance in this case that go beyond the immediate personal gains and losses of the principals. For example, issues of process and legitimacy influenced the behavior of the politicians involved. Menem won the right to run for reelection, but his strategic choices included a preference for processes that would increase the legitimacy of his actions. There were other ways of achieving his goals; trying to insist on a very loose interpretation of the constitution or calling a national plebiscite were two of these. Yet he agreed to put his advisers to work with those of Alfonsín and hammer out a constitutional reform. Why did he favor this approach? The constitutional history of Argentina must be invoked to provide an answer to this question; that history was riddled with constitutional changes that were imposed by one party or one faction on others and that subsequently were called into question on the basis of the very legitimacy they were supposed to establish. Menem preferred a two-party agreement to a plebiscitary fiat because of the public perception of the legitimacy of the changes he favored. In the end, he opted for a narrower definition of the process described in the constitution, negotiated a range of issues with the opposition, agreed to a set of changes that would curtail his control over political resources, and called a constitutional convention to give greater stability and legitimacy to the changes. Alfonsín, as we have seen, had a range of goals that included institutional arrangements that would not benefit him personally but which corresponded to principles of democratic governance that he had long held. Moreover, both leaders chose to break with a tradition of party confrontation by negotiating the nucleus of basic agreement. While simple power maximizing explains much about the timing of change, it does not fully explain the content of the agreement or the concern of participants with issues of legitimacy.

These motivations drew the two leaders to the table and made them amenable to the constitutional proposals hammered out by their advisers. Nevertheless, the story of the motivations of the politicians is incomplete without acknowledging the history of the working group that initially crafted the constitutional reform project. The agreement that was cobbled together reflected the work of legal scholars, constitutional experts, and political officials who had worked in concert since 1985 and who had their own ideas about how a constitution should be constructed and how Argentine political institutions should be structured and should function. Initially, these groups were given considerable room to address such a large issue when brought together in the Council for the Consolidation of Democracy. Their mandate was both broad and open-ended, and they were brought together as part of a broadly representative group of public intellectuals. This provided them ample space to serve as constitutional redesigners rather than as delegates of parties or particular politicians. As a consequence, the ideas that emerged from the council reflected a wide range of innovations, including the autonomy of Buenos Aires and the direct election of its mayor, that were not of immediate interest to the political leadership. Their role in setting the constitutional reform agenda was significant and was responsible for a broader range of proposals than probably would have been the case had only Menem and Alfonsín been consulted. Electoral calculations are important in explaining this case, but they cannot account for the range of the reforms introduced.

As in the cases of Venezuela and Bolivia, a design team played a central role in shaping the content of the reform. Clearly, much bargaining and conflict surrounded the work of these experts and contributed to the recommendations they made, but so too did their expertise as lawyers and constitutional specialists, and so too did their concern with basic problems of representation and responsiveness in democracies. Placing controls on the president, bringing greater balance to the relationships among the three branches of government, and bringing local government closer to citizens in the case of Buenos Aires were all issues that were approached not only from the perspective of political advantage but also from the perspective of good governance. The pact was preceded by considerable discussion of reform and a set of solutions for particular problems. The agreement was a negotiated one, but behind it there was a good deal of work in institutional design that had been carried out by the reformers. Action required the commitment of the two main protagonists, but the work of the commission and the subsequent discussions among participants in that process did much to define the content of the reform.

# Waiting for Godot?

## Constitutional Change in Argentine Practice

The constitutional reform of 1994 that, among other changes, altered the status of the capital city and allowed for the direct election of the mayor was widely dismissed as window dressing to permit Carlos Menem to run for a second term as president.[1] The new charter was also strongly attacked by FREPASO, which criticized the bossism implicit in the reform process and questioned the "smoke-filled room" negotiations that led to the nucleus of basic agreements. The opposition of FREPASO meant that the legitimacy of the constitutional reform was questioned by a political voice that was gaining strength and that had its largest base of support in the city of Buenos Aires. Within the Peronist Party, the powerful governor of Buenos Aires Province was opposed to the reforms because the reelection clause significantly curtailed his presidential aspirations. Similarly, some of the leaders of the Radical Party anticipated tougher electoral battles ahead when a Menem reelection bid could stymie their political opportunities. However, many in this party strongly supported the direct election of the Buenos Aires mayor because of Radical electoral strength in the city.

While debate continued on the appropriateness of constitutional reform, President Menem took immediate advantage of it. He won the nomination as presidential candidate for the Peronist Party and easily won the elections of May 1995. He polled 47.5 percent of the vote; the Radical Party candidate, Horacio Massaccesi, polled only 16.2 percent. FREPASO, in alliance with several other parties, claimed a surprising second place with 28.2 percent of the vote for its candidate, José Bordón.[2] In the capital city, Bordón won 44.1 percent of the vote, placing it first among the parties contesting the election in that arena.

The most important theme of the election for the voters was not the legitimacy of the constitutional reform. It was continuity—of the policies that had brought economic stability and a return of economic growth to the country, particularly since 1991, when Domingo Cavallo took over the Ministry of the Economy. The results of the election were generally interpreted in these terms also: Argentines voted for economic reform and stability.[3] Under the continuation of the Menem-Cavallo team, the reform policies were maintained and deepened in the wake of the "tequila crisis" provoked by economic disarray in Mexico at the end of 1994. In 1996, the economic growth rate climbed to 4.4 percent, and the economy continued to expand in 1997. Moreover, despite unemployment figures that reached unprecedented levels of more than 18 percent, public opinion demonstrated considerable approval of the management of the economy by the government.[4]

In other regards, however, the government received more criticism than support. Throughout 1996, 1997, and 1998, political debate and public commentary centered on unemployment, the prevalence of corruption in government, executive manipulation of the judiciary for political ends, low levels of public security, and the importance of improving public services, particularly education.[5] In terms of these particular concerns, Argentines were extremely critical. In a 1996 study, 66 percent of respondents stated that levels of corruption were very high in Argentina. Another 30 percent characterized the levels as high. Fifty percent of respondents believed that politicians were the most corrupt group in the country. Thirty-four percent believed that 50 percent or more of the national budget was lost through corruption.[6] The trust that Argentines had in their institutions of governance reached perilously low levels.[7]

More generally, as the economic situation improved, themes of institutional reform and government performance replaced demands that the government "do something" about the economy. And when Domingo Cavallo left government in mid-1996 and his replacement demonstrated that neoliberal policy continuity could be maintained without him, public attention further shifted to institutional issues and complaints about government performance. At the same time, few Argentines believed the government of Carlos Menem was at all interested in institutional reform. To underscore this point, they pointed to the fate of constitutional reform after it was adopted. While

the provision for reelection went into effect almost immediately, judicial reform—one of the most important changes that would constrain the power of
Argentina's presidents—did not, despite widespread demands that improving
the performance and autonomy of the judiciary was essential to effective
democratic governance. Similarly, new constitutional provisions for enhanced democratic accountability (the public ombudsman) and participation
(the plebiscite, referendum, and citizen initiative provisions) remained paper
changes only. Moreover, Carlos Menem continued to occupy center stage as
the initiator of policy and the manager of political dynamics. Many acknowledged that although the reforms were important in theory, they were of little
practical importance as long as Menem held the reins of power. Thus, an
eminent constitutional scholar commented that "Menem got what he wanted,
including the capacity to make what Alfonsín wanted worthless."[8]

Public skepticism affected even those constitutional reforms that were
put into effect, such as those that affected the city of Buenos Aires. Within
months, the city was planning for the election of its chief executive, a constitutional assembly, and its legislature. Despite rapid implementation of the
constitutional change, "giving up" the city was often dismissed as a throw-
away for Menem. The city of Buenos Aires had long been a stronghold of the
Radical Party. Thus, some argued that the president had really given away
very little in terms of presidential command of his support base. Typical of
this view was that of one observer of Argentine politics: "Menem was not
really giving up power. It was a trade-off. He wanted to be reelected and knew
that he would lose the vote of Buenos Aires anyway, so it did not cost him
much."[9]

Others dismissed political decentralization for Buenos Aires by arguing
that big cities always present major problems of governability and that in
providing for the direct election of the mayor, the president was taking advantage of an opportunity to shift the blame for poor service delivery, poor security, potholes in the streets, and corruption of city workers to someone else.
So, for example, one public official in the new city government argued,
"There is also a lot of discontent about government and the provision of services in Buenos Aires. . . . Now [the president] is relieved of responsibility
and does not have to take the blame for it. Let the Radicals assume responsibilities and take the blame."[10]

These explanations understate the extent to which the direct election of
the mayor and the autonomy of the city were politically significant institutional changes. Buenos Aires, with three million inhabitants, was home to
about 10 percent of the population and was the economic and social center

of the country and the headquarters of its major political parties.[11] The city generated about 24 percent of the country's GNP, provided employment for a significant portion of the labor force, and hosted most of the country's major educational and cultural institutions as well as its powerful media organizations.[12] It had a large public sector and the third-largest budget for government in the country, coming just after the national government and the provincial government of Buenos Aires. The city largely defined national culture and identity and was home to the most mobilized political groups in the country. Moreover, despite the widespread belief that the Peronists were giving up little, it is important to remember that in 1989 and 1995, as well as the 1993 mid-term elections, their party had come in ahead of the Radicals in the city, suggesting that the city was less the bastion of Radical support than generally believed. In fact, one analysis of urban voting in the late 1990s argued that the capital was "disputed territory" for the political parties.[13]

Buenos Aires was also important because it was a source of new political dynamics in the country. The return to democracy in 1983 encouraged the emergence of a number of parties that sought to compete with the Peronists and the Radicals by mobilizing citizens around issues of participation and good governance. These organizations focused their vote-getting campaigns through grass roots networks and the use of the print and broadcast media. For example, FREPASO, the center-left alliance, attracted primarily middle-class support through its pledges to improve the responsiveness and efficiency of government, increase citizen participation, eliminate widespread public corruption, and attend to the country's mounting social needs. A right-wing party, MODIN (Movimiento por la Dignidad y la Independencia Nacional), and the Frente Grande attracted social protest and ideological votes in elections in the late 1980s and early 1990s.[14] In 1993, the Frente Grande received 13.6 percent of the vote in the capital city. For the 1995 presidential elections, it formed an alliance with FREPASO and a number of small parties to garner almost 45 percent of the city's vote. For parties such as these, gaining positions in the Buenos Aires city council and capturing control of the mayor's office became important political prizes that could be used to strengthen their national profile. Control of city government was a way of demonstrating the capacity to put good governance and participatory pledges in action. Partisans of the newer political parties believed that with a bottom-up approach through local city government and by sophisticated strategies to take advantage of an expanding media, they might eventually be able to challenge the Peronists and the Radicals in national elections.[15] Thus, the man-

**TABLE 8.1**
VOTES FOR MAYOR AND CONSTITUTIONAL ASSEMBLY IN BUENOS AIRES CITY, 1996

| Party | Mayor (% of votes) | Assembly (% of votes) | Seats (no. of seats) |
|---|---|---|---|
| UCR | 39.8 | 27.3 | 19 |
| FREPASO | 26.6 | 34.8 | 25 |
| PJ | 18.1 | 15.0 | 11 |
| ND | 13.1 | 8.1 | 5 |

Source: La Nación, July 1, 1996.
Note: Unofficial results.

agement of the city had become very politically relevant by the mid-1990s, as this chapter indicates.

## City Government under Constitutional Reform

The mayor of Buenos Aires, when appointed, had been an important national political figure. At the same time, because it was the largest and most important city in the country as well as the seat of national government, it was important to the national executive that the capital city be managed reasonably well. It was also important that it be as politically quiescent as possible, a point well understood by military governments that gave considerable attention to monitoring and repressing the political behavior of urban residents. Certainly, in elite and middle-class neighborhoods and in the downtown business area, streets were generally well maintained, and trash was collected on a daily basis. City contracts helped maintain labor peace. The city budget was provided by the national government, so there was little connection between what city taxpayers paid and what they got in return. Among the most frequently criticized public services were police protection and traffic management, neither of which were provided by the city.

Thus, when Fernando de la Rúa, a Radical and former senator, became the first elected mayor of the city of Buenos Aires after elections on June 30, 1996, citizens had high expectations for city government.[16] His election, in which he won nearly 40 percent of the vote, demonstrated the continued strength of the Radical Party in the city, despite its declining fortunes more generally, and even though the FREPASO list took first place among votes for constitutional assembly (see Table 8.1). De la Rúa had been in outspoken opposition to the constitutional reform, but his career was now benefiting from it. Nevertheless, the demands on him and his government were considerable. There was little structure to the newly autonomous administration; even fixing the mayor's term of office had to wait for the meeting of a constitutional assembly that would write the charter for the city. Delegates to the sixty-member assembly were elected on the same day as the mayor. They were required by law to set to work by July 20 and produce a constitution within forty-five days. At that point, elections for city councillors would be scheduled.

In addition to setting up the institutions of self-government, including a constitution and legal codes to regulate the activities of government and citizens, the new government had to sort out the now-dual identity of Buenos Aires as an autonomous city and as capital of the country. What should city police be responsible for, and how should they be differentiated from the provincial and national police? What crimes should be city crimes, and which national or provincial ones? Which buildings of government belonged to the city, and which to the national government? What services were to be delivered by the city, and which by the central government? Who had responsibility for various hospitals in the city? Who employed those who worked in city government, hired under contracts in the past by the national government? How should these contracts be renegotiated? Which monuments belonged to the city, and which to the nation? What about the parks and the streets surrounding federal buildings? From the mayor's perspective, the answers to such questions were not obvious. In fact, the more contentious and problematic the issue, the more the mayor, who aspired to be the presidential candidate of the Radical Party for the 1999 elections, might wish to avoid taking responsibility for it.

The new mayor was cautious in responding to the challenges of his office. First, he worked hard to delay for 18 months the election of the city council, even though FREPASO and its supporters were pressing equally hard for early elections. His strategy, as it evolved between mid 1996 and 1998, was to begin to put in place some management infrastructure that would eventually contribute to better city governance, while at the same time delaying important institutional changes until a city constitution was in place and a city council elected.[17] Among his early initiatives were activities related to transportation and flooding in the city.[18] More broadly, he instituted a decentralization plan demonstrating this cautious approach. The city was divided into sixteen regions, and a team of planners and technocrats began designing a system to enhance responsiveness in services provided to citizens and to follow-up on complaints and needs. This "Government in Every

Neighborhood" program provided local residents with information, civil reg-
istries, offices for paying taxes and parking tickets, social workers to deal with
family-related problems, consumer-protection services, and crime-prevention
activities. It also provided professional city managers in each part of the city
and a computerized system for tracking service requests and complaints and
ensuring that the appropriate offices and officials were informed of needs and
that timely response was initiated.

The system was designed to accommodate the interests of local politicians, individual citizens, locally mobilized groups, and the mayor's political
concerns, as well as to set up the underpinnings needed for good governance.
According to the official in charge of decentralization, "Our strategic plan is
to reform the management system of the city and make it more accountable
to the citizens at the neighborhood level. . . . We are in the process of rein-
venting local government."[19] Nevertheless, the political infrastructure that
needed to be linked to this system to ensure that it would work—local politicians, political clubs, neighborhood associations, and other such organizations—was given second place to getting the technology up and running.
There was concern that this infrastructure might constrain the mayor's political "space." More pointedly, the city officials in charge of the decentralization
initiative were instructed to avoid a situation in which the new system might
be swamped with demands that it could not meet in the absence of a full
array of institutions and laws that the city council still had to design and pass.

The mayor was equally cautious in terms of a new constitution for the
city. The constitutional assembly began meeting in July 1996 and was led by
FREPASO, which had won twenty-five of its sixty seats in the June elections.
The constitution makers drafted a rights-oriented document reflecting the
influence of good governance concerns. This charter devoted some twelve
hundred words to the rights enjoyed by citizens of the city; four thousand
words to promised services in health, education, environment, culture, security, and housing; and twelve hundred words to the needs of particular groups
of citizens—children, adolescents, the elderly, women, those with special
needs, and consumers. It also detailed the organization of the city's government. Governing the city until an elected council could develop the institutional and legal infrastructure called for in the constitution was covered by a
series of transitional arrangements. Among these were a set of deadlines during which elections had to be held, basic legislation outlined, and specific
services provided for.

One issue raised by the constitution was that of police protection for
the city. Traditionally, the forty-five thousand police officers of Buenos Aires

Province, who also served in the city, were noted for being particularly corrupt and resistant to outside control, a mafia-like law unto themselves.[20] In a context in which failure was likely to be held against incumbents, the mayor might well prefer that the police for the city remain under the control of the governor of the province, himself a presidential hopeful of the Peronist Party.[21] Federal police also had jurisdiction in the city. At the same time, however, citizen demand for better security and an effective police force was high.[22] The constitution of the city mandated that the city government be responsible for the strategies and regulations to enhance public security, even while police protection continued under the purview of the provincial and national governments. The governor of the province—where 37 percent of the electorate lived—increasingly on the spot in the national media for the performance of the police, was torn between restricting the activities of the provincial police and the potential for enhancing his political claims through a successful reform of a high-profile public service.[23] By such logic, many of the decisions relating to the organization of city government became highly political issues.

The central activities of newly elected councillors when they took office at the end of 1997 was to set in place the structures and processes for new institutions that would govern the city. As indicated, this involved sorting out responsibilities and legislating basic laws and codes for the city. The council worked hard on these issues through the first six months of 1998; these activities had to be completed before the councillors could get on to dealing with issues of concern to their constituents and before they could begin thinking about their representative functions in the allocation of resources to various city responsibilities in ways that could be of benefit to them, to their parties, or to their constituents. The discussions about governance of the city, however, were affected by the national orientation of city government—the ways in which what occurred in the city was revealed through the media to the rest of the country and the ways in which the actions and decisions of city politicians reflected their national political aspirations. Just as in the case of the police, institutional design issues therefore became embroiled in larger political rivalries for turf, reputation, and avoidance of politically unattractive decisions.

The employment status and legal rights of city workers who had been hired under contract by the federal government prior to the constitutional change revealed the difficult situation facing parties and politicians. At the time of negotiating the constitutional change to give the city autonomy, these employees were assured that they would not lose their jobs, even though the right of contracting city workers would pass to the city. Clearly, newly empowered city officials wanted to hire their own employees, for political as well as efficiency and loyalty reasons. The city was also committed to reducing the overall number of people it employed. So what should be done with the employees already in place? This question was a difficult one for the city councillors: they risked losing valuable patronage opportunities if they took on employment contracts for the existing workers but they risked strikes, disruption, and serious labor disputes if they renounced the promise that existing workers would not be dismissed. The city councillors wanted the central government to take on responsibility to these workers and reassign them to national government positions; the central government wanted the city to assume responsibility for them. The mayor was reluctant to become involved in what appeared to be a no-win situation. The issue was finally resolved, not without considerable press coverage, demands from the workers, and discomfort on the part of the councillors when the city agreed to take on contractual responsibilities for the workers.

Conflict also emerged in the design and approval of a new municipal violations code. The councillors were required to legislate a code for offenses that would be adjudicated by the city. This involved separating out what kinds of crimes were defined as federal or municipal. It also involved devising a set of normative principles about what kinds of behavior should be considered criminal, what kinds would be misdemeanors, and what kinds of behaviors, though not necessarily approved, would be tolerated. Thus, for example, the councillors discussed the decriminalization of prostitution and public drunkenness as well as the imposition of punishments for vandalism, possession of unauthorized weapons, and gang-related disturbances. The orientation they eventually agreed upon was a liberal code that was permissive in terms of the range of behaviors considered acceptable. Behavior deemed worthy of punishment was that involving the violation of citizen rights, while prostitution and public intoxication, considered to be generally "victimless" crimes, would be decriminalized. Appropriate police behavior was also circumscribed by concerns for citizen rights.[24]

The discussions that led to the promulgation of this code were extensive and at times characterized by considerable divergence of opinion. Having eventually reached consensus, however, the councillors were unprepared for the extent of public outcry against the new code. The church spoke out against its permissiveness, the legal profession opined against it, and citizen groups expressed either approval or dismay about it. The mayor, conscious of his national political aspirations and of the role of the media in broadcasting this issue throughout the country, immediately backed away from the code and sought ways to put off signing the legislation, citing the need for citizen input and discussion. The city council, led by FREPASO, responded with opposition to the legislative initiatives of the mayor.[25] More generally, and despite a formal alliance between FREPASO and the Radical Party, the relationship between FREPASO and de la Rúa in the capital city became more problematic as the presidential elections of 1999 neared. FREPASO charged the mayor with corruption and politicking with city business.[26]

Thus, the new institutions of governance in the city were being politically constructed in a context of party rivalry and the infusion of national political aspirations and competition. In this context, the behavior of the councillors and the mayor were often at odds. The councillors wanted to move the process of institutional creation along so they could be in a better position to "do politics" in responding to their constituents, building their political reputations, or influencing the allocation of resources in politically advantageous ways. The mayor, on the other hand, sought to avoid making decisions, particularly those that involved conflict, and to avoid responsibilities for activities and services that could be used against him if they were not carried out well.

## Intertwining National and Local Politics

In the case of Argentina, in which national politics was dominated by a very strong, even authoritarian, president and in which conflict among political parties was extensive, local politics became national politics in important ways. This dynamic may have been inevitable in considering the impact of institutional changes that affected the city of Buenos Aires. As we have seen repeatedly, national politics was centered in the city. The political parties were headquartered there; a politicized population and virtually all the national media were also located in the city. Local politics were quickly absorbed in national political competition for office, and national political issues reso nated in local political competition.[27] This was true in terms of the electoral strategies of the parties, in terms of the issues that dominated elections, and in terms of the careers of aspiring politicians.

### Party Strategies

Did parties alter their electoral strategies as a result of political decentraliza tion? Clearly, city elections became a new arena for political competition in

Argentina. The Peronist and Radical Parties and FREPASO approached the elections for mayor, constitutional assembly, and city council as arenas in which they could appeal to national audiences and strengthen their positions for national elections. FREPASO in particular, because its base of support was principally within the city, used city elections as a platform for its national ambitions. It sought to capture votes that had usually gone to the Radical Party, as well as the votes of a growing number of people who claimed independence from all political parties. The Peronists, aware of their traditional weakness within the confines of the city, fought hard to gain as much of the vote as possible, so as not to be branded the loser in this important arena. President Menem publicly promoted his party's mayoral candidate. The Radical Party was under pressure not to decline further and saw FREPASO as cutting most significantly into its traditional base of support in the city.

Ten parties put forward candidates for mayor in June 1996. Opinion polls indicated that de la Rúa could be expected to come in first, followed by the candidate for FREPASO, in turn followed by the Peronist candidate.[28] The parties were intensely interested in the campaign and the vote, considering them to be indicators of the career expectations of the candidates at national levels. De la Rúa hoped to run for president and was under pressure to win in the capital city. One party leader, in fact, announced that "there will not be a Radical president in 1999 if we don't get at least 30 percent of the vote in Buenos Aires in 1997."[29] The future of the Peronist candidate for mayor, who had served in various national- and provincial-level positions before being appointed mayor by President Menem, would be significantly determined by his ability to pull in enough votes to match what the party had historically polled in the city. The head of the FREPASO ticket for constitutional assembly candidates had aspirations to the national legislature and eventually to the presidency; her vote was watched to see if she would maintain the strong showing she had when running for the senate a year earlier.[30] The national vice-president headed the Peronist candidates for the assembly and saw his career significantly harmed when the list polled only 15 percent of the vote.

The traditional parties, rooted in local machines that were kept alive through patronage and clientelism, campaigned by mobilizing these machines. FREPASO candidates, in contrast, campaigned at the neighborhood level, door to door and through local neighborhood meetings, as well as through extensive use of the media. In doing so, they were more agile and efficient than the other parties and were able to be more responsive to the increasingly mobilized organizations of civil society in the city.[31] As a new

**TABLE 8.2**
VOTES FOR CITY COUNCIL IN BUENOS AIRES, 1997

| Party | Percentage of Votes |
|---|---|
| Alianza UCR-FREPASO | 56.8 |
| PJ | 18.0 |
| APR | 17.1 |
| Others | 8.1 |

*Source: El Clarín,* October 28, 1997.
*Note:* Unofficial results.

organization, FREPASO was more an electoral movement than a membership party. It had little organizational infrastructure but a good understanding of how politics in the age of television and investigative journalism was played. As a result, a party that had polled 1.5 percent of the vote in 1991, 2.5 percent in 1993, and 21.2 percent in the 1995 elections for president, won 34.8 percent of the votes for constituent assembly members. Press commentary portrayed the electoral victories of the Radicals and FREPASO as an embarrassing defeat for Menem's government.[32]

The political parties also had significant stakes in the elections for city councillors in October 1997. The Peronist Party, after actively mobilizing its support among the unions and within working-class neighborhoods, was disappointed by a poor showing in the city. For the first time, a Peronist government lost an election while in power. The Radical Party contested the election in an alliance with FREPASO and took a clear lead by capturing almost 57 percent of the vote; this translated into control of thirty-seven out of the sixty seats in the city legislature (see Table 8.2). When the council met, therefore, three parties rather than two were serious players. The city elections helped cement the showing of FREPASO in the earlier presidential elections of 1995. The party captured serious national attention in terms of its potential showing in the 1999 presidential elections.[33] And, equally important, these elections, which included contests for national congress, were evaluated as an anti-Menem/anti-Peronist vote.[34]

The first initiatives of the new city council also revealed the strength of party affiliations and the jockeying for institutional advantage that was rooted in electoral politics. The councillors were organized into party blocs and sat down to negotiate initial issues as parties. All were conscious of the foundational role of the early legislative acts that would position the parties in power relationships in the future. As one councillor described it, "Creating new institutions means very carefully figuring out the impact of change on power relationships and the distribution of power. We can't be responsive [to our constituents] while we're thinking of our power bases at the same time."[35] The new institutions were thus put in place amid considerable conflict between the political parties as each jockeyed to claim or reclaim political advantage in a new political arena.

Moreover, national political concerns were paramount in the strategic decisions of political actors involved in getting city government up and running. The mayor was a leading contender for his party's nomination as a presidential candidate in 1999. The council, however, was dominated by FREPASO. FREPASO was locked in a conflict between its two most prominent leaders about who would be its presidential candidate. The situation was complicated by a formal alliance between FREPASO and the Radical Party to support each other in legislative matters at the national level.[36] This *Alianza* was observed at the city level also. In many ways it was a very sensible political arrangement, given strong anti-Peronist sentiment within FREPASO and the Radical Party, and given a bias toward a two-party system with Peronism in the ascendance. However, it was an alliance fraught with tension at both national and city levels. FREPASO was suspicious of the Radicals for their willingness to negotiate with the Peronists, as in the case of the Pacto de Olivos; the Radicals in turn had an extensive party bureaucracy that was reluctant to submerge its identity into that of the *Alianza*. Leaders of both parties continued to have strong political ambitions that worked against a common approach to the Peronists.[37]

Thus, formally committed to work together in legislative issues and in opposing Menem and the Peronist Party, there was at the same time intense rivalry between them over candidates for national political office. From the beginning, then, the alliance was vulnerable to tension and failure. An imminent split was widely reported to be in the works throughout 1998, although late that year the two parties agreed to back a common candidate for the presidential elections. Moreover, leaders of both parties recognized the national political relevance of the decisions they were making at the city level. Given a highly competitive situation, they preferred caution to boldness in taking on new responsibilities. Thus, much of the decision making about new institutions was slow, conflict-ridden, and often characterized by the desire to avoid responsibilities that could be turned into liabilities by the opposition.

*Electoral Issues*

The first elections carried out under the new constitution—those for mayor and constitutional assembly in 1996, and those for city councillors in 1997—might have focused on issues related to the management of the city and of local needs and participation in that government. Instead, they took on a national character. Long-term opposition to Peronism, always strong among the middle and upper classes of Buenos Aires, converged with growing dissatisfaction with Carlos Menem as president. While Menem continued to find support for his economic policies, opposition parties and growing numbers of groups in civil society increasingly focused on issues of corruption, mismanagement, and centralization of power. They were similarly concerned with issues of social protection in Argentina's new market-oriented economy. Within the Peronist Party, this debate was particularly strong, given the social welfare legacy of the party and the shift toward the market presided over by a Peronist president. Moreover, members of the party and its leadership were split over whether they should back Menem in a bid for a third term or support one of his rivals.

The campaigns appealed to citizen identity with the parties and to their positions on the pro-Menem/anti-Menem continuum. Corruption, insecurity, unemployment, and the traditional rivalries between the political parties combined with a focus on candidate personalities to underscore the extent to which local politics were national politics writ on a smaller scale.[38] In the mayoral race, personal attacks on opposing candidates featured significantly in what one candidate called "the lightest campaign in recent history" in terms of its issue content.[39] To the extent that local concerns were reported, they dealt with the probity of the candidates and the fiscal health of the city.[40] In the end, voting in both elections was as much about the fates of national political parties and their national futures as it was about local issues and local governance. In both cases, elections for national congress coincided with local elections, and during the June 1996 elections, those running for national office also headed the slates of candidates for constituent assembly of the city. Thus, both campaign rhetoric and election results were directly relevant to the national balance of power among the parties. As I have indicated, these national concerns affected the way the mayor and the new city council approached the challenges of governing the city and were important in shaping the decisions made by these political actors as they sought to define structures and processes of governance for the newly autonomous city.

*Political Careers*

Traditionally, the governor of the province of Buenos Aires or a governor of
Córdoba was in a strong position to become the Peronist candidate for president. In the 1980s, Antonio Cafiero, governor of Buenos Aires, was widely
expected to be the Peronist presidential candidate in 1989. In the 1990s, Eduardo Duhalde, governor of the same province, was locked in a fierce competition with Carlos Menem to head the ticket in 1995 and in 1999. For the
Radical Party, routes to national prominence depended on positions of power
within the party bureaucracy as well as demonstrated capacity to win elections. Raúl Alfonsín had assumed the leadership of the party during the military dictatorship of the 1970s and 1980s, after the death of Ricardo Balbín,
who had long occupied that position. In the 1990s, Fernando de la Rúa was
considered *presidenciable* (politically prominent enough to be nominated for
the presidency) by virtue of his centrist position within the party and his long
term loyalty to it. He competed against Alfonsín in 1983 to be nominated the
presidential candidate by the Radical Party, was elected a senator, ran again
and lost, became head of his party in the capital city, and then was elected
senator again. His political fortunes became more certain when he was
elected mayor of the largest and most politically significant city in the country. One presidential aspirant observed how new rules of the game could alter
candidate selection: "Helped along by the media, a person like de la Rúa can
show the whole country an alternative to Menem and this way, become a
natural candidate for the presidency. Always before, the natural candidates
for the presidency were the governors of Buenos Aires and sometimes the
governors of Córdoba—two very politically important positions. Now the
head of Buenos Aires is in a similar position."[41] In fact, in November 1998,
de la Rúa was overwhelmingly endorsed to be the presidential candidate of
the Radical Party in an alliance with FREPASO. He subsequently won the
1999 presidential elections. The FREPASO candidate, who lost out in the alliance with the Radicals, was selected to run for the governorship of the province of Buenos Aires.[42]

The constitutional reform of 1994 thus created a new platform for political career making. According to an observer of Argentine politics, "The position of *intendente* has created new ways of being *presidenciable*. De la Rúa will
be sharing power with Menem as soon as the election campaign gets started.
The campaign will focus attention on two people—the president and the
mayor."[43] The new position reshaped the view of political careers. "It is now
a position that opens up the opportunity to counterbalance the power of the

Province of Buenos Aires in national politics."[44] The dynamics of Argentine politics changed through the constitutional reform but in ways that accentuated the national rather than the local. Nevertheless, local politics clearly became a springboard to national prominence. Politicians in national office also ran for local office, and those in city government had opportunities to rise in prominence to national levels. Throughout the period in which the new institutions were being consolidated, however, older career paths continued to be of service to those who sought political office. Thus, for example, Menem made repeated efforts to introduce new rules to allow him to run for a third term. In this, he was locked in ongoing conflict with Governor Eduardo Duhalde, widely perceived as the most *presidenciable* among prominent Peronists.[45]

## Conclusions: Capturing Local Politics

National concerns continued to dominate political dynamics in the wake of constitutional change in Argentina. Elections for mayor and city councillors provided new opportunities to political parties opposed to the nationally dominant Peronists. Some of these political parties, eager to acquire power at national levels, adopted innovative techniques for campaigning and attempted to address the community-level concerns of citizens. The new rules of the game thus encouraged adaptive behavior among the parties. By and large, however, the issues they championed and contested were most relevant for national rather than local audiences. Long-term conflicts between the political parties and factions within them reemerged in the new institutions of government in the city. The new spaces were quickly filled with national political issues, campaigns, and ambitions. What might have become a thriving marketplace for local politics instead reiterated national politics. The new institutions in Argentina quickly became a context eliciting short-term electoral calculations among parties and politicians. Among the three cases, this one thus conforms most closely to the rational choice hypothesis about the consequences of institutional change.

Moreover, to a greater degree than was the case in Venezuela and Bolivia, the candidates who ran for office at the local level had their eyes on national positions. The Peronist and Radical parties vied for institutional places that would assist them in national elections; FREPASO rehearsed its national political strategies and objectives on a city-wide stage. The mayor assessed his mandate and policy objectives in terms of his national political future, and the council considered its institutional structures in terms of both governance and national power. The issues in local elections reiterated national concerns, and the media retold local politics to a national audience. Clearly, then, the consequences of institutional reform in Argentina were conditioned by the arena in which change was enacted: the national capital had long been the center of national politics and could not easily escape its history. In this way, and as in the cases of Venezuela and Bolivia, new institutions provided a way to revisit conflicts from the past.

C H A P T E R 9

# Democratizing Reforms
## Origins and Consequences

This book considered a series of democratizing reforms involving the creation of new institutions and asked, Why did politicians give up power? How did new institutions take shape? What were the political consequences of the creation of new institutions? The origin and consequences of institutional innovation are important, but not because they will illuminate broad patterns of regularities in political behavior. They are important because they are significant events in the political histories of countries. Most politics, most of the time, occurs within the context of relatively stable expectations and institutions. Sometimes, however, the introduction of new institutions alters the nature of everyday politics and shapes incentives for political behavior far into the future. While not as noticeable or dramatic as revolutions, civil wars, or military coups, these institutional inventions can alter history.

The events chosen for exploration here —institutional changes in Venezuela, Bolivia, and Argentina—established new rules of the game for politics. In Venezuela, the ways in which central government and centralized political parties related to the country's states and localities were altered fundamentally when citizens gained the right to elect their regional and municipal leaders and acquired an expanded range of voting choices through rewritten electoral rules. In Bolivia, the relationship between center and periphery was reordered when municipal governments were created, citizens were empowered to choose their leaders, and elected decision makers acquired new responsibilities and development resources. In Argentina, the political importance of the capital city increased when it became a center of independent decision making and when citizens had greater input into leadership choices. These were not marginal or incremental changes in existing political institutions; instead, they put in place rules that differed considerably from past practice. At the most general level, historical legacies of centralization gave way to more decentralized structures of power and authority.

These events raise puzzles about behavior that does not necessarily fit many basic assumptions about politics. In each of these cases, political leaders advocated and supported changing the rules in ways that would constrain their future capacity to wield power. They committed to new institutions to extend democracy more broadly in the political system, even though the risks of altering already fragile institutions were very high. Moreover, not only politicians but also political parties and citizens had to adjust to new ways of doing politics and take on new responsibilities in an uncertain environment. Politicians giving up power, deciding to take risks in an unstable environment, acting in the absence of reliable information about probable outcomes—is there a logic to such behavior?

In searching for responses to this question, I have posed a series of hypotheses derived from two competing approaches to the study of politics, one that is an extension of how economists understand behavior and another that is rooted in sociological explanations of conflict and group action. In this chapter, I use the findings of the case studies to reflect on the usefulness of contending explanations for what was observed. Although the assessment of the hypotheses is limited to three cases, it points to several conclusions: empirically, the motivations of politicians are complex, reflecting both personal ambitions and enduring political conflicts in their societies; political elites play a significant role in framing issues even while self-conscious institutional design plays a large role in the selection of new institutions; and new rules of the game encourage adaptation and new political dynamics at the same time that they provide an arena for revisiting old conflicts.

## The Motivations of Politicians

In presenting the cases of institutional change in Venezuela, Bolivia, and Argentina, I have not seriously questioned whether the politicians promoting reform were acting rationally, in the way that people generally understand rational behavior. I assumed that they were capable of identifying reasonable goals and understanding means-ends relationships in efforts to achieve these goals. Instead, the issues that interested me dealt with the content of the goals and how they were formed. What did politicians in Venezuela, Bolivia, and Argentina want, and why did they want it, when they backed proposals to alter the rules of the game for doing politics in their countries? Two approaches to explaining politics provided contrasting hypotheses for responding to these questions.

In explaining politics through the lenses of economic theory, politicians are most frequently assumed to be motivated by the desire to maximize their power, particularly in the short term. From the perspective of sociological approaches to politics, the motivations of politicians are understood to be shaped through specific historical experiences and institutions that determine how power is distributed in a society and how conflict is played out among groups.

Empirical evidence about what motivated politicians in the three cases includes some consideration of the short-term electoral consequences of ceding power. Only in the case of Argentina, however, can it be concluded that these concerns were a central motivation for action. Carlos Menem, an incumbent president, accepted a broad array of institutional innovations in exchange for the right to run for reelection. Indeed, in his willingness to accept a range of future constraints on his power for the chance to be president again, he seemed the epitome of the short-term utility maximizer in politics. At the same time, however, it is important to acknowledge that the price he paid for the possibility of reelection was very high in terms of the changes he agreed to: they would constrain his use of power when and if he were reelected. Menem explored other ways of achieving his reelection goal that would have meant ceding less power but chose instead the route of extensive and negotiated constitutional change. The bargain he made acknowledged the importance of the legitimacy of the process through which institutional reform was achieved. Similarly, Raúl Alfonsín backed a number of institutional changes with the apparent goals of strengthening his party in the future, or at least slowing the erosion of its importance, and enhancing his position within the party. But his preferences, as revealed during the negotiations, went far beyond institutional changes that could be linked to his own or his party's future power. They included a series of deeply held beliefs about how democratic government ought to work and how its institutions ought to be arranged.

In Venezuela, Carlos Andrés Pérez adopted political decentralization during his electoral campaign, an action consistent with a desire to acquire votes. At the same time, however, the case demonstrates that the campaign, and candidate Pérez, did not focus much attention on this proposal. In addition, he announced his commitment to the election of regional and local officials and then went on to join a broad commitment among the leading presidential candidates to support the same initiative. In fact, Pérez's behavior during the election confirms that there were other, and better, ways of winning votes than promising the direct election of state and local officials. The message of his campaign was a promise to Venezuelans that the country could return to the good old days of the petroleum bonanza. Explaining his adoption of political decentralization as a strategy to gain electoral support thus seems to underexplain this Venezuelan case.

In addition, Pérez could reasonably anticipate the negative reaction of the traditional leaders of his party as well as that of the principal opposition. Of course, he may have been convinced that political institutions in his country were so weak that his own immediate tenure as president might be curtailed through violence or regime change. But it is important to remember that he became a convert to political decentralization prior to the *caracazo* of February 1989, which took the entire political elite by surprise at the same time that it drove home the threat of a crisis of governance. Nor was the potential for a military coup viewed as an immediate threat by Pérez and others in 1988 and 1989, given thirty years of democratic government.

In Bolivia, the Plan de Todos, which included a proposal for the participation of communities in their own development, was forged by a team appointed by Gonzalo Sánchez de Lozada. When he became the MNR's presidential candidate, this proposal and several others were adopted as the party's campaign platform. As in the case of Venezuela, however, the election focused less on the promise to introduce institutional change than on the personalities of the candidates and the traditional rhetoric of the MNR. Moreover, as a strategy to win votes, it is not clear that promising greater community control over decision making was a very good one. Rural and indigenous communities might have been attracted to this pledge, but historically these groups had been marginalized in national politics. Their votes were usually mobilized through clientelist networks, not issue-based policy promises. Meanwhile, many of the rich and powerful wanted regional, not local, control of decision making and resources. From a vote-maximizing perspective, Sánchez de Lozada would have been better off making promises to the powerful elites who, from the base of well-organized civic committees, had long been advocating decentralization to regional levels. Instead, he sought to undermine the power of these elites. More broadly, the MNR might have expected to garner votes from a proposal to empower its rural constituents, but in fact its rural support base had been eroding and the majority of Bolivia's population had shifted to urban areas. Moreover, the MNR was not much involved in the elaboration of the Plan de Todos and had traditionally mobilized votes through clientelism and local bossism rather than through policy commitments. That an early version of what became the Popular Participation plan was part of an electoral platform is not sufficient evidence that either Sánchez de Lozada or the MNR adopted it primarily as a means of acquiring votes.

Further, by backing Popular Participation after he was elected, Bolivia's Sánchez de Lozada reaped the opposition of regional elites and unions convinced that the proposal robbed them of power. Nor does it seem likely that supporting changes that involved the redistribution of power would enhance his position within the MNR, because party leaders in this centralized organization would have had to give up considerable control over their membership under the presidential initiative. And the institutional changes in no way "locked in" the policy or political preferences of these leaders because policy change and more intense electoral competition became more likely after the reforms in all three countries.

If rational choice hypotheses do not provide robust explanations for the three cases, what about hypotheses derived from comparative institutionalism? It is interesting that in none of the cases was there strong evidence that the institutional innovations proposed were pushed upon the politicians by mobilized groups in society. Clearly, there were group interests at stake in each country. In Venezuela, centralized party organizations and neighborhood associations had conflicting interests in political decentralization; in Bolivia, the centralized parties, the unions, and the regional economic elites were concerned that they would be the losers in the president's plan for municipalization; in Argentina, the traditional parties would be affected in different ways by the political autonomy of Buenos Aires. Equally important, historical conflicts that characterized politics in each country were important in explaining why and how these groups supported or opposed change. In Venezuela, the advantages of the parties in dominating virtually all political dynamics in the country were acquired through a process of democratic institution building that had placed stability and growth at the center of national priorities. In Bolivia, the historical role of the MNR and the unions in contesting power as well as the tension between La Paz and the regions shaped the way these opponents of change organized their resistance. In Argentina, the symbolic and actual role of Buenos Aires in national politics, the ways in which the two main parties defined their historical missions, and the ways in which presidential power was exercised lay behind the negotiations over change.

But in none of these cases did the issue of institutional change get on the politicians' agendas primarily because of pressure from these groups or conflicts among them.[1] Although organized groups and their historical orientations formed a backdrop for the institutional change initiatives and were important in understanding the opposition and strategies chosen to resist change, there is no evidence that politicians supported the initiatives as a reflection of group pressures or solely to advance group causes. In Bolivia in particular, to the extent that group interests were engaged in the reform effort, they were active in opposition to it rather than appearing as its champions. Most beneficiaries of the proposed changes were not mobilized around support for change. There were proponents of reform in each case, and they influenced presidents and helped get reform proposals on leaders' agendas, but they were not acting primarily as representatives of mobilized group interests. In Venezuela, a small group of reformers had little audience prior to 1987. In Bolivia, the principal architect of Popular Participation was called a prophet in the wilderness prior to 1993 because he had an idea that no one seemed particularly interested in. In Argentina, reformers were engaged in a long process of consensus building about institutional change in which part of their role was to influence the groups they represented rather than to reflect their interests. Thus, there is little empirical support for the proposition that politicians were motivated to cede power as a response to group pressure and the conflict of group interests.[2] Rather, the reform agenda is best explained as the result of elite projects, in which the elites were called together—in each case, by political leaders—to make recommendations about how best to respond to problems of governance.

The action taken on these elite projects lends credence to the idea of institutional crisis as a factor that motivates politicians to advocate reform. In Venezuela, politicians were shocked into action by what they viewed as a clear and present danger to the sustainability of the political system. The unexpected and massive violence of the *caracazo* in early 1989 convinced them that the decline of institutional legitimacy and effectiveness that they had been witnessing for a number of years had finally reached the breaking point. Although Pérez championed political decentralization prior to this event, it was taken up more broadly as a serious solution to an identifiable problem when events forced the political class to face up to the possibility of the collapse of the political system. Certainly, in terms of the rhetoric that surrounded Pérez's initial adoption to political reform, he seemed convinced that the performance of democracy in the country needed to be improved. A similar case might be made in the case of Bolivia. Sánchez de Lozada and other reformers became convinced that the dysfunctional nature of public institutions threatened the sustainability of the political system. While there was nothing like the *caracazo* to focus political attention on these issues, centralization of decision making, unbridled corruption, and national security were issues that the reformers sought to fix through Popular Participation. Even in Argentina, reformers such as Raúl Alfonsín articulated concerns about the functioning of democratic institutions in the country.

In each case, then, there is evidence that some politicians were willing to cede power because they believed it would ensure the longer-term legitimacy and stability of institutions of governance in the country. Even in the absence of mobilized group pressure, concerns about governance went beyond calculations of the power and conflict situations of the protagonists. This evidence can be related to the historical context confronting these leaders. Because they were acting in an environment of weak institutions with records of such poor performance that the basic legitimacy of the political system was called into question, political leaders seemed to have been motivated to consider the creation of new institutions, even if it meant curtailing their own power.

At the same time, however, politicians in Venezuela, Bolivia, and Argentina arrived at these conclusions in different ways. Carlos Andrés Pérez and other politicians in Venezuela chose to devolve power, even though it would harm them personally, because of a series of clear, threatening, and tangible signs that the institutions of government were no longer widely respected and that the democratic system that had been so carefully constructed in the past was at risk. Even before the *caracazo*, Pérez and party leaders worried about increasing abstention rates in elections and diminishing levels of militancy within the parties. Institutional crisis was also important in convincing Bolivia's Gonzalo Sánchez de Lozada to devolve power, but belief in the crisis of governance emerged from his own experience and his own prior history; it was not brought home to him by the same kind of growing threat that culminated in violent political acts in Venezuela. In the case of Alfonsín and other reformers in Argentina, concerns about governance were similar to those in Bolivia in that they grew out of their accumulated experience with dysfunctional institutions and their worries about the fragility of the democratic system more generally.

However, the fact that one of the politicians, Carlos Menem, did not appear to have been concerned about governance issues in the same way as

Alfonsín, Pérez, and Sánchez de Lozada cautions against generalizing the institutional crisis hypothesis too broadly. Behind these specific issues of choice, the cases also indicate that analysts need to consider how and why history has shaped particular institutions and how conflict over institutional arrangements has emerged over time. This is consistent with a comparative institutionalist approach. History, however, will not necessarily provide answers to what politicians might do to change things or when they will propose to do it. In our cases, some leaders chose reform but others rejected it within similar contexts of institutional crisis and vulnerability. Leadership choices thus remain something of a "black box" analytically.

The central role of political leaders in framing issues, adopting (and rejecting) reform agendas, and determining the timing for action is clear in all three cases. In reflecting on the theoretical lenses of both economic and sociological approaches to politics, leadership in the sense of creative political action is underexplained. In particular, economic models of politics are deficient in understanding the kinds of system-changing decisions of concern here. At least in the case of efforts to explain the unexpected, it makes sense to adopt approaches that encourage empirical exploration of why political actors do what they do. A rational choice approach discourages exploration of motivations because of the requirement that preferences be asserted *ex ante*. Moreover, because rational choice theory is meant to be applied in stable institutional contexts and to explain normal politics, it may not be the most propitious way to inquire into the kinds of deeply significant political changes that are under consideration here. These kinds of institutional inventions, however, have not been uncommon events in the 1980s and 1990s, even though they are outside the realm of everyday political events. At a more general level, then, a rational choice approach to explaining the behavior of politicians may encourage the study of the conventional during a time in which developing countries are in the midst of profound changes. As an approach, it may blind us to what is most significant about the world of the politician in the 1990s.

Leadership choices, particularly in the context of weakly legitimized or malfunctioning institutions of governance, remain a topic for more empirical and theoretical research. Comparative institutionalism appears to provide some guidance for such research, even though the approach may overemphasize group conflict in political decision making and the link between leadership behavior and specific group interests. It does, however, provide analytic space for treating motivations as problematic and thus as worthy of inquiry.

# The Content of Institutional Creation

Whether politicians are seeking to maximize power, are responding to group interests, or are seeking to respond to institutional crisis and decay, they may have a variety of options for action. Why do they select some institutions rather than others as solutions to the particular problems they face? Economic and sociological approaches to politics suggest at least three possible responses to this question. Particular institutions might be selected because they promise to lower transaction costs, because they appear to provide solutions to principal-agent problems, or because they represent the results of conflicts among groups about the allocation of power in society.

The case studies of Venezuela, Bolivia, and Argentina tell an interesting and quite consistent story about the choice of institutions. In each case, the design for new institutions was the result of a small group or team that was charged with making recommendations about how political institutions could be made to work more effectively.[3] The composition and behavior of the designers suggest that the specific content of reforms emerged as elite projects. In Venezuela and Argentina, the process of institutional design was initiated and at least initially pursued within presidentially appointed commissions that were given broad scope to explore ideas for political reform and build consensus around them. In Bolivia, the design team was put together by an aspirant to political power who was interested in hearing a range of proposals about how the country could be made to function better. These reform teams took their responsibilities seriously and acknowledged few constraints on the range of changes they considered— even the test of political feasibility was initially given less attention than how, ideally, problems of governance might be solved. In Venezuela and Argentina, the reform recommendations languished until political leaders took up the initiatives, but in all cases it is clear that political leaders were led to support particular institutional innovations as a result of the work of the design teams.

The direct election of governors and mayors in Venezuela was the result of a five-year discussion among intellectuals and political, economic, and social elites in the country. In the process of discussion, centered in COPRE, intellectuals in leadership roles largely determined the strategy for generating recommendations and persuaded commission members that the reforms were important for shoring up the legitimacy of the political system. The team consulted widely and was very concerned about generating consensus for change, but the discussions within COPRE were not the focus of much public attention nor were the reforms hotly contested. Elite networks, broad consultation among opinion leaders in the country, and institutional design appear to have been key inputs of the COPRE experience.

In fact, what is interesting in the Venezuelan reforms is the extent to which they were the outcome of the work of a small group grappling with problems of public-sector performance and political-system legitimacy. COPRE members focused great attention to the ways in which citizens could participate more effectively in the political system, how they could have more information on who their elected officials were and what they were up to, and how mechanisms would work to ensure that citizens could hold public officials accountable for their behavior. They addressed fiscal relationships between the center and the periphery and the linkages between elected officials and public servants. They considered how public services could be delivered more efficiently and equitably. The institutional designs they generated can be easily understood as responses to transaction costs that citizens encounter when dealing with government, the efficiency costs of administering public programs through alternative institutional arrangements, or the principal-agent problems that bedevil the management of public affairs and the relationship between public officials and citizens. Empirically, these factors seemed to have been more important than the extent to which COPRE was an arena in which conflicts among groups and interests were played out. Technical discussion, problem solving, and the search for "workability" dominated the activities of the design team more than the clash of interests or the mediation of group positions on issues.

In Bolivia, a small team convened to consider what the basic problems of governance in the country were and, with input from an international board of experts, began considering issues related to the distribution of power within government and how decision making about development could result in more effective use of resources. Within the Fundación Milenio, there were few constraints on the kinds of institutional changes or policy preferences that the group could consider. The composition of the team, however, shaped its focus on ways to enhance local-level problem solving and decision making: Carlos Hugo Molina was an advocate of municipalization, and other members were familiar with the experience of indigenous and local community organizations.

After the presidential elections, a team composed of many of the same individuals reconvened to carry out confidential discussions on the workings of what was to become Popular Participation. The president was an active participant in this intensive work and became a convert to the idea of munici-palization. The discussions involved very detailed analysis of how particular mechanisms would affect the power relationships between citizens and gov-ernment, local groups and local officials, and central administrators and local decision makers. In this case also, issues of the transaction costs involved in getting government business done and principal-agent asymmetries that resulted in corruption and lack of accountability were squarely on the table in the design meetings. The resulting recommendations presented the group's assessment of how to resolve these problems. Team members were aware of the group interests at stake but did not interact as advocates of particular group positions.

Constitutional reform in Argentina featured more overt negotiation over the terms of institutional change. The initiative already had a long history when it appeared suddenly on the political agenda as a result of the Pacto de Olivos. In the mid-1980s, a presidentially appointed council spent consider-able time and effort in drafting new rules of the political game for the country and in building elite consensus on their importance to the future of demo-cratic government there. Although the Council for the Consolidation of De-mocracy, created by President Alfonsín, only initiated this process, its reports influenced an ongoing discussion among scholars, politicians, and other in-fluentials about the need to change the constitution in important ways. Nego-tiations within and between political parties in the late 1980s and early 1990s continued to revolve around the recommendations of the council. The nu-cleus of basic agreements that was eventually signed by Menem and Alfonsín closely reflected the work of the council.

Throughout the negotiation of change, legal scholars played a prominent role in discussing and drafting a variety of recommendations. Much of their concern centered on how incentive structures might affect the behavior of public officials. For example, regarding the direct election of the mayor of Buenos Aires, the evidence suggests that the constitutional experts paid par-ticular attention to the responsibilities for managing public services and the accountability of those who would provide such services. The drafters of the recommendations were very much aware that winners and losers might be created through new institutional structures, and they explicitly sought trade-offs among proposals in order to generate an overall consensus on the package of reforms they presented.

In these three cases, then, individuals gathered around a metaphorical table and self-consciously constructed institutions to solve widely perceived problems of governance. Transaction costs were important as the design teams set out to make government work better. More specifically, though, the reformers focused on a variety of principal-agent problems of transparency, accountability, and performance. In none of the cases was there clear evidence that a principal dynamic of the design teams was the reflection of group conflict. Instead, members appointed to these teams appeared to be well known to one another, to be committed to developing consensus around their proposals, and to develop good working relationships with one another to avoid overt conflict and to promote consensus, negotiation, and compromise.

Thus, the new institutionalism in economics appears to have considerable capacity to explain the content of the reform initiatives that emerged in Venezuela, Bolivia, and Argentina. This approach, which has generated both transaction costs and principal-agent explanations, does not account for why politicians picked up on the recommendations of the design teams, nor does it explain the timing of the introduction of institutional change proposals. In each case, however, the choices eventually made by the politicians were significantly shaped by the deliberations of those who took up the problem of institutional design and thought through classic problems of efficiency and performance in government. Politicians in these cases, confronted by particular problems of governance (how to make government work better and more responsively in Venezuela and Bolivia) and power (how to maximize it or how to control it in Argentina), found the recommendations produced by earlier design teams ready at hand.[4] Throughout this process of design and choice, conflict over institutional arrangements was not the dominant dynamic, nor did it appear that the solutions were primarily negotiated or imposed outcomes of contestation, as the comparative institutionalist approach hypothesizes.

More evidence of conflict over institutional change emerged after initial design ideas were developed within the largely consensual environment of the design teams. When it emerged, the teams and the politicians who advocated change attempted to negotiate away some of the conflict without, at the same time, undermining the impact that reform would have on the political system. In Venezuela, they initially experienced failure when President Lusinchi refused to support the proposals of COPRE and did his best to put distance between himself and the designers. In the other cases, designers were successful in countering opposition. The team in Bolivia, for instance, made a few alterations in the Popular Participation plan and signed agreements to reassure its opponents that their interests would not be jeopardized by the reform, but their plan was approved without major changes. In Argentina, the aftermath of the work of the Council for the Consolidation of Democracy involved negotiation and fine-tuning of the change recommendations, but these had more to do with horse-trading about the full package of proposals that would be part of the nucleus of basic agreements than with alterations in any specific proposals. There was considerable conflict over the process of change and about the inclusion of the reelection proposal, but most of the institutional changes were the subject of very little controversy.

The issue of selecting new institutions also raises the question of whether the range of possible reforms is significantly constrained by path dependencies. That is, can the dimensions of proposals for institutional change be predicted on the basis of current and past institutional arrangements? The new institutionalism in economics and the comparative institutionalist approach agree that institutions are sticky and tend to evolve over time. Disjunctures are possible but tend to be the result of cataclysms such as revolution or war.[5] In a very general way, the case studies support the existence of path dependency in the sense that changes were introduced within an overall context of democratic institutions; in large part, the purpose of reform was to enhance the workability, fairness, and responsiveness of such institutions. Similarly, the way in which new institutions were put in place reflected the hold of existing institutions on process. In each case, formal mechanisms of approval to legitimize change were observed, even in the case of Argentina, in which the power-maximizing objective of political leaders was most clear. Thus, path dependency constrained the process through which change was put in place.

At the same time, the content of the changes proposed and eventually adopted was much less narrowly constrained than path dependency would suggest. Each of the changes caused a reversal in historic trajectories toward increasing centralization of power. Although path dependency would result in changes at the margin of existing institutions, the cases of Venezuela, Bolivia, and Argentina represent major disjunctures with the past. History mattered in these cases, but more in the sense of a set of experiences and institutional arrangements to react against or to hold responsible for current problems than in the sense of creating the floor upon which institutional change would evolve. History mattered more because it helped bring people to the table to consider what issues to propose and helped them understand and diagnose the problems than because it narrowly constrained the options available for change.

## The Consequences of Creating New Institutions

The creation of new institutions in Venezuela, Bolivia, and Argentina had clear consequences for the strategies adopted by political parties, for the issues that emerged during electoral campaigns, and for the structure of political careers. Indeed, as we have seen, much of the conflict over institutional change emerged after the reforms were adopted and as political actors sought to understand the changes, adjust to them, or replace them with rules they liked better. There was considerable similarity among the cases in terms of the consequences of change, suggesting that political decentralization, even in distinct guises and distinct countries, can set off a series of similar dynamics.

In all three cases, political parties began to alter their strategies for contesting elections in light of the new rules. Interestingly, however, parties adjusted in different ways to the new competitive environment. Traditional parties—AD and COPEI in Venezuela; MNR, MIR, and ADN in Bolivia; Peronists and Radicals in Argentina—responded more slowly to change than other parties. This appears to have happened because these parties were burdened by large and entrenched bureaucracies and extensive clientelist networks and had long followed relatively successful rules about how to select candidates and contest elections. Newer, less institutionalized parties, particularly those cast in the mold of electoral rather than membership parties—La Causa R, MAS, and a variety of new parties in Venezuela; MBL, UCS, and CONDEPA in Bolivia; FREPASO and Nueva Dirigencia in Argentina—were quicker to understood the advantages of opportunities to contest elections at local and regional levels and were astute and efficient in enlisting candidates that appeared to have good potential to win votes at these levels.

After some initial experience of coming out behind in elections, the more institutionalized parties began to alter their behavior in ways that helped them become or remain competitive in local and regional contests. Leaders of these older parties, particularly in Venezuela and Bolivia but also in Argentina, complained that more extensive and less predictable electoral arenas meant changes in the traditional ways the parties mobilized voters. They were conscious that old ties of militancy and identities created through involvement in a historic movement, as well as the old clientelist networks, were being replaced by the need to woo voters through the mass media and on the basis of the personalities of individual candidates. Indeed, after the new institutions were in place, parties that were disadvantaged by the new rules initiated efforts to reestablish the old ways of doing politics, such as by negotiating alliances, reinforcing clientelist networks, or building local machines for distributing patronage and garnering votes. The old party bosses in all three cases were not pushed into oblivion by the institutional change but rose to fight again. Moreover, some of the younger parties were not able to sustain their new bases of support. In Bolivia, MBL virtually disappeared in the aftermath of presidential elections in 1998, and CONDEPA faced a similar threat. In Venezuela, neither the old nor the newer parties were able to sustain the national challenge of Hugo Chávez, even though several retained local and state level office.

Electoral campaigns in Venezuela and Bolivia affected not only the behavior of the political parties but also the issues that emerged as important. Local and regional elections in the first case and local elections in the second provided opportunities to make promises about solutions for problems such as sluggish regional development, garbage collection, road repair, the state of the local school or clinic, police protection, or the behavior of local officials. They could also promise particular benefits to particular constituencies now that decentralized political offices included control over resources. This was also a significant consequence of institutional change in countries in which electoral campaigns had focused almost exclusively on national issues. Under new rules in Venezuela and Bolivia, issues became more localized, and so did conflict over what to do about them.

The consequence of change in Argentina was somewhat more complex. The issues of relevance to campaigns in the capital city were affected by the hegemonic role that Buenos Aires had long played in national politics. Issues of national concern such as corruption and the responsiveness of government to citizen demands were also issues of local concern because citizens of the capital suffered significantly from national or provincial control over these factors. Moreover, given the size and influence of Buenos Aires, candidates for mayor could easily aspire to national office and therefore they pitched their campaigns to a national audience. From another perspective, local issues such as public security, traffic congestion, and air pollution became national issues because the media, located in the capital, reported them nationally. Thus, while local politics gained presence in Venezuela and Bolivia, national politics tended to absorb local politics in the wake of institutional change in Argentina.

New rules of the political game created new paths to political power in the three countries. For example, the election of local officials in Venezuela, Bolivia, and Argentina meant that achieving office as mayor of a significant city became a potential launching pad for those with presidential ambitions

In Venezuela, those who won election as state governors could also consider developing the political base for high-level national office. At lower levels on political totem poles, municipal councillors could imagine becoming mayors or deputies in congress, congressmen had opportunities to exchange national office for positions as municipal or regional leaders, and regional leaders could aspire to congressional positions as well as to the presidency. These new political career opportunities reflected the wider range of offices available for aspiring politicians.

Equally important, they reflected the loss of party control over candidate selection. In Venezuela in particular, but also in Bolivia and to some extent in Argentina, careers under the old rules of the game were largely determined by the hold that party bosses had over which candidates were listed on the ballots and in which order. Those who rose in political importance tended to be those who had worked long and hard within the party apparatus and who had demonstrated great loyalty to the party leadership. Under the new rules of the game, these attributes were no longer enough to win elections; the local or regional attractiveness of candidates to the voters opened up a variety of other ways to reach political office. Of course, this trend was given added impetus by another change that all parties were experiencing—that is, the growing role of the media and investigative journalism in electoral campaigns, which increased the incentives to find publicly attractive candidates.

Interestingly, then, the case studies support both the rational choice and the comparative institutionalist perspectives about the consequences of introducing new rules of the game. The evidence is clear that after institutional changes were made, narrowly rational political behavior was reasserted. That is, political parties and politicians adapted their behavior in ways consistent with efforts to win elections and maximize power in the short term. As I indicated above, this reaction was not immediate for the more traditional political parties because they had to overcome behavior embedded in their own institutional pasts before they could adapt to new rules of the game. But by and large, political actors sought to mobilize votes, identify issues, and build support bases in ways that would allow them to win current and subsequent elections.

At the same time, it is difficult to argue that this behavior represented a new equilibrium in the sense of a broadly accepted and stable institutional context for ongoing strategic decision making. Political actors were attempting to maximize their power, but many were doing so by attempting to impede the consolidation of new rules of the game. In Venezuela, for example, although new institutions were put in place in 1989, political and

party leaders in the mid-1990s were actively trying to undermine these institutions and return to older rules of the game that advantaged these leaders
more fully. In Bolivia, a new administration sought to counterbalance new
municipal institutions by shoring up the power of regional governments and
regional elites who had been clear losers in the earlier institutional changes.
In Argentina, city, provincial, and national governments locked horns over
who would assume responsibility for providing politically sensitive services,
and the city council sought to engineer new structures of power in ways that
revisited historic conflicts among political parties. In these cases, then, conflict about the rules reemerged in the wake of reform. In addition, new kinds
of conflicts developed as local, regional, and national governments sought
control over fiscal resources and as new actors, such as neighborhood and
community organizations, began to assert claims for resources and responsiveness from government. These conflicts were about the distributional consequences of institutional change and the acceptability of the new rules.

Thus, even though parties and politicians began to behave in ways that
conformed to the expectations of rational choice theorists, the context in
which they did so was far from one in which they could make reliable strategic calculations. Institutional change remained contested and unstable. More
generally, issues over which there was conflict had to do not only with individual efforts to acquire and maintain power but also with broader conflicts
of group interests and their claims to power and resources. From the perspective of alternative hypotheses, comparative institutionalist approaches are
helpful in understanding these consequences.

In Venezuela, Bolivia, and Argentina did new rules of the game result in
reduced transaction costs of doing politics or resolve some principal-agent
problems as proponents of the new institutionalism in economics predict? To
the extent that the reforms affected overall perceptions of the legitimacy of
the political system, they could certainly be said to have lowered the costs of
doing politics. Compliance with laws and public policies would presumably
be forthcoming more efficiently or with less investment in monitoring and
coercion. Moreover, the threat of violent acts to overthrow existing institutions might be diminished. In Venezuela, the failure of two attempted military
coups was partly laid at the door of political decentralization and the strength
of confidence in local and regional government. In Bolivia, rural communities
and organizations active among them often responded strongly and positively
to new institutions of governance at the municipal level. However, the impact
of the autonomy of Buenos Aires on legitimizing government in Argentina
appears to have been minimal.

Principal-agent problems for citizens decreased as policy decisions that affected their lives came increasingly under the responsibility of levels of government much closer and more visible to them. They could now reach public officials in their offices more easily and punish and reward them more effectively through their votes. This was particularly evident in Bolivia. Communities with strong grass-roots organizations were able to negotiate about the selection of candidates with national political parties. Municipalities with strong vigilance committees were able to demand more responsive public-investment decision making. Municipal councils became active in dismissing mayors from office.

More specifically, however, the impact of change on the transaction costs of doing politics and on principal-agent problems depended on the position of different actors within the new institutions. For example, both transaction costs and principal-agent problems probably increased for national-level politicians, administrators, and political parties as they lost direct mechanisms for acquiring information, controlling candidates, and holding candidates and officials accountable to national headquarters. Presidents were no longer able to appoint and remove many public officials from office. Party leaders could no longer fully control the selection of those running for office under the party label. They also had to focus much more time and effort on generating electoral strategies that would be effective in a much wider array of local and regional contexts. These factors certainly increased the costs of doing politics for them.

Similarly, although citizens may have gained in having more transparent and responsive local government, the transaction costs for voters may have increased as it became more important for them to acquire information about candidates for office at local, regional, and national levels. This was clearest in the case of Venezuela, in which the highly centralized parties no longer provided the single piece of information most voters had traditionally needed in order to make a decision—party affiliation.

As parties lost control of resources and candidacies, the choices voters faced became more complex. Moreover, parties faced increased principal-agent problems as candidates gained independent sources of power and became less dependent on the parties for ensuring their base of support. They also had to put much more effort into collecting information for a wide variety of local electoral contests and on how local officials representing their own or opposition parties were carrying out their responsibilities. Similarly, national administrators could no longer control how resources would be used at local levels. Thus, the cases point out the extent to which transaction costs and principal-agent problems accrue differentially to actors within a political system.[6]

## How Far the Reach of History and Conflict?

Two critical issues raised by distinct approaches to political explanation considered in this book are the role of history in institutional change and the role of conflict in generating responses to problems of governance. The new institutionalists who draw on economics argue that history matters because institutions evolve over time in path-dependent ways. Comparative institutionalists insist that history matters because it shapes problems and perceptions of problems, the goals of politicians, and the ways conflict is likely to emerge over institutional change. They insist that the dynamics of change cannot be abstracted from particular experiences and explained by generic forms of political behavior and that economic approaches to politics, particularly rational choice perspectives, do not take context seriously enough.[7] In addition, comparative institutionalists propose that the ongoing and historically embedded conflict of group interests is a centrally important engine of change, whereas those who adopt an approach rooted in economics are more likely to understand conflict as a situationally specific bargaining game.

Each case study included a discussion of the roots of major institutions of governance in the countries and of the traditions of conflict that characterized political interactions. Thus, in Venezuela, a legacy of conflict between central and regional power had been resolved in favor of centralism; a legacy of political instability had shaped political parties that were highly structured, disciplined, and centralized. Both trends had been further entrenched by the petroleum wealth that allowed the central government and the centralized parties to command extraordinary amounts of resources to exchange for political conformity to their power. In Bolivia, a weak state and a weak sense of national identity combined with confrontational union organizations, centralized and clientelistic political parties, and the aftermath of political revolution to create a situation of institutional instability and deep distrust of government. In Argentina, politics in the 1980s and 1990s was carried out in an environment in which separate parties each claimed to be unique bearers of national destiny, day-to-day party activity was pursued through clientelism, and extensive political instability had created a legacy of hyperpresidentialism and cynicism in politics. Given these histories, it is reasonable to ask at this point how important it was to know about these legacies in order to understand the process of institutional innovation in the case-study countries.

Certainly, history was essential in order to understand why existing institutions were problematic from the perspective of citizens, public officials, and politicians. In all three countries, history had to be invoked to explain the extensive centralization of power and decision making that came to be identified as major sources of problems in the political system. As a consequence, the history of institutional development in Venezuela, Bolivia, and Argentina was important for understanding how political actors diagnosed the nature of the problem they wanted to fix. When they criticized centralism, presidentialism, instability, or ineffectiveness, they offered explanations of how existing institutions came to reflect these characteristics. Sketching the backdrop of history in each case also made it possible to understand how design teams determined the groups and the conflicts that were important to discussions of institutional change. Which conflicts might be mediated through change? Which interests needed to be accommodated? Which might react strongly against proposals for change? Similarly, historical legacies, such as the ways in which traditional political parties were structured through clientelism or confronted each other over elections and the distribution of public resources, were important to assessing the power of different groups and understanding the room for negotiation, consensus, and conflict in the process of change.

Thus, the case studies provide considerable evidence to support the contentions of the comparative institutionalists. History was important for understanding the problems, the diagnoses of those problems, and the concerns that surrounded them in Venezuela, Bolivia, and Argentina. At the same time, however, the studies suggest that history does not provide a good predictor of what will be done about those problems or when it will be done. History did not dictate the solutions to the problems that politicians confronted in the three countries. This was true in two senses. First, as suggested above, the kinds of institutional changes proposed in each country were not confined to an evolutionary approach by path dependency or embeddedness. In each case, the institutions put in place represented a disjuncture with the past and an explicit effort to reverse the dynamics of that history. Second, projects to alter existing institutions did not clearly emerge from the historical conflicts of mobilized group interests in the countries.

In the cases, the conflict of group interests was important in understanding how institutional problems emerged in the history of each country—centralists and federalists, unions and parties, and local and national rivalries bequeathed complex legacies and symbols that influenced perceptions and assessments of wins and losses. The conflict of group interests was also important in responding to initiatives of change—who mobilized against the reforms and who supported them. And conflict reasserted itself in the wake of institutional change as groups sought to reposition themselves to benefit from the change or to reverse it to minimize their losses. Nevertheless, while each of the initiatives recognized historically rooted problems, their emergence as political agenda items cannot be clearly linked to overt conflicts in which groups sought to acquire benefits through change or resist the loss of power.

History and conflict matter, but they do not tell the whole story of institutional change. The analysis of Venezuela, Bolivia, and Argentina suggests that those who wish to account for institutional innovation must be able to account for the historical roots of problems that shape perceptions and diagnoses and that condition the behavior and goals of group actors. At the same time, explaining institutional innovation requires the ability to account for the particular goals of political actors who champion change and the problem-solving orientation of reform teams. This fact points to a series of conclusions about agency in political life.

## Lessons for Reformers?

In the three case studies explored in this book, I found considerable evidence that issues of governance and system legitimacy are important to political leaders who undertake institutional change. I also found consistent stories about how institutional changes were selected and what kinds of consequences resulted from them. The case studies indicate that politicians were concerned about the extent to which the authority of the state was accepted as legitimate and about the effectiveness of the state in responding to public problems. The studies also indicate that the process of institutional innovation began when political leaders empowered design teams to think broadly about such issues and to generate recommendations for change. In all the cases, the forthcoming recommendations were at the mercy of political leaders who chose to take them up, ignore them, or revive them in response to specific challenges they faced. Varying degrees of conflict and negotiation characterized the process of gaining approval for these changes, and once adopted, they tended to generate more conflict. The introduction of the reforms had significant consequences for how politics was done in each of the countries that influenced the behavior of politicians, political parties, and citizens. Politicians and political parties faced more complex arenas for political competition. Citizens gained more options for participating in politics, greater input into decision making about resource allocation, and more capacity to hold public officials accountable for their actions

Those committed to introducing democratizing reforms in Latin American countries may find some instruction in the case studies of Venezuela, Bolivia, and Argentina. Aspiring or actual politicians can take heart that statecraft clearly matters in the history of countries, that individuals can make a difference, that agency is possible. In each country, change would not have happened had political leaders not chosen to champion reform. Leaders also played important roles in generating strategies for marshaling political agreement and authorization for the changes. Equally important, political leaders appear to have been encouraged to take up the reform banner because they were influenced by personal experiences and ideas to view certain issues as important and problematic for the institutional health of their countries. Equally important, the leaders were receptive to the recommendations of design teams that were in turn influenced by ideas and problem-solving orientations.

For those who have access to aspiring or actual leaders, the cases suggest that opportunities exist for influencing politicians to take up problems of governance and to shape their diagnoses of the problems. Reformers may also find opportunities to shape institutional changes through work similar to that of the design teams. In the cases, these teams focused attention on specific problems of governance and engineered solutions that were then translated into recommendations for political action. In the cases, reformers were also able to promote democratizing change by developing consensus around the need for change and specific reform measures, anticipating resistance to change, and negotiating compensatory mechanisms in reform packages.

Although not fully presented in the case studies, my research also uncovered ways in which reformers continued to make a difference once the reforms were in place. My interviews revealed that some reformers went on to monitor the performance of newly autonomous local and regional governments, or became politically active in attempting to mobilize citizens at local levels to participate in the new institutions, or helped make the new institutions work effectively. Others continued to advocate changes in the distribution of power in their societies. All of these activities suggest ample room for reformers to make a difference in the institutional histories of their countries, regardless of whether academics can ever fully appreciate their experiences at the level of political theory.

# Notes

## Chapter One: Democratizing Latin America

1. In Latin America, municipalities (*municípios*) are territorial units below the state or provincial level of government. They correspond most closely to counties in the United States and thus contain both urban and rural areas. In some Latin American countries, municipalities are administrative units; in some countries they are both administrative and political units. See, in particular, Nickson (1995) for a review of local government structures and history.

2. See, for example, Schmidt (1989a, 1989b); Manor (1999); and Nickson (1995).

3. In this definition, I follow North (1990:3), the "rules of the game in society or, more formally, . . . the humanly devised constraints that shape human interaction." For similar definitions, see Calvert (1995:217), "any of the rules of the game by which individuals in society find themselves confronted when contemplating action"; and Riker and Weimer (1995:82), "more or less agreed upon and relatively stable rules that guide people in carrying out their transactions." Institutions thus provide a relatively ordered environment and offer information about norms for acceptable (and therefore predictable) behavior through the ways that they structure the costs and benefits of individual and group action. Institutions reduce uncertainty in undertaking such action

4. See, for example, Haggard and Kaufman (1995); Huntington (1991); Nonneman (1996); Markoff (1996); O'Donnell, Schmitter, and Whitehead (1986); and Smith, Acuña, and Gamarra (1994).

5. See Romero (1996); Remmer (1985–86); and Karl (1990).

6. See Grindle (1996); Malloy (1989); Williamson (1994); Grindle and Thoumi (1993); Geddes (1995b); and Naím (1995).

7. See Romero (1996); Haggard and Kaufman (1995); and Remmer (1985–86).

8. See Grindle (1996:ch. 2).

9. For a description of the new vitality of local government in Latin America, see Fiszbein (1997); Fox (1994); Friedland (1997); Campbell (1997); Tendler (1997); Willis, Garman, and Haggard (1999); and Peterson (1994).

10. See Bates and Krueger (1993); Drazen and Grilli (1993); Frieden (1991); Haggard and Kaufman (1992); Nelson (1990); Nelson and Contributors (1989); Nelson and Contributors (1994); Rodrik (1993); Schamis (1999); Smith, Acuña, and Gamarra (1994); and Tommasi and Velasco (1996).

11. A good review of this literature is found in Geddes (1995b).

12. See, for examples, Bates and Krueger (1993); Geddes (1995b); Nelson and Contributors (1989, 1994), Nelson (1990); and Smith, Acuña, and Gamarra (1994).

13. See Huntington (1991); Karl (1990); Markoff (1996); O'Donnell, Schmitter, and Whitehead (1989).

14. See Agüero Stark (1998); Linz and Valenzuela (1994); Graham and Naím (1998); Tulchin (1995).

15. See especially North (1990) and Alston, Eggertsson, and North (1996). The literature on market-oriented reforms has spawned a rich discussion of the kinds of institutions that are needed if markets are to perform well, as well as a theoretically interesting literature about institutional choice that deals with the issue of what kinds of consequences can be anticipated from particular institutional structures. This literature does not, however, deal with the issue of how and when choices about institutional innovation are made. See Horn (1995); Borner, Brunetti, and Weder (1995); and Knott and Miller (1987).

16. See, for example, Lipjhart and Waisman (1996).

17. The difference between chosen and pressing reforms is found in Hirschman (1981).

18. These are official estimates of the number of dead and wounded and of economic losses. Unofficial figures were much higher (see *VenEconomy Monthly* [March 1989]).

19. These data are taken from UNDP (1998).

## Chapter Two: Explaining the Unexpected

1. The theoretical chapters of Evans (1995b) and Geddes (1994a) suggest some of the heat of the underlying debates about how to do social science.

2. A useful overview of rational choice political economy is Geddes (1995a). For a critique, see Green and Shapiro (1994). On the new institutionalism in economics, see North (1990) and Banks and Hanushek (1995).

3. On institutionalism in sociology, see the discussion of historical institutionalism in Steinmo, Thelen, and Longstreth (1992) and the defense of "embeddedness" as an explanatory approach in Evans (1995b).

4. On the issue of preferences, see Geddes (1995a:83). Within rational choice theory, individuals are acting rationally when their actions "can be shown (*ex ante* rather than *ex post*) to be the best actions possible to satisfy the agent's preferences given his or her beliefs, that the beliefs are rational given the evidence available, and, finally, that the amount and quality of the evidence available can be justified in terms of cost/benefit ratios" (Caporaso and Levine, 1992:130).

5. See, for example, Geddes (1995a:84) and Ames (1987:3).

6. Geddes (1995a:82).

7. Thus, Geddes (1995a:89) argues that "individual action is assumed to be an optimal adaptation to an institutional environment, and interaction between individuals is assumed to be an optimal response to each other. Therefore, the prevailing institutions . . . determine the behavior of the actors, which in turn produces political or social outcomes" (90). Bates and Weingast (1995:4) concur that "the greatest achievement of rational choice theory has been to provide the tools for studying political outcomes in stable institutional settings."

8. Geddes (1994a) and Ames (1987) argue that this is particularly true for politicians in Latin America, who face the threat of being ousted from office by the military.

9. The classic statement of this situation in developing countries is Bates (1981).

10. See Olson (1965) and Olson (1982).

11. See especially Persson and Tabellini (1994), Root (1989), Taliercio (1996), and Weingast (1995).

12. See Horn (1995:especially ch. 8).

13. See, for example, North and Weingast (1994).

14. The term *comparative institutionalism* is taken from discussions of a symposium on theory and comparative politics presented in *World Politics* 48 (1995). In Steinmo, Thelen, and Longstreth (1992), this approach is referred to as "historical institutionalism." Among those who are often cited as leaders in this tradition are Theda Skocpol, Peter Katzenstein, Peter Evans, and Peter Hall.

15. See especially Thelen and Steinmo (1992) as well as a series of case studies in Steinmo, Thelen, and Longstreth (1992) for discussions of the importance of institutions, conflict, and history in comparative analysis. See also contributions to "The Role of Theory in Comparative Politics: A Symposium," *World Politics* 48 (October 1995).

16. Thelen and Steinmo (1992:6).

17. Evans (1995b) uses the concept of embeddedness to explore why some governments are more able to encourage efficient industrial development than others.

18. See, for example, Immergut (1992). King (1992) provides a comparative analysis of welfare policy in the United States and Britain through an institutionalist approach.

19. Thelen and Steinmo (1992:8). Institutions influence the ideas, values, perceptions, and preferences of political actors; part of the research task is to demonstrate the "social construction" of preferences, strategies, and actions.

20. Indeed, a recurring theme in critiques of rational choice theory is that the theory itself is not able to explain how individual preferences are aggregated into organizations or institutions or history that are meaningful at a level beyond the aggregation of individual preferences. For example, Geddes (1994a:1n.1) defines the state—a central concept in comparative institutionalism—as "a shorthand way of talking about the actions of individuals whose power derives from their positions in government."

21. See especially North (1990).

22. For analysis of a new institutionalist approach that focuses on imperfect information, see Bardhan (1989).

23. North (1990:16).

24. Thus, North (1990:68) argues that due to the differential distribution of bargaining power, "only when it is in the interest of those with sufficient bargaining strength to alter the formal rules will there be major changes in the formal institutional framework. . . . At the same time, the complex of informal and formal constraints [of existing institutions] makes possible continual incremental changes at particular margins."

25. North (1990:6). "If, however, [the case of the Northwest Ordinance] sounds like an inevitable, foreordained account, it should not. At every step along the way there were choices—political and economic—that provided the real alternatives. Path dependency is a way to narrow conceptually the choice set and link decision making through time. It is not a story of inevitability in which the past neatly predicts the future" (North 1990:98–99). See also Alston, Eggertsson, and North (1996) for case studies demonstrating how and why "history matters." See also Root (1989).

26. Moe (1984:756).

27. See, for example, Calvert (1995).

28. See, in particular, Horn (1995) for a description of this approach and its relevance to

restructuring government in New Zealand. Much of the discussion of the need for institutional reform that has been produced within international development agencies, such as the World Bank and regional development banks, rests on the assumption that institutions can be rationally designed to resolve certain problems of economic development, such as credibility, principal-agent problems, transparency, or incentives.

29. "The relative underdevelopment of explicit theorizing about the reciprocal influence of institutions and politics is also clear when one considers the question of institutional formation and change. Although arguably one of the most important issues in comparative politics, this issue has received relatively little attention in most of the literature to date. Again, one reason for this deficit is that institutionalists generally focus on constraints and offer explanations of continuity rather than change" (Thelen and Steinmo, 1992:15). Krasner (1984), however, is frequently cited for exploring moments of institutional creation and periods of institutional stability and incremental change. Rothstein (1992:35) argues that "at certain *formative moments* in history, [new] institutions are created with the object of giving the agent (or the interests the agent wants to further) an advantage in the future game of power." He thus introduces the important question about the intentionality of the design of new institutions that is present in the institutional design approach in economics.

30. See, for example, Weir (1992:192).

31. For example, Libecap (1996) explains the evolution of laws to structure mining rights as a result of successive adjustments to uncertainties about ownership rights.

### Chapter Three: Institutional Invention in Venezuela

1. See *Gaceta Oficial No. 4153 Extraordinario de 28-12-89* for the text of the basic law.

2. For a basic overview of decentralization in Venezuela, see González Cruz (1996); see de la Cruz (1992) for greater detail.

3. For an overview of state and municipal government in Venezuela, see Nickson (1995:259–68).

4. Nickson (1995:259).

5. Interview, January 16, 1997, Caracas. Most interviews were confidential and names of most interviewees are therefore not provided.

6. See Martz (1992:102).

7. Indeed, one student of Venezuelan politics has dubbed the system a "partyarchy" to capture the extent of party centralization and control over politics. "In Venezuela," he writes, "political parties monopolize the electoral process, dominate the legislative process, and penetrate politically relevant organizations to a degree that violates the spirit of democracy" (Coppedge 1994b:2).

8. Gran Colombia extended through a large area in northern South America currently divided among Colombia, Ecuador, and Venezuela.

9. The Liberal and Conservative Parties were formed in the ten years following the demise of Gran Colombia in 1830 and persisted as loose coalitions of elites for nearly a century.

10. Blank (1973:8).

11. See Blank (1973:13–14); see also Martz (1992:93).

12. In fact, the national government needed the consent of state governments to move troops within states (Lattanzi Arévalo 1996:19–21).

13. See Tugwell (1975) for a history of the petroleum industry in Venezuela and its impact on the country's development up to the early 1970s.

14. Interview, January 16, 1997, Caracas.

15. See Karl (1986) for this view. For reviews of distinct perspectives on the character of Venezuelan democracy, see Ellner (1997), and McCoy, Smith, Serbin, and Stambouli (1995). See also Crisp (1994), Coppedge (1994b), and Levine (1973, 1994).

16. Guerón (1993:3). The extensive growth of the 1970s was fueled in part by petroleum revenues but also by international credit.

17. In February 1928, students organized Student Week, whose original non-political purpose was transformed into a confrontation between students and the Gómez regime, later joined by a wider popular protest. Those leading the movement and arrested or exiled by the regime became the nucleus of the Generation of '28, which later initiated mass political mobilization for new parties that would, along with the military, become the central forces of national politics in the 1940s.

18. Prior to this, the president had been selected by an electoral college, senators had been elected by state legislatures, and deputies had been elected by municipal councils.

19. AD is part of the International Social Democrats, and COPEI is part of the International Christian Democrats.

20. Those attending the meeting at the Plaza Hotel were the leader of Acción Democrática, Rómulo Betancourt; COPEI's leader, Rafael Caldera; Jóvito Villalba, who led the URD; and Eugenio Mendoza and Mario Diez, representing the more progressive wing of the urban business elite. For a discussion of this meeting and of the nature of a pacted democracy, see Karl (1986).

21. Coppedge (1992:34–35).

22. In the 1960s, the exclusionary character of the pact and the extent to which AD and COPEI dominated political positions and power led the radical left to abandon the constitutional road to power for armed insurgency posing yet another threat to the coherence and unity of the country.

23. Coppedge (1994b:24) reports that "the normal procedure in the Congress is for the Speaker to have a bill read; debate is opened, at which time one designated spokesman for each party states his party's position on the bill; the Speaker then closes debate with the ritual statement, 'Deputies who are in favor of approving [this bill], please indicate it with the customary sign'; and without counting votes, often without even looking up, he brings down his gavel and announces, 'Approved.'"

24. See Coppedge (1994a:402). Many social organizations select their leaders through elections based on party slates; others "belong" to the parties that organized them.

25. The party bosses of AD meet formally as the National Executive Committee (CEN) and are popularly known as a cogollo (the heart or apex of an organization).

26. Coppedge (1994a:402).

27. Coppedge (1992:35).

28. Coppedge (1994a:397)

29. Romero (1997).

30. The capacity for gridlock between executive and legislative branches was troublesome, however, when the legislature was not controlled by the party of the president. See Coppedge (1994a, 1994b) for discussions of presidentialism and the problems it creates for governing effectively. He argues that the governing party (almost always Acción Democrática) is regularly fac-

tionalized between those who support the incumbent president and those who are planning for the next election. At the same time, this factionalism does not affect the policy making process.

31. Coppedge (1994b) has identified a characteristic tension between "Ins" and "Outs" when parties are in power; these conflicts, however, revolve around candidatures for the next presidential election. He identifies factionalism as a problem that afflicts the party in power; parties not in power tend to unify in order to compete effectively in elections.

32. Interview, January 23, 1997, Caracas.

33. Naím (1993:23).

34. Karl (1986:215).

35. Interview, January 13, 1997, Caracas.

36. Article 22.

37. Sometimes administration over government functions has been deconcentrated by creating subnational units of national ministries and agencies; sometimes it has been devolved to become the responsibility of more local levels of government; and sometimes it has been delegated to semi-autonomous agencies or organizations.

38. Defenders of political decentralization as a way of encouraging administrative decentralization, however, argue that it creates a demand for administrative decentralization that would not necessarily exist otherwise and that this form of decentralization results in a demand-driven process of capacity-building more robust and enduring than the typical supply-driven process.

39. See Kelly (1986:7–11). A good source on the first four years of activities of COPRE is Gómez Calcaño and López Maya (1990). See also Willis, Garman, and Haggard (1999) and Bland (1998).

40. Decree No. 403, *Gaceta Oficial* No. 33,127, December 17, 1984.

41. See Decree No. 403, *Gaceta Oficial* No. 33,127, December 17, 1984.

42. See Gómez Calcaño and López Maya (1990:82–88).

43. See Kelly (1986:11).

44. Kelly (1986:41).

45. Interview, January 13, 1997, Caracas.

46. According to Janet Kelly (1986:11), the focus on the state signaled a need for "a root and branch effort. . . . Limiting efforts to mere fiddling with organization charts or training bureaucrats or gathering statistics would be doomed to failure, because such fiddling would not alter the relation between the citizen or civil society, and the State."

47. These reforms, however, were vaguely defined in the plan. See Gómez Calcaño and López Maya (1990:86).

48. See de la Cruz (1988:147).

49. See, for example, de la Cruz (1995:4–5) and Romero (1997:7). See also Coppedge (1994b:159–60), and Gómez Calcaño and López Maya (1990:ch. 3).

50. Gómez Calcaño and López Maya (1990:ch. 2).

51. Much of the debate, then, focused on the continued viability of the country's political and economic institutions. See Gómez Calcaño and López Maya (1990:ch. 3).

52. See, for example, the link drawn between corruption and economic deterioration in Naím (1993:125–28) and Romero (1997:19–21).

53. See Gómez Calcaño and López Maya (1990:53–55).

54. Interview, January 14, 1997, Caracas.

55. The number of people on the commission was a source of concern, according to Janet Kelly: "The insiders preferred the idea of a small commission in order to avoid the likely possibil-

ity of the group being turned into a microcosm of the political system, with all the conflict and opposition that this would entail. . . . Apparently President Lusinchi preferred assuring that the commission be as representative as possible. Instead of choosing a smaller number from among the candidates, he chose 25 names. Such generosity had a perverse result. Indeed, since so many people made the cut, there were many more that felt offended at not being included. To the horror of some, the government responded to the criticisms by naming an additional ten members, broadening representation to include such 'groups' as the women, the armed forces, and the left" (1986:14). Among those selected, there was a predominance of central administrators, national and regional legislators, academics, business association representatives and union leaders. AD and COPEI adherents occupied fourteen seats; independents of the left and right occupied eighteen. The remaining seats were filled by representatives of smaller parties. See Gómez Calcaño and López Maya (1990:91).

56. Interview, January 23, 1997, Caracas.

57. Gómez Calcaño and López Maya (1990:201).

58. The working-group issues were (a) political reforms; (b) public administration; (c) decentralization; (d) economic strategy; (e) social policy; (f) administration of justice; (g) education; (h) science and technology; and (i) change-oriented culture. The final report followed this organization also (Gómez Calcaño and López Maya [1990:95]).

59. Interview, January 23, 1997, Caracas.

60. Kelly (1986:19-20).

61. Kelly (1986:21), citing El Nacional, February 16, 1986.

62. Blanco (1993:101); Naím (1993:23) has termed the Venezuelan state "rich in oil but poor in efficient institutions."

63. Gómez Calcaño and López Maya (1990:98-108).

64. De la Cruz (1995:7).

65. Overall, the reforms proposed were more "radical" than changes supported by Acción Democrática (see Gómez Calcaño and López Maya [1990:156]).

66. There were twenty states at the time.

67. Interview, January 23, 1997, Caracas.

68. Interview, January 23, 1997, Caracas.

69. Gómez Calcaño and López Maya (1990:162); see also Bland (1998), and Willis, Garman, and Haggard (1999).

70. See Gómez Calcaño and López Maya (1990:98-108).

71. Bland (1998:25-26).

72. The party leaders and Lusinchi backed Octavio Lepage but could not marshal enough support within the party to withstand those supporting Pérez. Factional struggles within AD about who will be the standard bearer in the presidential elections are a commonplace feature of Venezuela's parties (see especially Coppedge [1994b]).

73. Interview, January 23, 1997, Caracas; see also El Universal, October 14, 1987, and El Nacional, October 23, 1987.

74. See El Nacional, January 23, 1988.

75. Stambouli (1993:119).

76. According to Stambouli (1993:119), "But for anyone who had read the government programs of both candidates—and very few voters had done so—the similarities of the offerings stood out: less of a state role, more market mechanisms, privatization, decentralizing political reforms, export-oriented economy, and so forth. The problem was that neither candidate elabo-

rated on the magnitude of the economic problems their programs were based on." In fact, Pérez declared himself a populist and a foe of the IMF during the elections (see Romero 1996:393–96).

77. The municipal reform law was passed on August 9 and announced in the *Gaceta Oficial No. 4054 Extraordinario* on October 9, 1988. The direct election of governors was announced in the *Gaceta Oficial No. 34039,* August 29, 1988.

78. Gómez Calcaño and López Maya (1990:186).

79. See Romero (1997) and Naím (1993).

80. Psacharopoulous et al. (1997).

81. Naím (1993:47).

82. See Naím (1993:ch. 7).

83. The fares were raised by government but independent operators raised them more. Naím (1993:31–32) indicates that the shock to workers was increased because the fares were put in place at the end of the month, when most of the workers were low on cash. He argues that the failure to communicate the content and rationale for economic reforms was a "systematic flaw" of the management of policy reform under Pérez.

84. Coppedge (1994b:160).

85. The law was signed the following day by President Pérez. See *Gaceta Oficial No. 4086 Extraordinario,* April 14, 1989, for the text of the law.

86. See *Gaceta Oficial No. 4409 Extraordinario,* June 15, 1989, for the text of the law.

87. Interview, January 17, 1997, Valencia.

88. Interview, January 20, 1997, Caracas.

89. Interview, January 13, 1997, Caracas.

90. Interview, January 15, 1997, Caracas.

91. Interview, January 21, 1997, Caracas.

92. Naím (1993:46–47), citing Foreign Broadcast Information Service, *Daily Report: Latin America,* March 15, 1993:53.

93. Interview, January 26, 1996, Caracas.

## Chapter Four: Consequences of Change in Venezuela

1. Cordiplan (1996).

2. De la Cruz (1997:Annex 3:2).

3. According to Aníbal Romero (1997:15), 1989 was critical to the attitudes that Venezuelans held about their country: "For several years prior to 1989, most Venezuelans thought that 'the country is in bad shape, but I am fine.' The events of early 1989 shifted their focus. In the new context of aggravated frustrations, Venezuelans perceived that 'the country is in bad shape and that is the reason why I too am suffering.'"

4. See especially Naím (1993:ch. 7), who argues that three decades of an expanding and interventionist state overwhelmed the capacity to deliver public services effectively: "As the public sector was burdened with added functions and responsibilities, the deterioration of its performance accelerated. The chronic fiscal crises made it impossible to sustain the appropriate funding levels required for the expanded public functions. An underpaid and poorly trained civil service plagued by turnover, corruption, congestion, and politicization severely eroded the capacity of public agencies to do their jobs" (130–31).

5. Although some have interpreted the riots as a spontaneous outbreak of anger over the Pérez government's economic stabilization and structural adjustment package, they occurred

only eleven days after the reform package was announced and before it was implemented, with the exception of the devaluation and increases in petroleum prices that were passed on to users of public and private transportation facilities in the capital city.

6. See Crisp (1998), Hernández (1995:26–28), Naím (1993), and Zambrano Sequín (1995).

7. Naím (1993:50–53).

8. Naím (1993:61–62), however, points out that crime rates escalated during this period, a trend he ascribes to increased poverty, unemployment, inflation, and the deterioration of social services, police, and judiciary.

9. Rumors of an anticipated coup circulated freely in the months leading up to the coup but were apparently not taken seriously by the government.

10. One report is that the president was hidden on the floor of an unofficial car and covered by a coat to make his escape (see Naím [1993:99]). See Philip (1992) for an assessment of the coup attempt in the context of Venezuela's democracy and also Hillman (1994:ch.7).

11. Philip (1992:456).

12. Quoted in Naím (1993:101).

13. Translated text presented in Naím (1993:157, app. 2).

14. The president made some adjustments in response to the coup and the protests. He appointed COPEI politicians to his cabinet and removed some of the technocrats who had designed the Great Turnaround, diluted some of the policies, and took initial actions to weed out corruption at high levels (see Philip [1992]).

15. Corrales (1996:21) refers to a "collision course between party and government by early 1991." Many of the technocrats named to the Pérez cabinet and other high-level positions had been deeply involved in the activities of COPRE in the 1980s.

16. Data from Consultores 21 poll of May 1992. Total sample – 2,000 respondents. For additional evidence of public opinion about the performance of the Pérez administration and the legitimacy of the political system, see Myers (1995).

17. Quoted in Naím (1993:108).

18. Consultores 21, national polls conducted in May 1989, January 1990, May 1992, and January 1993. Total sample = 2,000 respondents in each poll.

19. Ten percent had no opinion, and 6 percent said all three levels of government functioned best (Consultores 21, May 1992).

20. Six percent chose the state level, 9 percent chose the local level, 15 percent had no opinion, and 6 percent replied that all three performed worst (Consultores 21, May 1992).

21. Consultores 21, May 1992.

22. Consultores 21, January 1993.

23. Interview, January 17, 1997, Valencia.

24. Interview, January 13, 1997, Caracas.

25. Coppedge (1994b:180–81).

26. See his statement to El Nacional, May 31, 1996, as well as a series of interviews by Caupolicán Ovalles in Ovalles (1996).

27. Latin American Newsletters, Andean Group Report, April 8, 1997.

28. Brewer-Carías (1994a:22) wrote in his official report of activities accomplished by the ministry under his command, "My mission as Minister of State for Decentralization, from the beginning and in those few months, was not, of course, to undo a hundred years of state centralism, which obviously cannot be accomplished nor will it be accomplished in a few months

or a few years. My mission, in those months of the transitional government, was to take the largest number of public policy decisions possible, so that the process of decentralization would become increasingly irreversible. Moreover, [it was my mission] that each decision that the government took . . . would make new decisions necessary, so that the process of decentralization would acquire its own dynamic, not just as something that was the responsibility of the national government, but also as something that the states and municipalities were concerned with. My mission . . . was to construct all the legal and institutional infrastructure necessary so that from the beginning of the presidential period of 1994–1999, the governors and mayors would have an arsenal of policy mechanisms that would enable them to demand that the new administration continue the decentralization process" (author's translation).

29. The distribution for states was based on a formula in which 35 percent of the funds were allotted on the basis of interstate compensation (poverty levels) and 65 percent of the funds were allotted on the basis of population and territory. Within this 65 percent, the formula weighted population as 98 percent and territory as 2 percent of the total. The problem, according to the president of FIDES, was that the government lacked good measures for poverty and good data on the distribution of population and territory among the states (interview, Caracas, January 15, 1997).

30. Navarro (1997:246).

31. A series of case studies prepared by Venezuela Competitiva, a think tank and consulting firm dedicated to investigating and improving the competitiveness of the Venezuelan economy, provides insight into the structure and accomplishments of many of the innovations listed in this paragraph (see Venezuela Competitiva [1994, 1995, 1996]). Other innovations mentioned here are from interviews with ex-governors and those who worked with them carried out in January 1997 (see also Navarro [1997]).

32. Alvarez (1998:269–71).

33. See Navarro (1997) and Alvarez (1998:270–71).

34. On problems related to the transfer of functions to the states and municipalities, see Barrios (1997).

35. This statement was made by the secretary of state to two governors who were widely known for their commitment to good government and to the decentralization process (interview, January 17, 1997, Valencia).

36. Barrios (1997:122).

37. For an overview of the weaknesses of the decentralization process, see de la Cruz (1995). He argues that the tortuousness of the process reveals the doubts that legislators had about the process of decentralization when they passed the law.

38. Alvarez (1998:256).

39. Cordiplan (1996) and Barrios (1997:121).

40. Interview, January 16, 1997, Caracas.

41. De la Cruz (1997:Annex 2-A:13); Garzón (1997:299–301) gives a figure of 242,494 state employees and an additional 80,000 municipal employees for 1996.

42. In the presidential elections of 1998, the abstention rate was 35.2 percent. For gubernatorial elections that year, it was 41.35 percent.

43. Alvarez (1998:264–65).

44. Stambouli (1993:121–22).

45. Coppedge (1992:39); see also Salamanca (1995).

46. Coppedge (1992:39).

47. Alvarez (1998:253).

48. Alvarez (1998:259–64).

49. This electoral outcome was assisted by a split within COPEI in which COPEI leader Rafael Caldera ran under another party label, in alliance with MAS.

50. *Latin American Weekly Report,* May 19, 1998.

51. Interview, January 24, 1997, Caracas.

52. *Latin American Weekly Report,* December 8, 1998.

53. Interview, January 23, 1997, Caracas.

54. See Kelly (1996:29); see also Alvarez (1998:274–75).

55. Alvarez (1988:260).

56. Consultores 21, January 1993.

57. Naím (1993:114).

58. Alvarez (1998:259).

59. The fourth candidate was Rafael Caldera, the traditional leader of the COPEI who had split from his party and pasted together an electoral coalition of seventeen parties to campaign under the banner of the Covergencia Party (an alliance, really). Prior to backing Caldera, MAS considered backing the twice-elected governor of Aragua state (Alvarez 1998:267). Caldera's platform included an indictment of traditional party politics and of political parties themselves. In the event, he won by a 6.9 point margin over his AD rival, Claudio Fermín, and by a 7.8 point margin over the COPEI candidate, Oswaldo Alvarez Paz. Once elected, he was relatively free of the claims of COPEI leaders.

60. Coppedge (1994b:134–135).

61. See, for example, Alvarez (1998:271).

62. Alvarez (1998:268).

63. Interview, January 20, 1997, Caracas.

64. Interview, January 23, 1997, Caracas.

## Chapter Five: Political Engineering in Bolivia

1. Good descriptions and analyses of the Popular Participation law can be found in Graham (1994), Gray Molina and Molina (1997), and Booth et al. (1997).

2. Elective local government at the municipal level was incorporated into a constitutional revision of August 12, 1994.

3. Republic of Bolivia, *Ley de Participación Popular* (1995:3).

4. In 1996, the proportion was changed to no more than 15 percent on operating costs and no less than 85 percent on investments.

5. Law No. 1654, July 28, 1995.

6. Republic of Bolivia, *Ley de Participación Popular* (1995:3) (author's translation).

7. Urban areas are defined as population settlements of two thousand inhabitants or more.

8. Local organizations have a long history in Bolivia. Many were the descendants of precolonial practice among indigenous people and had at their core a territorial concept of community or representation. Their function was primarily that of providing local-level social control, conflict resolution, and the regulation of community life and ritual. Others emerged from the agrarian struggle of the 1940s and 1950s and were organized as unions or rural syndicates and were part of the Confederación Sindical Unica de Trabajadores Campesinos de Bolivia (CSUTCB). Their concept of community was functional and sectoral, although in many peasant communities

they had emerged as the central organization for governance. In urban communities, *juntas veci-nales* (neighborhood councils) organized local communities and acted as intermediaries to government and party leaders. These organizations were often highly politicized and part of the clientelist system that characterized Bolivian national politics. Under the Popular Participation law, such organizations would petition for the right to represent the community and then would select representatives to the municipal-level vigilance committees in accordance with local practice (by appointment or election, for example).

9. An OTB had to petition for the right to represent a community or neighborhood. Once granted this official status, no other OTB could represent for the same territorial unit.

10. On the tradition of local self-government of Amerindian communities in Bolivia, see Ticona, Rojas, and Albó (1995).

11. Nickson (1995:108). Between 1878 and 1942, mayors were appointed by the president, based on nominations by elected municipal councils. A municipal code of 1942 allowed for some local autonomy, but this legislation was never effectively implemented.

12. Each year, municipal development plans were to be elaborated by local groups that were to meet to discuss local needs and investment projects. These would then be incorporated into annual operating plans through meetings among mayors, councils, and vigilance committees, and approved by the vigilance committees and the national finance ministry before being incorporated into the national budget. Municipal budgets were then to be elaborated by officials from the municipality on the basis of allocations from the national budget.

13. The law allowed vigilance committees to claim that local governments were not being responsive or were misusing funds, through appeals to the National Secretariat for Popular Participation, the Ministry of Finance, or the congress. In these cases, fund transfers would be suspended while an investigation was being carried out. When the council elected the mayor (because no party gained an absolute majority in the council), it had the right to censure the mayor in the first year of his or her administration and to hold new elections.

14. Graham (1994:5).

15. PRONAGOB (1996:155).

16. See *Latin American Weekly Report,* August 8, 1996, and August 15, 1996.

17. The first president of the country, José de Sucre, held office for two and a half years of unsustainable reformism. The second president filled that office for five days. The third president, Andrés de Santa Cruz, remained in office for ten years and established the basis of the Bolivian state—a legal code, public education, fiscal control, and a rudimentary bureaucracy. He was succeeded by chaotic rivalries among regional *caudillos* for the next several decades, and their activities undermined these nascent institutions.

18. Nickson (1995:107–8).

19. Malloy (1970:28).

20. Malloy (1970:19).

21. In the elections of 1898, an estimated 35,785 citizens voted for president, out of a population of approximately 1.82 million (1900). Thirteen percent of the population was characterized as "white" in the census of 1900. At that time, the illiteracy rate for the country was 83 percent. Only about 7 percent of the population lived in centers of 20,000 inhabitants or more (see Mesa Gisbert [1990], Contreras [n.d.:19], and Klein [1982:166–67]).

22. Liberals promised to deliver land and greater autonomy in exchange for service in this army. At the conclusion of the war, however, the peasant leaders were shot and land taken away from their followers (Malloy [1970:19] and Klein [1982:ch. 6]).

23. The growth of the state was significant in the first three decades of the twentieth century. A national bank was established in 1911, the Central Bank in 1929, and the government's accounting agency (*contraloría*) in 1930. The government invested heavily in railroads and established the basis for a national education system (Contreras [n.d.:1–2, 19–21]).

24. This was about a quarter of those mobilized for the war (see Klein [1982:ch. 7]).

25. Malloy (1970:88–90) and Klein (1982:163–70).

26. Article 44, constitution of 1938.

27. Mesa Gisbert (1990), assuming a population of 2.3 million people.

28. The MNR had won the presidential elections of May 1951, and the traditional elites, claiming the need to protect the country from communism and Nazism, declared a state of siege and enlisted the support of the military (see Malloy [1970:156–58]).

29. See Klein (1982:ch. 8).

30. With universal adult suffrage, registered voters jumped from 204,649 in 1951 to 1,119,047 in the first elections with expanded suffrage in 1956.

31. See especially Whitehead (1974–75).

32. Whitehead (1974–75:98).

33. Malloy (1970:291) sums up this situation vividly: "When Paz assumed the presidency for the second time in 1960, the general situation of the national authorities was nothing short of absurd. It is not too much of an exaggeration to say that national authority was roughly coterminous with the city limits of La Paz. Sandoval Morón and Ruben Julio effectively ruled almost half the existing territory of the country between them. The bulk of the altiplano was under the thumb of Toribio Salas. José Rojas held sway in the Valley. . . . Northern Potosí was in a state of anarchic inter-tribal warfare. The major mining camps were indisputably controlled by local sindicatos [unions]. The overall situation had deteriorated to such a point that national officials, including the president, could not safely travel throughout large sections of the country without the express permission and protection of local bosses."

34. See Conaghan and Malloy (1994) on the development of regional economic elites in the 1970s; on the role of the Santa Cruz entrepreneurs, see Mayorga U. (1996).

35. See Conaghan and Malloy (1994:66–67).

36. Gill (1987:197–99).

37. These events are important to the eventual development of Popular Participation because one of the most important leaders of the CEPB was Gonzalo Sánchez de Lozada, later to be president of Bolivia.

38. Malloy (1970) provides a useful overview and analysis of this period.

39. Malloy (1970:133).

40. In a national survey in 1993, 16 percent of respondents (N = 4,250) indicated that their labor union best represented their interests, following 23.4 percent who chose the media. The third most popular choice was the church, with 11.4 percent (see PRONAGOB [1996:161]).

41. On political parties in Bolivia, see *Opiniones y Análisis* (1998) and CIDES-PNUD (1997).

42. See Malloy (1970:185–6).

43. See n. 33.

44. See Whitehead (1974–75).

45. Interview, La Paz, February 28, 1997.

46. The underground economy related to coca growing and cocaine production was estimated to amount to some $1.9 billion in 1990 (Paz Zamora 1990:327).

47. The state of political conflict had reached a point that the National Conference of Bishops of the Catholic Church called contending groups together to craft an agreement to call for elections in June 1985, a proposal adopted by Siles Zuazo.

48. See Mayorga U. (1996:57).

49. The ADN candidate, Hugo Banzer Suárez, had actually come in ahead in the popular vote. The MNR, however, was able to create an alliance with the MIR to win the constitutionally mandated congressional vote for president when no candidate receives an absolute majority of the popular vote. Banzer had polled 32.8 percent of the popular vote and Paz Estenssoro, 30.4 percent (Corte Nacional Electoral 1997:5).

50. Sánchez de Lozada had become active in the CEPB (the peak organization of the private sector) and was elected to congress as a deputy and then as a senator. He was president of the senate before being appointed to serve in the Paz Estenssoro government.

51. The experience of the economic team is described in Morales (1994). The relationship with Harvard began under the auspices of the ADN, which sent a group of advisers to the Kennedy School of Government for a seminar on Bolivian development strategy. As a result of that seminar, attended by KSG graduates Ronald Maclean and David Blanco, Mario Mercado, Juan Cariaga, and others, Sachs traveled to Bolivia at the invitation of the newly elected Paz Estenssoro government. Juan Cariaga later became an important member of the economic team that was put together by the MNR. The ADN, therefore, claimed credit for the intellectual core of the Paz Estenssoro economic package. Sánchez de Lozada took over the Ministry of Planning in January 1986 (see Conaghan and Malloy [1994:127–29, 189–90]).

52. For a report by a participant in this working group, see Cariaga (1996).

53. See Sachs (1987).

54. Gonzalo Sánchez de Lozada, quoted in Morales (1994:134). Morales argues that they were not so much liberals as reformers opposed to the "klepto-patrimonialism" of the Bolivian state.

55. See especially Graham (1994). Many of the funds of the Social Emergency Fund (ESF) were distributed through a large and active NGO sector; Graham credits the program with substantially altering the relationship between the NGOs and the government (see also Jorgensen, Grosh, and Schacter [1992]).

56. The ADN had been created in 1979 as an electoral vehicle for former president General Hugo Banzer.

57. See especially Gamarra (1994).

58. In January 1990, Decree 22407 committed the government to follow the main lines of the NPE and to deepen the reforms aimed at privatization of state-owned enterprises and at attracting foreign capital. The exchange of congressional support for ministerial and government positions actually added to the size of the government, despite NPE commitment to a much smaller state.

59. According to one observer of Bolivian politics, the "logic of the pact took hold and this has lead to greater democracy. The political class has come to depend on the political pact to solve problems rather than the golpe" (interview, February 26, 1997).

60. Morales (1994:131); see also Cariaga (1996) and Conaghan, Malloy, and Abugattas (1990).

61. Gamarra (1994:116) points out that an important difference between the Pacto por la Democracia and the Acuerdo Patriótico is that the former was an agreement between a governing

party and the principal party in opposition, whereas the latter was an agreement about sharing government between two parties that were relatively equal in power.

62. Gamarra (1994:107).

63. Gamarra (1994:108).

64. He was referred to as a "prime minister" in the Paz Estenssoro government (interview, February 26, 1997, La Paz).

65. Sánchez de Lozada owned and managed COMSUR, a large mining company in Bolivia. In the 1970s, he had become active in representing business groups through the CEPB.

66. See Mayorga U. (1996).

67. The maintenance of the NPE was particularly important to Paz Estenssoro, and his support of Sánchez de Lozada was not only an effort to strengthen the modernizing wing of the party but also to see his economic program carried out in the future. On the internal party conflicts between the modernizers and technocrats on one hand and the traditional populist leaders on the other, see Mayorga U. (1996). The former claimed the traditional politicians were an anachronism while they in turn called the modernizers "antinationalists" (Mayorga U. 1996:109–10, 139).

68. On the electoral system, see Mayorga (1997:79–81).

69. This rule was later changed to a congressional run-off between the top two vote-getters, in order to avoid the kind of result that occurred in 1989.

70. Gamarra (1994:109–110). Moreover, the MNR had broken a secret agreement with the ADN made in 1988 to support Banzer's presidential bid.

71. Interview, February 27, 1997, La Paz.

72 Interview, February 28, 1997, La Paz.

73. According to Carlos Hugo Molina, "The participation of Goni . . . was always relevant and positive. When he didn't have in-depth knowledge of a particular theme, he asked questions and listened His open and receptive attitude allowed him to gain much from the discussions and from people like me, who didn't agree much with neoliberal propositions. We worked with pleasure, without political pressures or party annoyances. In fact, because of the varied professional backgrounds and experiences of the members of the group, we all learned" (personal correspondence, September 2, 1998, author's translation).

74. The experience of the foundation is discussed in Molina Monasterios (1997), see also Grebe López (1997).

75. According to the 1992 National Population and Housing Census, 55 percent of the population speaks an Indian language, although a large portion of these people are bilingual in Spanish and an indigenous language. In rural areas, 27.4 percent of the population speaks only Spanish, 45.8 percent are bilingual, and 26 8 percent speak only an Indian language (reported in UNDP 1998:164).

76. Interview March 4, 1997, La Paz.

77. His father was an early supporter of the MNR who, while living in Washington in the 1940s, was actively engaged in influencing U.S. policy toward the country. In 1952, he was named ambassador to Washington by the new revolutionary government. Sánchez de Lozada returned to Bolivia in 1951 to attempt a career as a filmmaker and then became a successful mine operator. Details on his life are found in Molina Monasterios (1997:ch. 8).

78. As an entrepreneur, he referred to himself as an "expert in the management of experts" (Mayorga U. 1996:70).

79. The campaign slogan of the MNR, "Goni listens," contributed to the image of the candidate as a modernizer open to new ideas.

80. The UCS had won 13.77 percent of the popular vote, and the MBL, 5.36 percent. The MNR-MRTKL coalition signed separate governing pacts with each of these parties in July 1993, giving the new government an absolute majority in both houses of congress. The costs of these pacts was the distribution of cabinet and subcabinet positions and a considerable amount of instability in the composition of the government. Nevertheless, they permitted an impressive amount of reform legislation to be passed by the MNR government.

81. Cárdenas was an Aymara Indian, and the election marked the first time that a high-level office had been held by any indigenous Bolivian. The electoral alliance with the MRTKL delivered a large indigenous vote to the MNR, particularly from the highland area of the country.

82. See Molina Saucedo (1994, originally published in 1990), which lays out his perspectives on decentralization.

83. Arauco and Belmont (1997) provide a history and overview of the MBL as a reformist party.

84. Interview, March 7, 1997, La Paz.

85. Carlos Hugo Molina, quoted in Molina Monasterios (1997:201), author's translation.

86. See Molina Saucedo (1990; 2nd ed., 1994).

87. Interview, La Paz, February 27, 1997. On the issue of indigenous and peasant community governance, see Ticona, Rojas, and Albó (1995). In 1989, the MBL Party drafted a "community law" in which it proposed legal recognition for traditional and indigenous forms of local government and block grants for them. The party proposed a law to this effect in 1991; it was subsequently rejected by congress.

88. See Molina Monasterios (1997:ch. 15).

89. The presence of the president in the meetings of the working group, which generally began at six in the evening and lasted until one or two in the morning, had a significant impact on the plan that eventually emerged. It was more detailed and more radical than the planning team would have designed without his presence, according to those who served on the team. They focused on details: "We met all the time with the president. But what did we talk about? Not so much about municipalization, but about the mechanics of how it would be done and local absorptive capacity. The choices were at this level, they were never at the level of should we do it or not" (interview, February 26, 1997, La Paz). According to another participant, "We were concerned above all to come up with a model that worked. We had already become comfortable with the idea of ceding power and this issue didn't play much of a role in our discussions at all, although the president used to joke that we were creating a Frankenstein" (interview, March 4, 1997, La Paz).

90. Interview, March 4, 1997, La Paz.

91. Interview, March 4, 1997, La Paz.

92. See, for example, Ardaya Salinas (n.d.).

93. Interview, March 7, 1997, La Paz. According to those who worked with the president on the plan, he often said that "even if drunks take charge at the municipal level, it will be better than what the central government is doing now."

94. Interview, March 7, 1997, La Paz.

95. In fact, in 1988, the Paz Zamora government attempted to decentralize social services to the departments, but without success. This initiative was credited to IMF conditionalities, and although not anticipated by the coalition partner ADN, it had support from some cabinet officials.

Decentralization to the departmental level was extensively discussed throughout his administration. In 1990, for example, the government proposed decentralizing government to the departments. In 1992, a senate commission sought to generate consensus on this form of decentralization. Prior to the 1993 elections, the senate voted for decentralization to the departmental level; there were insufficient votes in the chamber of deputies to approve the law, however.

96. Interview, February 26, 1997, La Paz.

97. Interview, February 26, 1997, La Paz.

98. See Molina Saucedo (1994).

99. Interview, March 7, 1997, La Paz.

100. Interview, February 26, 1997, La Paz. On this perspective, see, in particular, Barbery Anaya (1996) and Molina Saucedo (1994).

101. Molina Monasterios (1997:205).

102. The letter is reproduced in Secretaría Nacional de Participación Popular (1995:3-4).

103. See Secretaría Nacional de Participación Popular (1995) for a compilation of opinions voiced and published during this period of debate and discussion. Some two thousand newspaper articles, letters, and op ed pieces about the new law appeared during this time.

104. Interview, February 28, 1997, La Paz.

105. See Secretaría Nacional de Participación Popular (1995).

106. Urioste and Baldomar (1996:30-35).

107. Ayo Saucedo (1998).

108. Molina Monasterios (1997:204).

109. The decision-making process that produced Popular Participation was not unique to this reform. The major reforms of the Sánchez de Lozada administration were the work of technical teams that, often in meetings with the president, focused minutely on the laws and called in groups to consult but did not encourage public discussion or debate. Indeed, throughout much of this presidency, the COB was in fierce opposition, calling strikes and demonstrations against measures such as the capitalization plan and the education reform. For the rest of the population, though, "Because the concept of municipalization was so new, people kind of sat back and said, well, let's see what kind of an animal gets passed and then they said let's see if it gets implemented. There was a certain amount of inertia in the opposition to the Popular Participation law" (interview, February 27, 1997, La Paz).

110. In contrast, the Administrative Decentralization Law of 1995 was more clearly designed with MNR electoral objectives in mind. It reaffirmed presidential appointment of prefects, instituted cabinets of centrally appointed ministers at the departmental level, and expanded the range of public-employment opportunities in deconcentrated bureaucracies. In recognition of regional pressures, it instituted elected councils. MNR and MRTKL leaders were more involved in the drafting of this legislation while they were excluded from the Popular Participation design team (see Gray Molina, Pérez de Rada, and Yañez [1998:7-8]).

## Chapter Six: National-Local Politics in Bolivia

1. The early days of Popular Participation, including the problems that had to be sorted out, are discussed in Urioste and Baldomar (1996) and Fuchschneider (1996). For a later analysis of the strengths and weakness of the Popular Participation and Administrative Decentralization laws, see Galindo Soza (1998).

2. PRONAGOB (1996:157).

3. An interministerial commission on boundaries was given responsibility for creating the new municipalities. Although conflicts arose over setting boundary lines, all were resolved or referred to the congress for settlement (personal correspondence, September 2, 1998).

4. Ministerio de Desarrollo Humano (1997:50, 52–53). This percentage remained nearly constant over the next two years.

5. Ministerio de Desarrollo Humano (1996:9–10). At the same time, the percentage of women councilors dropped from 231 elected in 1993 to 135 in 1995.

6. Secretaría Nacional de Participación Popular, "Registro de Personería Jurídica de Comunidades Urbanas y Rurales," www.snpp.gov.bo.

7. Gray Molina (1996:3).

8. In the capital cities of the departments, Popular Participation funds accounted for 29 percent of investments; in the rest of the country, they accounted for 64 percent of investments. Thus, rural municipalities were much more dependent on Popular Participation than those that were primarily urban. The decentralization law of 1995, which transferred operations of many ministries to the departmental level, rapidly increased the proportional weight of investment at that level. It more than tripled between 1995 and 1997.

9. See especially Ardaya Salinas (n.d.:87–95).

10. Ministerio de Desarrollo Humano (1997:23).

11. The population-based formula created a series of problems because 1992 census data was inaccurate and municipalities contested the numbers.

12. UNDP (1998:93, 174), citing 1992 census data.

13. Private correspondence, June 25, 1998.

14. Gray Molina (1996:5).

15. Gray Molina (1996:6).

16. Gray Molina and Molina (1997:11).

17. Gray Molina (1996:14).

18. UNDP (1998:125).

19. Booth et al. (1997).

20. Gray Molina and Molina (1997:6).

21. Campero Nuñez del Prado and Pérez de Rada (1997:44).

22. See, for example, Booth et al. (1997).

23. Gray Molina and Molina (1997:11)

24. Booth et al. (1997:31–32).

25. Rojas (1998).

26. Gray Molina and Molina (1997:19). The authors found the vigilance committees to be particularly effective when they were acting as countervailing powers to traditional political elites in the municipality.

27. The constitution of 1967 extended the franchise to all citizens 21 years of age or older and to those between 18 and 21 years who were married.

28. In 1987, 1989, 1991, and 1993 there were also municipal elections, but they were limited to areas of the country in which municipalities existed. In the 1993 municipal elections, 53.3 percent of those registered voted, or 1.2 million people (Ministerio de Desarrollo Humano 1996:7). The country's legacy of exclusionary politics is important in assessing voting behavior. In 1996, the Bolivian government estimated that about 29 percent of eligible voters were not registered. Given geography and history, most of these unregistered people are likely to be found in rural areas, to be from indigenous groups, and to be women (see Booth et al. 1997: 36).

29. See, for example, UNDP (1998:128).

30. In the MNR, for example, Gonzalo Sánchez de Lozada and his followers headed the more progressive and internationalist wing; the traditional party militants continued to follow the leadership of Guillermo Bedregal, its president during the Sánchez de Lozada presidency. Certainly, the reforms of that administration tested the internal coherence of the MNR, calling on the party to back such neoliberal reforms as privatization of state-owned industries and restructuring the relationship between the state and the private sector.

31. UNDP (1998:124).

32. See Ardaya Salinas (1996:38–39).

33. After its local candidates were claimed to be "on loan" to the party by the press, the MBL claimed to be leading a new civic-community movement in which parties represent organizations of civil society rather than selecting their candidates from among party militants (see Ministerio de Desarrollo Humano [1996:13–14] and Rivera Santiváñez [1996]).

34. The 1995 elections are compared with those of the presidential election of 1993 because both were national elections. The 1993 municipal elections excluded much of the population because they were held only in the municipalities that exited at that time.

35. Interview, La Paz, February 26, 1997.

36. Data from Calla Ortega and Calla Ortega (1996:25).

37. In the first agreement, the MNR-MRTKL electoral coalition signed a pact (Pacto por la Gobernabilidad) with UCS in July 1993. Very soon afterward, a separate agreement was signed between MNR-MRTKL and the MBL (Pacto por el Cambio).

38. Details of the local negotiations are found in Calla Ortega and Calla Ortega (1996:32–113); see also Berthin Siles (1996).

39. One example is the mobilization of coca growers in the Chapare region, whose peasant-union movement "adopted" a small party, Izquierda Unida (IU), in the elections and won seven mayorships in that region, along with four others that resulted from post-election political pacts. This left the "party" in control of a quarter of the municipalities in the department (Ministerio de Desarrollo Humano [1996:14–15], and Booth et al. [1997:52–53])

40. Booth et al. (1997:53).

41. Booth et al. (1997:54), citing a survey by the Secretaría Nacional de Participación Popular.

42. Ardaya Salinas (n.d.:137), Berthin Siles (1997).

43. Interview March 7, 1997, La Paz.

44. Booth et al. (1997:52).

45. Ardaya Salinas (1996:39). In 1999, the impetus to reform the party was strengthened through the introduction of party primaries.

46. Interview, March 7, 1997, La Paz.

47. Ministerio de Desarrollo Humano (1996:14).

48. See the New York Times, June 13, 1998, A4, for a portrait of Evo Morales, leader of the cocalero movement.

49. The UNDP (1998:124) referred to this scenario as the local-level "reproduction of the patrimonialist state."

50. Interview, February 26, 1997, La Paz.

51. Interview, February 25, 1997, La Paz.

52. In an interview, the leader of the MNR argued that "this is a historical moment in which people's attitudes have changed. You see people who have been beat down for five hundred years

now looking you in the eye with pride. It is a wonderful thing. But the party hasn't figured it out yet" (March 7, 1997, La Paz).

53. See *Latin American Weekly Report,* December 2, 1997.

54. See Ministerio de la Presidencia et al. (1998).

### Chapter Seven: Pacting Institutional Change in Argentina

1. In Argentina, *intendente* (intendent or superintendent) is more commonly used than the term mayor (*alcalde*). Similarly, the city council is frequently referred to as the city legislature. In this book, I have used the terms *mayor* and *city council* to avoid any confusion about the roles or duties of the chief executive and legislature of the city. The constitutional change gave Buenos Aires "special status" with powers similar to those of a province but with restrictions to safeguard the interests of the national government.

2. The city had had an elective "deliberative council" prior to the constitutional change.

3. These reforms are described in Rosatti et al. (1994), Ministerio del Interior (1996), and García Lema (1994). See also De Riz (1996).

4. As an example, the electoral college overrepresented peripheral provinces with low populations; abolishing it shifted the weight of regions of the country in national elections. The addition of a third senator was to be from a minority party, thus undercutting the historical dominance of the Peronist Party in the senate (see Gibson and Calvo [n.d.b]).

5. This constitution is often referred to as the constitution of 1853–60, recognizing revisions that occurred between these two dates. In fact, the constitution was significantly revised on several occasions. It was the constitution under which Argentina had returned to democratic government in 1983 and was accepted by most in Argentina as the most democratic of its many constitutions, as well as its most legitimate. It was also widely recognized to be deficient as an instrument to structure government and state-civil society relations.

6. For an analysis from this perspective, see Acuña (1995); see also De Riz (1996:153).

7. Throughout his two terms of office, Menem frequently sought to alter laws to meet his own political convenience. Public opinion was frequently critical of his political maneuvering with the constitution and other "rules of the game" of Argentine politics. See McGuire (997:253–60) for a discussion of some such initiatives.

8. The process leading up to the Pacto and its signing are detailed in García Lema (1994).

9. García Lema (1994:131).

10. The year 1810 is generally adopted by Argentines as the date of its independence, even though the official declaration of independence did not come until 1816.

11. In 1820, an effort to establish a monarchy sparked a revolution, the only outcome of which was increased autonomy for provincial *caudillos* and more internecine fighting among them.

12. Quadri (1986:42–46); Whitaker (1964:22). The total population of the country in 1820 is estimated at about 700,000, with 55,000 people settled in Buenos Aires (Béliz 1996:33).

13. Whitaker (1964:37).

14. See Quadri (1986:43–47).

15. Whitaker (1964:28–29). Rosas was elected governor of the province of Buenos Aires in 1829 and reelected in 1835.

16. Customs from the city were the largest source of revenue in the country.

17. Scobie (1971:104).

18. Quadri (1986:83).

19. Between 1821 and 1932, Argentina received 6,405,000 immigrants, far more than any other country in Latin America and second only to the United States during that period (Whitaker [1964:53-54]).

20. See Béliz (1996).

21. In 1914, 49 percent of the population of the city of Buenos Aires was foreign born.

22. Béliz (1996:59).

23. Porto (1996:167).

24. Confederación General Económica (1993:40, 52); Béliz (1996). Most of the workers were in the education and health sectors.

25. On Alfonsín's years in office, see Epstein (1992a).

26. On Menem's political career and relationship with Peronism, see McGuire (1997:207-217).

27. On the relationship between Menem and the Peronist Party in the neoliberal reforms of the early 1990s, see Corrales (1996), Palermo and Novaro (1996), McGuire (1997:ch. 7), and Smith (1991).

28. In 1892, the Civic Union split, with the larger faction adopting the name Unión Cívica Radical.

29. This compares with some 9 percent who voted in 1910 (Whitaker [1964:49]).

30. See Whitaker (1964:ch. 4).

31. See Epstein (1992b:15) and Corrales (1996).

32. See especially McGuire (1997).

33. The party was established by Peron as the Partido Unico de la Revolución, renamed the Peronist Party in 1947. In 1959, the Partido Justicialista was formed but without legal recognition by the government, and it vied with a number of other Peronist and neo-Peronist parties for the mantle of the movement's leadership.

34. See Gibson and Calvo (n.d.a).

35. See McGuire (1997).

36. McGuire (1997) argues that the Peronist Party is best understood as a movement rather than as a party. Movements have overarching commitments to a few specific goals that bring together people who may diverge significantly on other dimensions. Movements also rely on minimal levels of institutionalization. Because movements tend to shy away from institutionalized procedures and rules for organizational management, they tend to emphasize the role of the leader within the organization.

37. In electoral campaigns in the 1980s and 1990s, the party could probably count upon 25-30 percent of the electorate as its committed base of support, which puts it far ahead of other parties. The Radicals, for example, could probably count on a 15-20 percent base of support, regardless of election issues or candidates. With the exception of 1983 and the two elections when the Peronist Party was proscribed (1958, 1963), the "iron law" held firm: if elections are fair, Peronists will win (see Corrales [1996:12]).

38. See Cavarozzi and Grossi (1992:187-94).

39. The pact of 1993 was preceded by a pact made in 1972 between the parties as a platform for the reintroduction of democratic government, but pactmaking between the two parties is rarer than their tendency to define themselves in opposition to each other.

40. FREPASO included the Frente Grande parties, the Unidad Socialista and Democracia Cristiana Parties, and elements of the Partido Intransigente and UCR (see McGuire [1997:250]).

41. Nino (1996:165).

42. Nino (1996:165).

43. In the federal capital, the president had the power to suspend the city council, which President Menem exercised in 1989.

44. Nino (1996:166–67).

45. Confederación General Económica (1993:40, 52).

46. Cavarozzi and Grossi (1992:180–85).

47. Prior presidents had used the decree power about thirty times; in his first four years in office, Menem used it more than three hundred times (McGuire 1997:255–26).

48. On Menem as a public figure, see McGuire (1997).

49. Although Alfonsín's interest in constitutional reform while he was president was linked to his own reelection ambitions, he argued in an interview that his own tenure was plagued by the responsibilities that created bottlenecks in his office: "When I was president, I had far too many functions. I suffered from hyperpresidentialism." Nevertheless, his party was deeply split over the signing of the pact because it made a Menem reelection bid possible. Accordingly, he argued, "In terms of the pact, I have no regrets. I would do exactly the same again. I have no regrets even though the pact cost me and Radicalism a lot. There was real division in the party" (interview, March 11, 1998, Buenos Aires).

50. García Lema (1994) links the constitutional reforms of 1994 to discussions initiated in 1974 under the second Perón era.

51. Alfonsín (1987:107–9).

52. See Alfonsín (1996b:13–14); see also Alfonsín (1994).

53. Decree 2446/85.

54. Perón's initiative was the result of a series of discussions with the leader of the Radical Party, Ricardo Balbín, foreshadowing the negotiations between Menem and Alfonsín almost twenty years later.

55. Alfonsín (1987:108).

56. Cavarozzi and Grossi (1992:183). During the same period, a number of provincial constitutions had been revised to allow for the reelection of governors.

57. See García Lema (1994:40).

58. García Lema (1994:43).

59. García Lema (1994:44–45).

60. García Lema (1994:48, and documents reproduced on pp. 305–8).

61. See García Lema (1994:45–46).

62. Cavarozzi and Grossi (1992:185–87).

63. Documents reproduced in García Lema (1994:308–310).

64. Documents reproduced in García Lema (1994:311–14).

65. Public-opinion polls carried out in urban areas of the country indicated that Alfonsín had a positive rating of 82 percent early in his administration; by early 1989, it had dropped to 38 percent. The approval rating for the government had dropped to 12 percent by that time. Even at the end of his administration, however, he continued to be widely respected for his commitment to human rights and democratic processes; criticism focused on his management of the economy (see Catterberg [1991:91, 93]).

66. García Lema (1994:152–54); see also the September 20, 1988, statement in García Lema (1994:314–16). The Peronists were also concerned to assure provincial governments—the great majority of which the party controlled—that they would retain many of their traditional powers.

67. Documents reproduced in García Lema (1994:314–30).

68. Documents reproduced in García Lema (1994:331–34).

69. In 1988, there were 541 strikes, and 3 general strikes were declared. In the first six months of 1989, 580 strikes were called (see Epstein [1992c:135–36])

70. For this history, see McGuire (1997:208–13).

71. Buenos Aires was torn by riots and looting that continued throughout May and June of 1989 (see Cavarozzi and Grossi [1992:196–97]).

72. See McGuire (1997:218–26), Palermo and Novaro (1996:ch. 3), De Riz (1996), Gerchunoff and Torre (1996), Corrales (1996), and Murillo (1997).

73. Gerchunoff and Torre (1996:736).

74. Document reproduced in García Lema (1994:334–35).

75. Cavallo was appointed minister of the economy in January 1991, after three other ministers had come and gone in the preceding eighteen months.

76. García Lema (1994:79–80).

77. García Lema (1994:80–82).

78. See Corrales (1996:18–21).

79. García Lema (1994:85–86). Public skepticism about President Menem's support of the constitutional reform were deepened in August 1993, when Béliz resigned as minister of the interior, citing activities of the government and the Peronist Party to buy support for the constitutional reform (see McGuire [1997:259–60]).

80. See Alfonsín (1996b:14–16).

81. The Radicals did score some victories in traditional Peronist territory, however (see De Riz [1996:152]).

82. García Lema (1994:119).

83. García Lema (1994:120).

84. Interview, March 5, 1998, Buenos Aires.

85. García Lema (1994:121).

86. The centrality of the nucleus of basic agreements to the work of the constitutional convention is well documented in Rosatti et al. (1994).

87. This law reiterated the nucleus of basic agreements from the pact

88. Interview, March 10, 1998, Buenos Aires.

89. See Acuña (1995).

90. See Pupik (1997)

## Chapter Eight: Constitutional Change in Argentine Practice

1. In 1997 and 1998, Menem began a campaign to seek authorization to run for a third presidential term, a move that increased public skepticism of his political motives in the constitutional reform. In mid-1998, his political supporters were involved in an initiative to have the constitution declared unconstitutional by the Menem-packed supreme court, thus permitting him to run for a third term. This issue split the Peronist Party seriously. Public opinion was also

split over the issue but became more critical of Menem as almost continuous scandal surrounded his presidency. By July 1998, with approval ratings down to 17 percent, he announced that he would not run for a third term (see *Latin American Weekly Report,* July 28, 1998).

2. The alliance of FREPASO, the Frente Grande, the Socialist Unity Party, the Christian Democrats, and the Social Integration Party was primarily an alliance against Menem. Bordón had been a Peronist and senator from the Province of Mendoza (see De Riz [1998:142–45]).

3. See De Riz (1998) for an analysis of the 1995 elections.

4. See, for example, McGuire (1997:ch. 8).

5. Carballo de Cilley (1997: 195).

6. Carballo de Cilley (1997: 202, 203, 216). This Gallup survey was carried out among 1,037 respondents in urban areas of the country.

7. In mid-1998, for example, opinion polls indicated that only about 10 percent of Argentines had any confidence in the supreme court, a result of Menem's 1991 "stacking" of justices and his subsequent use of the court for political purposes (see *Latin American Weekly Report,* June 9, 1998:254). On a series of scandals and corruption charges that pointed to the president's office, his cabinet, the supreme court, and the legislature, see McGuire (1997:257–60).

8. Interview, Buenos Aires, March 26, 1997.

9. Interview, Buenos Aires, March 25, 1997.

10. Interview, Buenos Aires, March 25, 1997.

11. The province of Buenos Aires had a population of 12.6 million people in 1991, or 39 percent of the total for the country. Thus, the capital district and the province surrounding it accounted for almost 50 percent of the population of the country. The metropolitan area of Greater Buenos Aires had a population of 7.9 million in 1991.

12. Confederación General Económica 1993:18.

13. Calvert (1998:4). The Peronist win in the capital in 1993 was the first since the reintroduction of democracy in 1983.

14. De Riz (1998:135–137).

15. In fact, however, disagreement over FREPASO's approach to the mayoral election led to a split within this new coalition in early 1996.

16. De la Rúa was an important figure in the Radical Party. In the party primary prior to the 1983 elections, he ran against Alfonsín to be the presidential candidate.

17. Interview, Buenos Aires, March 25, 1997.

18. See *La Nación,* July 4, 1996.

19. Interview, Buenos Aires, March 25, 1997.

20. See *Latin American Regional Report, Southern Cone and Brazil,* June 24, 1997.

21. The governor, Eduardo Duhalde, argued that he was the "natural" successor to Menem and became increasingly critical of the president for his efforts to run for a third term. He became the head of the party in late 1997.

22. For a variety of proposals to increase the quality of life in Buenos Aires, see Béliz (1996). The author, who had been minister of the interior until resigning in protest over possible corruption in the process of the constitutional reform, ran for mayor in the 1996 elections, as a candidate of the Nueva Dirigencia (ND, New Leadership) party.

23. On the governor's relationship to the police, see *Latin American Regional Report, Southern Cone and Brazil,* June 24, 1997, and *Latin American Weekly Report,* January 6, 1998.

24. The new code prohibited detention without trial and required suspects to be brought immediately to court (see *Buenos Aires Herald,* March 11, 1998).

25. *Latin American Weekly Report*, July 28, 1998.

26. *Latin American Weekly Report*, June 8, 1998.

27. See especially Calvert (1998).

28. *La Nación*, June 30, 1996.

29. *La Nación*, July 1, 1996. This newspaper reported the appearance of "de la Rúa 99" signs the evening of the election.

30. *La Nación*, June 30, 1996, and July 1, 1996.

31. FREPASO's electoral strategy became a model for other new parties to emulate, such as Frente para la Justicia, the party formed by former economy minister Domingo Cavallo and former interior minister Gustavo Béliz, in mid-1997 (interview, Buenos Aires, March 5, 1998).

32. *La Nación*, July 1, 1996. On July 4, the same newspaper referred to the Peronist showing in the election as "a disaster."

33. See *La Nación*, July 1, 1996, October 14, 1997, and October 28, 1997.

34. See, for example, *Clarín*, October 27, 1997, and *La Nación*, October 31, 1997.

35. Interview, Buenos Aires, March 6, 1998.

36. On the shaping of the *Alianza* and its troubled history, see *Latin American Weekly Report*, August 5, 1997, and June 9, 1998.

37. By mid-1998, these ambitions were strong enough that the leaders of FREPASO were publicly charging the mayor of Buenos Aires with involvement in corrupt activities (see *Latin American Weekly Report*, June 9, 1998).

38. See, for example, *La Nación*, June 30, 1996.

39. *La Nación*, June 9, 1996. A debate among candidates in mid-June centered on the municipal fiscal deficit (see *La Nación*, June 14, 1996).

40. See, for example, *La Nación*, June 14, 1996, and June 15, 1996.

41. Interview, Buenos Aires, March 5, 1998.

42. *Latin American Weekly Report*, December 1, 1998.

43. Interview, Buenos Aires, March 26, 1997.

44. Interview, Buenos Aires, March 26, 1997.

45. See *Latin American Weekly Report*, December 8, 1998, and March 2, March 9, March 16, and March 23, 1999.

## Chapter Nine. Democratizing Reforms

1. This is consistent with most of the case-study findings about the politics of economic reform; for a review, see Geddes (1995b).

2. Again, this does not mean that there were no group interests at stake but that empirically, it is not possible in the cases to demonstrate a link between what politicians did and specific and observable pressures upon them to behave in certain ways. This is a critical link that must be made in empirical research. In fact, analysts frequently reason backward from results in the sense of arguing that if particular interests benefited from change, these interests must have promoted it or somehow caused politicians to adopt their favored positions. My book suggests that such reasoning can be fallacious.

3. This is consistent with evidence from case studies about economic reforms; see, in particular, Waterbury (1992), and Grindle (1996:ch. 5).

4. Thus, solutions to problems do not always emerge as responses to issues getting on politicians' agendas but may exist prior to their emergence on such agendas. Kingdon (1995:ch.

6), in exploring the policy process in the United States, considers how ideas may float in a "primeval soup" within a policy community before they are taken up as solutions. In the case of the United States, the policy community tends to be rooted in the executive branch of government; in the Latin American cases reviewed here, those concerned about particular issues tended to be located outside of the executive branch and often outside of government. Moreover, while there were people concerned with particular problems of governance, it is difficult to consider them a policy community in the sense of a group of people who interacted on a fairly regular basis around discussions of the particular issues. In the three cases, the "community" was created when political leaders put together commissions or think tanks around the problems.

5. In the case of the literature on institutional design that raises issues of principal-agent asymmetries, path dependence is not problematic because new institutions are viewed as artifacts resulting from rational problem-solving activities. Institutional design is an engineering problem, not a result of historical evolution.

6. It may be even clearer in politics than in economics that transaction costs are not a generalized condition with universal implications. Organization theorists certainly understand that whether principal-agent issues are problematic depends on where one sits in the accountability chain; institutional inefficiencies create winners and losers, as do institutional changes. Given that transaction costs and principal-agent issues are not universally or equally distributed, the cases again suggest that the idea of ongoing conflict is helpful in understanding the consequences of institutional change.

7. Rational choice theorists see context as an arena in which individuals and groups make strategic decisions about how to achieve their preferences. Comparative institutionalists see context as a complex historical milieu in which goals and actions are shaped by experiences specific to particular contexts.

# Bibliography

Aberbach, Joel D., and Bert A. Rockman. 1992. "Does Governance Matter—And If So, How? Process, Performance, and Outcomes." *Governance: An International Journal of Policy and Administration* 5, no. 2 (April): 135–53.

Acuña, Carlos H. 1995. "Algunas notas sobre los juegos, las gallinas y la lógica política de los pactos constitucionales (Reflexiones a partir del pacto constitucional en la Argentina)." In Carlos Acuña, ed., *La nueva matriz política Argentina*. Buenos Aires: Nueva Visión.

Agüero, Felipe, and Jeffrey Stark. 1998. *Fault Lines of Democracy in Post-Transition Latin America*. Miami: North South Center Press.

Albánez Barnola, Teresa. 1994. "Towards a Social Agenda." In Colin Bradford, Jr., ed., *Redefining the State in Latin America*. Paris: Organization for Economic Cooperation and Development.

Alfonsín, Raúl. 1996a. *Democracia y consenso: A propósito de la reforma constitucional*. Buenos Aires: Fuali.

———. 1996b. "Conferencia inaugural sobre la reforma de la Constitución Nacional." In Ministerio del Interior, *La constitución reformada: Primer seminario sobre la reforma de 1994*. Buenos Aires: Ministerio del Interior.

———. 1994. *La reforma constitucional de 1994*. Buenos Aires: Tiempo.

———. 1987. *El poder de la democracia*. Buenos Aires: Fundación Plural.

Alston, Lee J., Trainn Eggertsson, and Douglass C. North, eds. 1996. *Empirical Studies in Institutional Change*. Cambridge: Cambridge University Press.

Altshuler, Alan A., and Marc D. Zegans. 1997. "Innovation and Public Management: Notes from the State House and City Hall." In Alan A. Altshuler and Robert D. Behn, eds., *Innovation in American Government: Challenges, Opportunities, and Dilemmas* Washington, D.C.: Brookings Institution Press.

Alvarez, Angel E. 1998. "Venezuelan Local and National Elections, 1958–1995." In Henry A. Dietz and Gil Shidlo, eds., *Urban Elections in Democratic Latin America*. Wilmington, Del.: Scholarly Resources.

Ames, Barry. 1987. *Political Survival: Politicians and Public Policy in Latin America*. Berkeley: University of California Press.

Arauco, Isabel, and Ana María Belmont. 1997. "El Movimiento Bolivia Libre: La gobernabilidad y la democracia en Bolivia." In CIDES-PNUD, *Gobernabilidad y partidos políticos*. La Paz: CIDES-PNUD.

Ardaya Salinas, Rubén. n.d. (1995?). *La construcción municipal de Bolivia.* La Paz: Strategies for International Development.

———. 1996. "Elecciones municipales y la Participación Popular." *Opiniones y Análisis* (La Paz). (February).

Aslund, Anders. 1994. "The Case for Radical Reform," *Journal of Democracy* 5, no. 4 (October).

Ayo Saucedo, Diego. 1998. "Los partidos políticos en la coyuntura de la descentralización." *Opiniones y Análisis* (La Paz). (January).

Banco Central de Venezuela. 1995. *Series estadísticas de Venezuela de los útimos cincuenta años.* Vol. 1. Caracas.

———. 1985, 1988. *Anuario de estadísticas, precios y mercado laboral.* Caracas.

Banks, Jeffrey S., and Eric A. Hanushek, eds. 1995. *Modern Political Economy: Old Topics, New Directions.* Cambridge: Cambridge University Press.

Barbery Anaya, Roberto. 1996. "Una revolución en democracia." In Ministerio de Desarrollo Humano, Secretaría Nacional de Participación Popular/UNDP, *Apre(he)ndiendo la Participación Popular: Análisis y reflexiones sobre el modelo boliviano de descentralización.* La Paz: Ministerio de Desarrollo Humano/UNDP.

Bardhan, Pranab. 1989. "The New Institutional Economics and Development Theory: A Brief Critical Assessment." *World Development* 17, no. 9.

Barrios R., Armando. 1997. "Las finanzas públicas de los estados en Venezuela." In Rafael de la Cruz, ed., *Federalismo fiscal y descentralización: Una nueva relación entre la sociedad y el estado.* Caracas: Instituto de Estudios Superiores de Administración.

Bates, Robert. 1981. *Markets and States in Tropical Africa.* Berkeley: University of California Press.

Bates, Robert, and Anne O. Krueger, eds. 1993. *Political and Economic Interactions in Economic Policy Reform.* Cambridge, Mass.: Blackwell Publishers.

Bates, Robert H., and Barry R. Weingast. 1995. "A New Comparative Politics: Integrating Rational Choice and Interpretivist Perspectives." Working Paper No. 95-3, Center for International Affairs, Harvard University (April).

Béliz, Gustavo. 1996. *Buenos Aires vale la pena: Propuesta para la ciudad que viene.* Buenos Aires: Planeta.

Berthin Siles, Gerardo. 1996. "El proceso electoral municipal en Bolivia: El caso de la democracia negociada?" *Opiniones y Análisis* (La Paz). (February).

Blanco, Carlos. 1993. "The Reform of the State in Latin American Perspective." In Joseph S. Tulchin, ed., with Gary Bland, *Venezuela in the Wake of Radical Reform.* Boulder, Colo.: Lynne Rienner.

Bland, Gary. 1998. "Building Political Will: The Decision to Decentralize in Chile and Venezuela." Paper presented at the meeting of the Latin American Studies Association, Chicago, September 23–26.

———. 1996. "Introduction" and "Notes from Further Discussion at the Seminar." Prepared as summaries for the conference report "Back to the Ballot Box: Evaluating Venezuela's 1995 State and Local Elections." Working Paper No. 218, Woodrow Wilson International Center for Scholars, Latin America Program, Washington, D.C. April.

Blank, David Eugene. 1973. *Politics in Venezuela*. Boston: Little, Brown.

Booth, David, et al. 1997. "Popular Participation: Democratizing the State in Rural Bolivia." Report to SIDA, Development Studies Unit, Department of Social Anthropology, Stockholm University.

Borner, Silvio, Aymo Brunetti, and Beatrice Weder. 1995. *Political Credibility and Economic Development*. New York: St. Martin's Press.

Bratton, Michael. 1994. "Peasant-State Relations in Postcolonial Africa: Patterns of Engagement and Disengagement." In Joel Migdal, Atul Kohli, and Vivienne Shue, eds., *State Power and Social Forces: Domination and Transformation in the Third World*. Cambridge: Cambridge University Press.

Brewer-Carías, Allan R. 1994a. *Informe sobre la descentralización en Venezuela, 1993*. Caracas: Editorial Arte.

———. 1994b. "Bases legislativas para la descentralización política de la federación centralizada." In Allan R. Brewer-Carías, Carlos Ayala Corao, Jorge Sánchez Melean, Gustavo J. Linare Benzo, and Humberto Romero Muci, *Leyes para la descentralizacion política de la federación*. Caracas: Editorial Jurídica Venezolana.

*Buenos Aires Herald*. March 1998.

Calla Ortega, Ricardo, and Hernando Calla Ortega. 1996. *Partidos políticos y municipios: Las elecciones municipales de 1995*. La Paz: Friedrich Ebert Stiftung/ILDIS.

Calvert, Peter A. 1998. "Urban Electoral Politics in Argentina." In Henry A. Dietz and Gil Shidlo, eds., *Urban Elections in Democratic Latin America*, Wilmington, Del.: Scholarly Resources.

Calvert, Randall L. 1995. "The Rational Choice Theory of Social Institutions, Cooperation, Coordination, and Communication." In Jeffrey S. Banks and Eric A. Hanushek, eds., *Modern Political Economy: Old Topics, New Directions*. Cambridge: Cambridge University Press.

Campbell, Tim. 1997. "Innovations and Risk Taking: The Engine of Reform in Local Government in Latin America and the Caribbean." World Bank Discussion Paper No. 357. Washington, D.C.: World Bank.

Campero Núñez del Prado, José Carlos, and Francisco Ernesto Pérez de Rada. 1997. "Equidad en la planificación de la inversión en municipios rurales de La Paz." Unpublished manuscript, Catholic University of Bolivia, La Paz (December).

Caporaso, James A., and David P. Levine. 1992. *Theories of Political Economy*. Cambridge: Cambridge University Press.

Carballo de Cilley, Marita. 1997. "La voz de la gente." In Gustavo Béliz, ed., *No Robarás: ¿Es posible ganarle a la corrupción?* Buenos Aires: Editorial de Belgrano.

Cariaga, Juan I. 1996. *Estabilización y desarrollo*. La Paz: Los Amigos del Libro.

Catterberg, Edgardo. 1991. *Argentina Confronts Politics: Political Culture and Public Opinion in the Argentine Transition to Democracy*. Boulder, Colo.: Lynn Rienner.

Cavarozzi, Marcelo, and María Grossi. 1992. "Argentine Parties under Alfonsín: From Democratic Reinvention to Political Decline and Hyperinflation." In Edward C. Epstein, ed., *The New Argentine Democracy: The Search for a Successful Formula.* Westport, Conn.: Praeger.

Cavarozzi, Marcelo, and Oscar Landi. 1992. "Political Parties under Alfonsín and Menem: The Effects of State Shrinking and the Devaluation of Democratic Politics." In Edward C. Epstein, ed., *The New Argentine Democracy: The Search for a Successful Formula.* Westport, Conn.: Praeger.

CIDES-PNUD. 1997. *Gobernabilidad y partidos políticos.* La Paz, Bolivia: CIDES-PNUD.

Conaghan, Catherine M., and James M. Malloy. 1994. *Unsettling Statecraft: Democracy and Neoliberalism in the Central Andes.* Pittsburgh: Pittsburgh University Press.

Conaghan, Catherine M., James M. Malloy, and Luis A. Abugattás. 1990. "Business and the 'Boys': The Politics of Neoliberalism in the Central Andes." *Latin American Research Review* 25, no. 2.

Confederación General Económica. 1993. *Libro Azul de las Provincias.* Buenos Aires: Confederación General Económica.

Consejo Supremo Electoral. n.d. "Elecciones 1995 Perfil." Mimeo. Caracas: Consejo Supremo Electoral.

Consultores 21. 1989–96. *Public Opinion on Current Politics.* Unpublished data. Caracas: Consultores 21.

Contreras, Manuel E. n.d. (1997?). "Bolivia in the First Four Decades of the 20th Century: The Mining and Railway Industries and Education." Unpublished paper, Harvard Institute for International Development, La Paz, and the Catholic University of Bolivia.

Coppedge, Michael. 1996. "Venezuela: The Rise and Fall of Partyarchy." In Jorge I. Domínguez and Abraham F. Lowenthal, eds., *Constructing Democratic Governance: South America in the 1990s.* Baltimore: The Johns Hopkins University Press.

————. 1994a. "Venezuela: Democratic despite Presidentialism." In Juan J. Linz and Arturo Valenzuela, eds., *The Failure of Presidential Democracy.* Baltimore: The Johns Hopkins University Press.

————. 1994b. *Strong Parties and Lame Ducks: Presidential Partyarchy and Factionalism in Venezuela.* Stanford: Stanford University Press.

————. 1992. "Venezuela's Vulnerable Democracy." *Journal of Democracy* 3, no. 4:32–44.

Cordiplan. 1996. "Situación actual del proceso de transferencia de competencias en Venezuela." Caracas: Dirección de Descentralización, Cordiplan (February 2).

Corrales, Javier. 1996. "State-Ruling Party Relations in Argentina and Venezuela, 1989–1993: Neoliberalism through Party Building." Paper prepared for the conference "Economic Reform and Civil Society in Latin America," Harvard University, April 12.

Corte Nacional Electoral. 1997. *Estadísticas electorales, 1985–1995*. La Paz: Corte Nacional Electoral.

Crisp, Brian. 1998. "Lessons from Economic Reform in the Venezuelan Democracy." *Latin American Research Review* 33, no. 1:7–41.

———. 1994. "Limitations to Democracy in Developing Capitalist Societies: The Case of Venezuela." *World Politics* 22, no. 10:1491–1509.

De la Cruz, Rafael. n.d. "Razones para votar: Un balance de la descentralización." *Debates IESA: ¿Para que votar?* Caracas: IESA.

———. 1995. "Decentralization and Democratic Governance in Venezuela." Paper prepared for the seminar "Is Small Always Better? Political Decentralization and Democracy in Latin America," Woodrow Wilson Center, Latin America Program, Washington, D.C., June 7.

———. 1988. *Venezuela en busca de un nuevo pacto social*. Caracas: Alfadil Ediciones.

De la Cruz, Rafael, ed. 1997. *Federalismo fiscal y descentralización: Una nueva relación entre la sociedad y el estado*. Caracas: Instituto de Estudios Superiores de Administración.

———. 1992. *Descentralización, gobernabilidad, democracia*. Caracas: Editorial Nueva Sociedad.

De la Cruz, Rafael, and Armando Barrios, eds. 1994. *El costo de la descentralización en Venezuela*. Caracas: Editorial Nueva Sociedad.

De Riz, Liliana. 1998. "From Menem to Menem: Elections and Political Parties in Argentina." In Joseph S. Tulchin with Allison M. Garland, eds., *Argentina: The Challenges of Modernization*. Wilmington, Del.: Scholarly Resources.

———. 1996. "Argentina: Democracy in Turmoil." In Jorge Domínguez and Abraham Lowenthal, eds., *Constructing Democratic Government in South America in the 1990s*. Baltimore: The Johns Hopkins University Press.

Domínguez, Jorge I., and Abraham F. Lowenthal, eds. 1996. *Constructing Democratic Governance: Latin America and the Caribbean in the 1990s*. Baltimore: The Johns Hopkins University Press.

Dos Reis Velloso, Joao Paulo. 1994. "Governance, the Transition to Modernity, and Civil Society." In Colin Bradford, Jr., ed., *Redefining the State in Latin America*. Paris: Organization for Economic Co-operation and Development.

Drazen, Allen, and Vittorio Grilli. 1993. "The Benefit of Crises for Economic Reforms." *American Economic Review* 83.

Echevarría, Oscar. 1995. *La economía venezolana, 1944–1994*. Caracas: Fedecámaras

Ellner, Steve. 1997. "Recent Venezuelan Political Studies: A Return to Third World Realities." *Latin American Research Review* 32, no. 2.

Epstein, Edward C., ed. 1992a. *The New Argentine Democracy: The Search for a Successful Formula*. Westport, Conn.: Praeger.

———. 1992b. "Democracy in Argentina." In Edward C. Epstein, ed., *The New Argentine Democracy. The Search for a Successful Formula*. Westport, Conn.: Praeger.

———. 1992c. "Labor State Conflict in the New Argentine Democracy: Parties, Union

Factions, and Power Maximizing." In Edward C. Epstein, ed., *The New Argentine Democracy: The Search for a Successful Formula.* Westport, Conn.: Praeger.

Escobari, Martin, and Erwin Landívar. 1996. "Key Problems in Implementation of Social Public Investments in Bolivia." Paper prepared for UDAPSO and Harvard Institute for International Development, November 4.

Evans, Peter. 1995a. Contribution to "The Role of Theory in Comparative Politics: A Symposium." *World Politics* 48 (October).

————. 1995b. *Embedded Autonomy: States and Industrial Transformation.* Princeton: Princeton University Press.

Ferejohn, John. 1995. "Law, Legislation, and Positive Political Theory." In Jeffrey S. Banks and Eric A. Hanushek, eds., *Modern Political Economy: Old Topics, New Directions.* Cambridge: Cambridge University Press.

Fiszbein, A. 1997. "The Emergence of Local Capacity: Lessons from Colombia." *World Development* 25, no. 7.

Fox, Jonathan. 1994. "Latin America's Emerging Local Politics." *Journal of Democracy* 5, no. 2.

Fraga, Rosendo. 1995. *Argentina en las urnas, 1916–1994.* Buenos Aires: Editorial Centro de Estudios Unión para la Nueva Mayoría.

————. 1992. *Argentina en las urnas, 1931–1991.* Buenos Aires: Editorial Centro de Estudios Unión para la Nueva Mayoría.

————. 1989. *Argentina en las urnas, 1916–1989.* Buenos Aires: Editorial Centro de Estudios Unión para la Nueva Mayoría.

Frieden, Jeffry A. 1991. *Debt, Development, and Democracy: Modern Political Economy and Latin America, 1965–1985.* Princeton: Princeton University Press.

Friedland, Jonathan. 1997. "Los alcaldes, el nuevo rostro de la política latinoamericana." *The Wall Street Journal Americas,* August 28.

Frischtak, Leila. 1994. *Governance Capacity and Economic Reform in Developing Countries.* World Bank Technical Paper No. 254. Washington, D.C.: World Bank.

*Gaceta Oficial de la República de Venezuela.* 1987–1997, various.

Galindo de Ugarte, Marcelo. 1991. *Constituciones Bolivianas Comparadas.* La Paz: Los Amigos del Libro.

Galindo Soza, Mario. 1998. "La participación popular y la descentralización administrativa." In Juan Carlos Chávez Corrales, ed., *Las reformas estructurales en Bolivia.* La Paz: Fundación Milenio.

Galindo Soza, Mario, and Fernando Medina Calabaceros. 1996. "Ley de Participación Popular: Aspectos económico-financieros." In Ministerio de Desarrollo Humano, Secretaría Nacional de Participación Popular/UNDP, *Apre(he)ndiendo la Participación Popular: Análisis y reflexiones sobre el modelo boliviano de descentralización.* La Paz: Ministerio de Desarrollo Humano/UNDP.

Gamarra, Eduardo. 1994. "Crafting Political Support for Stabilization: Political Pacts and the New Economic Policy in Bolivia." In William C. Smith, Carlos H. Acuña, and Eduardo A. Gamarra, eds., *Democracy, Markets, and Structural Reform in Latin America*. New Brunswick, N.J.: Transaction Publishers.

Garcia, Maria Pilar. 1992. "The Venezuelan Ecology Movement: Symbolic Effectiveness, Social Practices, and Political Strategies." In Arturo Escobar and Sonia E. Alvarez, eds., *The Making of Social Movements in Latin America*. Boulder, Colo.: Westview Press.

García Lema, Alberto Manuel. 1994. *La reforma por dentro: La defícil construcción del consenso constitucional*. Buenos Aires: Planeta.

Garretón, Manuel Antonio. 1994. "New State-Society Relations in Latin America." In Colin Bradford, Jr., ed., *Redefining the State in Latin America*. Paris: Organization for Economic Co-operation and Development.

Garzón, Blanca. 1997. "Características del personal empleado por los gobiernos estadales y municipales." In Rafael de la Cruz, ed., *Federalismo fiscal y descentralización: Una nueva relación entre la sociedad y el estado*. Caracas: Instituto de Estudios Superiores de Administración.

Geddes, Barbara. 1995a. "Uses and Limitations of Rational Choice." In Peter Smith, ed., *Latin America in Comparative Perspective: New Approaches to Methods and Analysis*. Boulder, Colo.: Westview Press.

———. 1995b. "The Politics of Economic Liberalization," *Latin American Research Review* 30, no. 2.

———. 1994a. *Politician's Dilemma: Building State Capacity in Latin America*. Berkeley: University of California Press.

———. 1994b. "Challenging the Conventional Wisdom." *Journal of Democracy* 5, no. 3.

Gerchunoff, Pablo, and Juan Carlos Torre. 1996. "La política de liberalización económica en la administración de Menem." *Desarrollo Económico* 36, no. 143 (October-December): 733–68.

Ghio, José María, and Sebastián Etchemendy. 1997. "The Politics of Administrative Reform in Menem's Argentina." Paper prepared for presentation at the conference "The Political Economy of Administrative Reform in Developing Countries," Brasilia, November 24–25.

Gibson, Edward L. 1997. "The Populist Road to Market Reform: Politics and Electoral Coalitions in Mexico and Argentina. *World Politics* 49 (April 1997).

Gibson, Edward L., and Ernesto Calvo. n.d.(a). "Electoral Conditions and Market Reforms: Evidence from Argentina." Unpublished paper.

———. n.d.(b). "Federalism, Public Spending, and Electoral Coalitions: Making Market Reform Politically Viable in Argentina." Unpublished paper.

Gill, Lesley. 1987. *Peasants, Entrepreneurs, and Social Change*. Boulder, Colo.: Westview Press.

Gómez Calcaño, Luis, and Margarita López Maya. 1990. *El tejido de Penélope: La reforma del estado en Venezuela, 1984–1988*. Caracas: CENDES, APUCV-IPP.

Gonzalez Cruz, Francisco. 1996. *El abc de la descentralización.* Caracas: FIDES Biblio-
teca para la Descentralizacion.

Graham, Carol, and Moisés Naím. 1998. "The Political Economy of Institutional Reform in Latin America." In Nancy Birdsall, Carol Graham, and Richard Sabot,
eds., *Beyond Trade-offs: Market Reform and Equitable Growth in Latin America.*
Washington, D.C.: Inter-American Development Bank and Brookings Institution Press.

Graham, Carol. 1994. *Safety Nets, Politics, and the Poor.* Washington, D.C.: Brookings
Institution.

Gray Molina, George. 1996. "Social Investments under Popular Participation in Bolivia: Explaining Municipal Investment Choices." Unpublished paper. Harvard
Institute for International Development and Unidad de Análisis de Políticas Sociales, La Paz, November 18.

Gray Molina, George, and Carlos Hugo Molina. 1997. "Popular Participation and Decentralization in Bolivia: Building Accountability from the Grassroots." Paper
prepared for the seminar "Assessing Bolivia's Reforms, 1993–1997." Harvard Institute for International Development, Cambridge, April 30.

Gray Molina, George, Ernesto Pérez de Rada, and Ernesto Yañez. 1998. "La economía
política de reformas institucionales en Bolivia." Unpublished paper, Fundación
Diálogo, La Paz, March.

Grebe López, Horst. 1997. "La reforma del poder ejecutivo: Diseño, aplicación y en-
señanzas primordiales." Unpublished paper, La Paz.

Green, Donald P., and Ian Shapiro. 1994. *Pathologies of Rational Choice Theory: A Critique of Applications in Political Science.* New Haven: Yale University Press.

Grindle, Merilee S. 1996. *Challenging the State: Crisis and Innovation in Latin America
and Africa.* Cambridge: Cambridge University Press.

Grindle, Merilee S., and Francisco E. Thoumi. 1993. "Muddling Toward Adjustment:
The Political Economy of Policy Change in Ecuador." In Robert Bates and Anne O.
Krueger, eds., *Political and Economic Interactions in Economic Policy Reform.* Cam-
bridge, Mass.: Blackwell Publishers.

Guerón, Carlos. 1993. "Introduction." In Joseph S. Tulchin, ed., with Gary Bland,
*Venezuela in the Wake of Radical Reform.* Boulder, Colo.: Lynne Rienner.

Haggard, Stephan. n.d. "The Reform of the State in Latin America." Unpublished
manuscript.

Haggard, Stephan, and Robert R. Kaufman. 1995. *The Political Economy of Democratic
Transitions.* Princeton: Princeton University Press.

————. 1994. "Democratic Institutions, Economic Policy and Performance in Latin
America." In Colin Bradford, Jr., ed., *Redefining the State in Latin America.* Paris:
Organization for Economic Co-operation and Development.

————, eds. 1992. *The Politics of Economic Adjustment.* Princeton: Princeton University Press.

Hall, Peter A. 1992. "The Movement from Keynesianism to Monetarism: Institutional

Analysis and British Economic Policy in the 1970s." In Sven Steinmo, Kathleen Thelen, and Frank Longstreth, eds., *Structuring Politics: Historical Institutionalism in Comparative Analysis.* Cambridge: Cambridge University Press.

Hausmann, Ricardo. 1994. "Sustaining Reform: What Role for Social Policy." In Colin Bradford, Jr., ed., *Redefining the State in Latin America.* Paris: Organization for Economic Co-operation and Development.

Healey, John, Richard Ketley, and Mark Robinson. 1993. "Will Political Reform Bring about Improved Economic Management in Sub-Saharan Africa?" In Mick Moore, ed., *Good Government.* Special Issue, *IDS Bulletin* 24, no. 1 (January): 31–38.

Hernández, Carlos Raúl. 1995. *El motín de los dinosaurios.* Caracas: Editorial Panapo.

Hillman, Richard S. 1994. *Democracy for the Privileged: Crisis and Transition in Venezuela.* Boulder, Colo.: Lynne Rienner.

Hirschman, Albert O. 1981. "Policymaking and Policy Analysis in Latin America—A Return Journey." In Albert O. Hirschman, *Essays in Trespassing: Economics to Politics and Beyond.* Cambridge: Cambridge University Press.

Horn, Murray J. 1995. *The Political Economy of Public Administration: Institutional Choice in the Public Sector.* Cambridge: Cambridge University Press.

Huber, Evelyne. 1995. "Assessments of State Strength." In Peter Smith, ed., *Latin America in Comparative Perspective: New Approaches to Methods and Analysis.* Boulder, Colo.: Westview Press.

Huntington, Samuel. 1991. *The Third Wave: Democratization in the Late Twentieth Century.* Norman: University of Oklahoma Press.

Immergut, Ellen M. 1992. "The Rules of the Game: The Logic of Health Policy-Making in France, Switzerland, and Sweden." In Sven Steinmo, Kathleen Thelen, and Frank Longstreth, eds., *Structuring Politics: Historical Institutionalism in Comparative Analysis.* Cambridge: Cambridge University Press.

Jorgensen, Steen, Margaret Grosh, and Mark Schacter. 1992. *Bolivia's Answer to Poverty, Economic Crisis, and Adjustment: The Emergency Social Fund.* Washington, D.C.: World Bank.

Karl, Terry. 1990. "Dilemmas of Democratization in Latin America." *Comparative Politics* 23, no. 1.

———. 1986. "Petroleum and Political Pacts: The Transition to Democracy in Venezuela." In Guillermo O'Donnell, Philippe C. Schmitter, and Laurence Whitehead, eds., *Transitions from Authoritarian Rule: Latin America.* Baltimore: The Johns Hopkins University Press.

Katzenstein, Peter J. 1995. Contribution to "The Role of Theory in Comparative Politics: A Symposium." *World Politics* 48 (October).

Keech, William R. 1995. *Economic Politics.* Cambridge: Cambridge University Press.

Kelly, Janet. 1996. "Comments on the Preceding Papers." In "Back to the Ballot Box: Evaluating Venezuela's 1995 State and Local Elections: A Conference Report." Working Paper No. 218, Woodrow Wilson International Center for Scholars, Latin American Program, Washington, D.C., April.

————. 1986. "Reform without Pain: The Commission on State Reform in the Lusinchi Administration." Paper prepared for the Thirteenth International Meeting of the Latin American Studies Association, Boston, October.

King, Desmond S. 1992. "The Establishment of Work-Welfare Programs in the United States and Britain: Politics, Ideas, and Institutions." In Sven Steinmo, Kathleen Thelen, and Frank Longstreth, eds., *Structuring Politics: Historical Institutionalism in Comparative Analysis.* Cambridge: Cambridge University Press.

Kingdon, John W. 1995. *Agendas, Alternatives, and Public Policies.* New York: Harper Collins College Publishers.

Klein, Herbert S. 1982. *Bolivia: The Evolution of a Multi-Ethnic Society.* New York: Oxford University Press.

Knott, Jack H., and Gary J. Miller. 1987. *Reforming Bureaucracy: The Politics of Institutional Choice.* Englewood Cliffs, N.J.: Prentice-Hall.

Kohli, Atul. 1995a. Introduction to "The Role of Theory in Comparative Politics: A Symposium." *World Politics* 48 (October).

————. 1995b. Conclusion to "The Role of Theory in Comparative Politics: A Symposium." *World Politics* 48 (October).

Kohli, Atul, and Vivienne Shue. 1994. "State Power and Social Forces: On Political Contention and Accommodation in the Third World." In Joel Migdal, Atul Kohli, and Vivienne Shue, eds., *State Power and Social Forces: Domination and Transformation in the Third World.* Cambridge: Cambridge University Press.

Kornblith, Miriam. n.d. "Elecciones 95: Nuevos actores, reglas y oportunidades." *Debates IESA: Para que votar?* Caracas: IESA.

Krasner, Stephan D. 1984. "Approaches to the State: Alternative Conceptions and Historical Dynamics." *Comparative Politics* 16, no. 2 (January): 223–46.

*La Nación* (Buenos Aires). 1996–98.

*Latin American Regional Report, Andean Group, Southern Cone.* London: Latin American Newsletters, Various, 1994–97.

*Latin American Weekly Report.* London: Latin American Newsletters, various, 1994–97.

Lattanzi Arvelo, Roxana. 1996. "La descentralizacion del estado venezolano." M.A. thesis, Universidad San Bolivar, Venezuela, October.

Leonard, David K. 1993. "Professionalism and African Administration." In Mick Moore, ed., *Good Government?* Special Issue of *IDS Bulletin* 24, no. 1 (January): 74–79.

Levine, Daniel H. 1994. "Good-bye to Venezuelan Exceptionalism." *Journal of Interamerican Studies and World Affairs* 36, no. 4 (Winter).

————. 1973. *Conflict and Political Change in Venezuela.* Princeton: Princeton University Press.

Libecap, Gary D. 1996. "Toward an Understanding of Property Rights." In Lee J. Alston, Thráinn Eggertsson, and Douglass C. North, eds., *Empirical Studies in Institutional Change.* Cambridge: Cambridge University Press.

Linz, Juan J. and Arturo Valenzuela, eds. 1994. *The Failure of Presidential Democracy*. Baltimore: The Johns Hopkins University Press.

Lipjhart, Arend, and Carlos Waisman, eds. 1996. *Institutional Design in New Democracies*. Boulder, Colo.: Westview Press.

López-Maya, Margarita. 1997. "The Rise of Causa R in Venezuela," In Douglas A. Chalmers et al., eds., *The New Politics of Inequality in Latin America: Rethinking Participation and Representation*. New York: Oxford University Press.

Malloy, James M. 1989. "Policy Analysts, Public Policy and Regime Structure in Latin America." *Governance: An International Journal of Policy and Administration* 2, no. 3 (July).

———. 1970. *Bolivia: The Uncompleted Revolution*. Pittsburgh: Pittsburgh University Press, 1970.

Manor, James. 1999. *The Political Economy of Democratic Decentralization*. Washington, D.C.: World Bank.

Markoff, John. 1996. *Waves of Democracy: Social Movements and Political Change*. Thousand Oaks, Calif.: Pine Forge Press.

Martz, John D. 1992. "Party Elites and Leadership in Colombia and Venezuela." *Journal of Latin American Studies* 24.

———. 1966. *Acción Democrática. Evolution of a Modern Political Party*. Princeton: Princeton University Press.

Mayorga, René Antonio. 1997. "Bolivia: Electoral Reform in Latin America." In Andrew Reynolds and Ben Reilly, *The International IDEA Handbook of Electoral System Design*. Stockholm: International Institute for Democracy and Electoral Assistance.

Mayorga U., J. Antonio. 1996. *Gonismo: Discurso y poder*. Cochabamba, Bolivia: UMSS.

McCoy, Jennifer, William C. Smith, Andrés Serbin, and Andrés Stambouli, eds. 1995. *Venezuelan Democracy under Stress*. Miami: North-South Center Press.

McGuire, James W. 1997. *Peronism without Perón: Unions, Parties, and Democracy in Argentina*. Stanford: Stanford University Press.

Mesa Gisbert, Carlos D. 1990. *Presidentes de Bolivia: Entre urnas y fusiles*. La Paz: Editorial Gisbert.

Migdal, Joel. 1994. "The State in Society: An Approach to Struggles for Domination." In Joel Migdal, Atul Kohli, and Vivienne Shue, eds., *State Power and Social Forces: Domination and Transformation in the Third World*. Cambridge: Cambridge University Press.

Migdal, Joel S., Atul Kohli, and Vivienne Shue, eds. 1994. *State Power and Social Forces: Domination and Transformation in the Third World*. Cambridge: Cambridge University Press.

Ministerio de Desarrollo Humano (Bolivia). 1997. *Bolivia: Participación Popular en cifras*. La Paz: Ministerio de Desarrollo Humano.

———. 1996. *Las primeras elecciones: Directorio de alcaldes y consejales de la Participación Popular*. La Paz: Ministerio de Desarrollo Humano.

Ministerio de Energía y Minas (Venezuela). 1970–91. *Petróleo y otros datos estadísticos.* Caracas: Ministerio de Energía y Minas, various years.

Ministerio del Interior (Argentina). 1996. *La Constitución Reformada.* Buenos Aires.

Ministerio de la Presidencia, Ministerio de Desarrollo Sostenible y Planificación, Viceministerio de Participación Popular y Fortalecimiento Municipal, Viceministerio de Coordinación Gubernamental (Bolivia). 1998. *Descentralización y Participación Popular: El desafío del Plan de Acción 1998–2002.* La Paz.

Moe, Terry M. 1984. "The New Economics of Organization." *American Journal of Political Science* 18, no. 4 (November): 735–77.

Molina Monasterios, Fernando. 1997. *Historia de la participación popular.* La Paz: Ministerio de Desarrollo Humano, Secretaría Nacional de Participación Popular.

Molina Saucedo, Carlos Hugo. 1994. *La decentralización imposible y la alternativa municipal.* 2nd ed. Santa Cruz de la Sierra, Bolivia: Ediciones de EL PAIS.

Montgomery, John D. 1995. "Beyond Good Policies." In John D. Montgomery and Dennis A. Rondinelli, eds., *Great Policies: Strategic Innovations in Asia and the Pacific Basin.* Westport, Conn.: Praeger.

Moore, Mick. 1993. Introduction to Mick Moore, ed., *Good Government?* Special Issue of *IDS Bulletin* 24, no. 1 (January): 1–5.

Morales, Juan Antonio. 1994. "Democracy, Economic Liberalism, and Structural Reform in Bolivia." In William C. Smith, Carlos H. Acuña, and Eduardo A. Gamarra, eds., *Democracy, Markets, and Structural Reform in Latin America.* New Brunswick, N.J.: Transaction Publishers.

Murillo, M. Victoria. 1997. "Union Politics, Market-Oriented Reforms, and the Reshaping of Argentine Corporatism." In Douglas A. Chalmers et al., eds., *The New Politics of Inequality in Latin America: Rethinking Participation and Representation.* New York: Oxford University Press.

Myers, David J. 1995. "Perceptions of a Stressed Democracy: Inevitable Decay or Foundation for Rebirth?" In Jennifer McCoy, William C. Smith, Andrés Serbin, and Andrés Stambouli, eds., *Venezuelan Democracy under Stress.* Miami: North-South Center Press.

Naím, Moisés. 1995. "Latin America's Journey to the Market: From Macroeconomic Shock to Institutional Therapy." Occasional Paper No. 62, International Center for Economic Growth. San Francisco: ICS Press, 1995.

———. 1993. *Paper Tigers and Minotaurs: The Politics of Venezuela's Economic Reforms.* Washington, D.C.: The Carnegie Endowment for International Peace.

Navarro, Juan Carlos. n.d. "El día después: Temas y variaciones sobre las consecuencias de las elecciones regionales y locales." *Debates IESA: Para que votar?* Caracas: IESA.

———. 1997. "Descentralización, gasto social, y políticas sociales en Venezuela." In Rafael de la Cruz, ed., *Federalismo fiscal y descentralización: Una nueva relación entre la sociedad y el estado.* Caracas: Instituto de Estudios Superiores de Administración.

Nelson, Joan M., ed. 1990. *Economic Crisis and Policy Choice: The Politics of Adjustment in the Third World*. Princeton: Princeton University Press.

Nelson, Joan M., and Contributors. 1994. *Intricate Links: Democratization and Market Reforms in Latin America and Eastern Europe*. New Brunswick, N.J.: Transaction Publishers.

————. 1989. *Fragile Coalitions: The Politics of Economic Adjustment*. New Brunswick, N.J.: Transaction Books.

Nickson, Andrew R. 1995. *Local Government in Latin America*. Boulder, Colo.: Lynne Rienner.

Nino, Carlos Santiago. 1996. "Hyperpresidentialism and Constitutional Reform in Argentina." In Arend Lipjhart and Carlos Waisman, eds., *Institutional Design in New Democracies*. Boulder, Colo.: Westview Press.

Nonneman, Gerd, ed. 1996. *Political and Economic Liberalization: Dynamics and Linkages in Comparative Perspective*. Boulder, Colo.: Lynn Rienner.

North, Douglass C. 1990. *Institutions, Institutional Change and Economic Performance*. Cambridge: Cambridge University Press.

North, Douglass C., and Barry R. Weingast. 1994. "Constitutions and Commitment: The Evolution of Institutions Governing Public Choice in Seventeenth-Century England." In Torsten Persson and Guido Tabellini, eds., *Monetary and Fiscal Policy*. Cambridge: MIT Press.

O'Donnell, Guillermo. 1994. "Some Reflections on Redefining the Role of the State." In Colin Bradford, Jr., ed., *Redefining the State in Latin America*. Paris: Organization for Economic Co-operation and Development.

O'Donnell, Guillermo, Philippe Schmitter, and Laurence Whitehead, eds. 1986. *Transitions from Authoritarian Rule: Latin America*. Baltimore: The Johns Hopkins University Press

Olson, Jr., Mancur. 1982. *The Rise and Decline of Nations*. New Haven: Yale University Press.

————. 1965. *The Logic of Collective Action: Public Goods and the Theory of Groups* New York: Schocken Books.

*Opiniones y Análisis* (La Paz). 1998. Special Issue, "Partidos Políticos en Bolivia."

Ovalles, Caupolicán. 1996. *Usted me debe esa cárcel: Conversaciones en La Ahumada*. Caracas. Rayuela Taller de Ediciones.

Palermo, Vicente, and Marcos Novaro. 1996. *Política y poder en el gobierno de Menem*. Buenos Aires: Grupo Editorial Norma.

Paz Zamora, Jaime. 1990. "Estrategia Nacional de Desarrollo Alternativo." In ILDIS-CEDIB, *Coca-Cronología*. La Paz: ILDIS-CEDIB.

Persson, Torsten, and Guido Tabellini, eds. 1994. *Monetary and Fiscal Policy*. Cambridge: MIT Press.

Peterson, G. E. 1994. *Decentralization Experience in Latin America: An Overview of Lessons and Issues*. Washington, D.C.: Urban Institute.

Philip, George. 1992. "Venezuelan Democracy and the Coup Attempt of February 1992," *Government and Opposition* 27, no. 4.

Pierson, Paul. 1996. "The New Politics of the Welfare State." *World Politics* 48 (January): 143–79.

Pinango, Ramon. n.d. "¿Para que votar?" *Debates IESA: ¿Para que votar?* Caracas: IESA.

PNUD (Programa de las Naciones Unidas Para el Desarrollo). 1998. *Desarrollo Humano en Bolivia 1998.* La Paz: Artes Gráficas Latina.

Popik, Sebastian. 1997. "Politicians Letting Go? Institutional Change and Democratizing Reform in Argentina." Unpublished paper, John F. Kennedy School of Government, Harvard University.

Porto, Guido G. 1996. *Las economías regionales en la Argentina.* Buenos Aires: Nuevohacer.

PRONAGOB (Programa Nacional de Gobernabilidad), PNUD (Programa de las Naciones Unidas para el Desarrollo), and ILDIS (Instituto Latinoamericano de Investigaciones Sociales). 1996. *La seguridad humana en Bolivia: Percepciones políticas, sociales, y económicas de los bolivianos de hoy.* La Paz: PRONAGOB, PNUD, ILDIS.

Psacharapoulos, George, Samuel Morley, Ariel Fiszbein, Haeduck Lee, and Bill Wood. 1997. *Poverty and Income Distribution in Latin America: The Story of the 1980s.* Washington, D.C.: World Bank.

Quadri, Mario. 1986. *La Argentina descentralizada.* Buenos Aires: EUDEBA.

Remmer, Karen L. 1993. "The Political Economy of Elections in Latin America." *American Political Science Review* 87, no. 2 (June).

———. 1991. "The Political Impact of Economic Crisis in Latin America in the 1980s." *American Political Science Review* 85, no. 3 (September).

———. 1985–86. "Exclusionary Democracy." *Studies in Comparative International Development* 20, no. 2.

República de Bolivia. 1995. *Ley de Participación Popular.*

Riker, William H., and David L. Weimer. 1995. "The Political Economy of Transformation: Liberalization and Property Rights." In Jeffrey S. Banks and Eric A. Hanushek, eds., *Modern Political Economy: Old Topics, New Directions.* Cambridge: Cambridge University Press.

Rivera Santivañez, José Antonio. 1996. "Seleccion de candidatos: MBL." *Opiniones y Análisis* (La Paz), February.

Rodrik, Dani. 1993. "The Positive Economics of Policy Reform," *American Economics Association Papers and Proceedings* 83, no. 2 (May).

Rojas, Gonzalo. 1998. "Censura constructiva: Inestabilidad y democracia municipal." *Serie Decentralizacion y Participacion,* no. 1. La Paz: ILDIS.

Romero, Aníbal. 1997. "Rearranging the Deck Chairs on the Titanic: The Agony of Democracy in Venezuela." *Latin American Research Review* 32, no. 1.

———. 1996. "Condemned to Democracy (with Adjectives): Latin America in the 1990s." Unpublished manuscript, Harvard University.

Rondinelli, Dennis A. 1995. "Processes of Strategic Innovation: The Dynamics of Decision Making in the Evolution of Great Policies." In John D. Montgomery and Dennis A. Rondinelli, eds., *Great Policies: Strategic Innovations in Asia and the Pacific Basin*. Westport, Conn.: Praeger.

Root, Hilton L. 1989. "Tying the King's Hands: Credible Commitments and Royal Fiscal Policy during the Old Regime." *Rationality and Society* 1, no. 2 (October): 240–58.

Rosatti, Horacio D. et al. 1994. *La reforma de la constitución explicada por miembros de la comisión de redacción*. Buenos Aires: Rubinzal-Culzoni Editores.

Rothstein, Bo. 1992. "Labor-Market Institutions and Working-Class Strength." In Sven Steinmo, Kathleen Thelen, and Frank Longstreth, eds., *Structuring Politics: Historical Institutionalism in Comparative Analysis*. Cambridge: Cambridge University Press.

Sachs, Jeffrey. 1987. "The Bolivian Hyperinflation and Stabilization." *American Economic Review* 77, no. 2.

Salamanca, Luis. 1995. "The Venezuelan Political System: A View from Civil Society." In Jennifer McCoy, William C. Smith, Andrés Serbin, and Andrés Stambouli, eds., *Venezuelan Democracy under Stress*. Miami: North-South Center Press.

Sánchez de Lozada, Gonzalo. 1995. "Bolivia debe cambiar." In Secretaría Nacional de Participación Popular, *Debate nacional sobre la Ley de Participación Popular*. La Paz: Secretaría Nacional de Participación Popular.

Sánchez Melean, Jorge. 1992. *Reforma del estado y descentralización*. Maracaibo, Venezuela: Imprenta del Estado Zulia.

Sawyers, Larry. 1996. *The Other Argentina: The Interior and National Development*. Boulder, Colo.: Westview Press.

Schamis, Hector. 1999. "Distributional Coalitions and the Politics of Economic Reform in Latin America." *World Politics* 51, no. 2 (January).

Schmidt, Gregory D. 1989a. "Political Variables and Governmental Decentralization in Peru, 1948–88." *Journal of Inter-American Studies and World Affairs* 31, nos. 1–2 (Spring–Summer).

———. 1989b. *Donors and Decentralization in Developing Countries: Insights from AID Experience in Peru*. Boulder, Colo.: Westview Press.

Scobie, James R. 1971. *Argentina: A City and a Nation*. 2nd ed. New York: Oxford University Press.

Scott, James. 1995. Contribution to "The Role of Theory in Comparative Politics: A Symposium." *World Politics* 48 (October).

Secretaría Nacional de Participacion Popular. 1995. *Debate nacional sobre la Ley de Participación Popular*. La Paz: Secretaría Nacional de Participación Popular.

Smith, William C. 1991. "State, Market and Neoliberalism in Post-Transition Argentina: The Menem Experiment." *Journal of Interamerican Studies and World Affairs* 33, no. 4:45–82.

Smith, William C., Carlos H. Acuña, and Eduardo A. Gamarra, eds. 1994. *Democracy,*

*Markets, and Structural Reform in Latin America: Argentina, Bolivia, Brazil, Chile, and Mexico.* New Brunswick, N.J.: Transaction Publishers.

Smulovitz, Catalina. 1995. "Constitución y poder judicial en la nueva democracia Argentina: La experiencia de las instituciones." In Carlos H. Acuña, ed., *La nueva matriz política argentina.* Buenos Aires: Nueva Visión.

Stambouli, Andres. 1993. "An Evaluation of the First Year of the Government of Carlos Andrés Pérez." In Joseph S. Tulchin, ed., with Gary Bland, *Venezuela in the Wake of Radical Reform.* Boulder, Colo.: Lynne Rienner.

Steinmo, Sven, Kathleen Thelen, and Frank Longstreth, eds. 1992. *Structuring Politics: Historical Institutionalism in Comparative Analysis.* Cambridge: Cambridge University Press.

Taliercio, Robert. 1996. "Administrative Reform as Credible Commitment: Taxpayers, Politicians, and the State in Guyana, Peru, and Venezuela." Paper prepared for the conference "Economic Reform and Civil Society in Latin America," Harvard University (April 12).

Tendler, Judith. 1997. *Good Government in the Tropics.* Baltimore: The Johns Hopkins University Press.

Thelen, Kathleen, and Sven Steinmo. 1992. "Historical Institutionalism in Comparative Politics." In Sven Steinmo, Kathleen Thelen, and Frank Longstreth, eds., *Structuring Politics: Historical Institutionalism in Comparative Analysis.* Cambridge: Cambridge University Press.

Ticona A., Esteban, Gonzalo Rojas O, and Xavier Albó C. 1995. *Votos y wiphalas: Campesinos y pueblos originarios en democracia.* La Paz: Fundación Milenio/ CIPCA.

Tomassini, Luciano. 1994. "The IDB and the Modernization of the State." In Colin Bradford, Jr., ed., *Redefining the State in Latin America.* Paris: Organization for Economic Co-operation and Development.

Tommasi, Mariano, and Andrés Velasco. 1996. "Where Are We in the Political Economy of Reform?" *Policy Reform 1.*

Touraine, Alain. 1994. "From the Mobilizing State to Democratic Politics." In Colin Bradford, Jr., ed., *Redefining the State in Latin America.* Paris: Organization for Economic Co-operation and Development.

Tuchschneider, David. 1996. "Una visión desde la planificación participativa municipal." In Rojas Ortuste, Gonzalo, ed., *La Participación Popular: Avances y obstáculos.* La Paz: Grupo DRU/SNPP.

Tugwell, Franklin. 1975. *The Politics of Oil in Venezuela.* Stanford: Stanford University Press.

Tulchin, Joseph S., ed., with Bernice Romero. 1995. *The Consolidation of Democracy in Latin America.* Boulder, Colo.: Lynne Rienner.

Tulchin, Joseph S., ed., with Gary Bland. 1993. *Venezuela in the Wake of Radical Reform.* Boulder, Colo.: Lynne Rienner Publishers.

Unidad de Políticas Económicas. 1992.

UNDP (United Nations Development Program). 1998. *Desarrollo humano en Bolivia, 1998.* La Paz: UNDP.

Urioste, Miguel, and Luis Baldomar. 1996. "Ley de Participación Popular: Seguimento crítico." In Rojas Ortuste, Gonzalo, ed., *La Participación Popular: Avances y obstáculos.* La Paz: Grupo DRU/SNPP.

Valenzuela, J. Samuel. 1994. "Recasting State-Union Relations in Latin America." In Colin Bradford, Jr., ed., *Redefining the State in Latin America.* Paris: Organization for Economic Co-operation and Development.

*VenEconomy Monthly.* 1989. Vol. 6, no. 6 (March).

Venezuela Competitiva. 1994, 1995, 1996. *Gobiernos Locales,* nos. 1–3. Caracas: Venezuela Competitiva.

Waterbury, John. 1992. "The Heart of the Matter? Public Enterprise and the Adjustment Process." In Stephan Haggard and Robert R. Kaufman, *The Politics of Economic Adjustment.* Princeton: Princeton University Press.

Weingast, Barry R. 1995. "The Political Foundations of Limited Government: Parliament and Sovereign Debt in 17th and 18th [Century] England." Paper prepared for the conference "The Frontiers of Institutional Economics, Washington University," March 17–19

Weir, Margaret. 1992. "Ideas and the Politics of Bounded Innovation." In Sven Steinmo, Kathleen Thelen, and Frank Longstreth, eds., *Structuring Politics: Historical Institutionalism in Comparative Analysis.* Cambridge: Cambridge University Press

Weyland, Kurt. 1996. "Risk Taking in Latin American Economic Restructuring: Lessons from Prospect Theory." *International Studies Quarterly* 40:185–208.

Whitaker, Arthur P. 1964. *Argentina.* Englewood Cliffs, N.J.: Prentice Hall.

Whitehead, Laurence. 1974–75. "El estado y los intereses seccionales: El caso Boliviano." *Estudios Andinos* 4, no. 1:85–118.

Williamson, John. 1994. "In Search of a Manual for Technopols." In John Williamson, ed., *The Political Economy of Policy Reform.* Washington, D.C.: Institute for International Economics.

Willis, Eliza, Christopher Da C. B. Garman, and Stephan Haggard. 1999. "The Politics of Decentralization in Latin America." *Latin American Research Review* 34, no. 1.

World Bank. 1997. *World Tables.*

———. 1996. "Partnership for Capacity Building in Africa." Unpublished paper, Office of the Vice President, Africa Region, World Bank, January 31.

———. 1992. *Governance and Development.* Washington, D.C.: World Bank, 1992.

*World Politics.* 1995. Vol. 48.

Yee, Albert. 1996. "The Causal Effects of Ideas on Policies." *International Organization* 50, no. 1 (Winter), 69–108.

Zambrano Sequín, Luis. 1995. "What We Have Done and What We Can Still Do in

Economic Policy." In Jennifer McCoy, William C. Smith, Andrés Serbin, and Andrés Stambouli, eds., *Venezuelan Democracy under Stress*. Miami: North-South Center Press.

Zbar, Agustín. 1988. "El Pacto de Olivos y la reforma constitucional argentina de 1994: Los desafíos institucionales de la segunda república." Unpublished paper.

# Index

Grindle, Merilee Serrill.
    Audacious reforms : institutional invention and democracy in Latin America / Merilee S.
Grindle.
        p.   cm.
Includes bibliographical references and index.
    ISBN 0-8018-6420-8 (hardcover : alk. paper) — ISBN 0-8018-6421-6
(pbk. : alk. paper)
    1. Local elections—Latin America—Case studies.   2. Decentralization in government—
Latin America—Case studies.   3. Central-local government relations—Latin America—Case
studies.   4. Democracy—Latin America—Case studies.   5. Political participation—Latin
America—Case studies.   I. Title.
    JS2061 .G73 2000
    320.98—dc21
                                                                        00-008002